BLITZ ON CHESHIRE

Rose and Paul Hurley

Blitz on Cheshire

A Photographic Record of Bomb Damage across Wirral, Cheshire and South Manchester

The History Press

Front cover: Damage caused by HE bombs at the Stanton Estate, Lower Bebington.
Rear cover: Mayfield Estate, New Ferry, 12 March 1941.

First published 2026

The History Press
97 St George's Place, Cheltenham,
Gloucestershire, GL50 3QB
www.thehistorypress.co.uk

British Library Cataloguing in Publication Data.
A catalogue record for this book is available from the British Library.

ISBN 978 1 80399 949 4

Typesetting and origination by The History Press
Printed and bound in Great Britain by TJ Books, Padstow, Cornwall.

MIX
Paper | Supporting responsible forestry
FSC® C013056
FSC
www.fsc.org

The History Press proudly supports
Trees for Life
www.treesforlife.org.uk

EU Authorised Representative: Easy Access System Europe
Mustamäe tee 50, 10621 Tallinn, Estonia
gpst.request@easproject.com

Contents

Introduction 7

1 Maps, Starfish Sites and Bombs 9

2 South Cheshire 15

3 Mid Cheshire 41

4 North Cheshire and South Manchester 57

5 The Wirral and West Cheshire 87

6 The War's Final Days 149

Notes 155

Bibliography and Sources 157

Acknowledgements 158

About the Authors 159

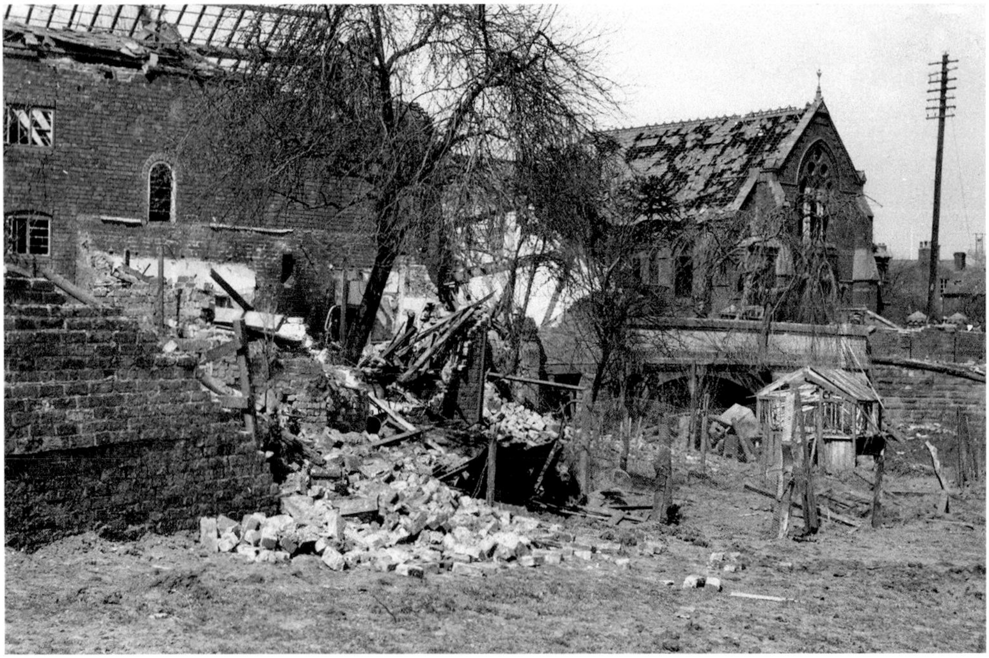

The incident at Wheelock on 26 April 1941 was caused by a parachute mine.

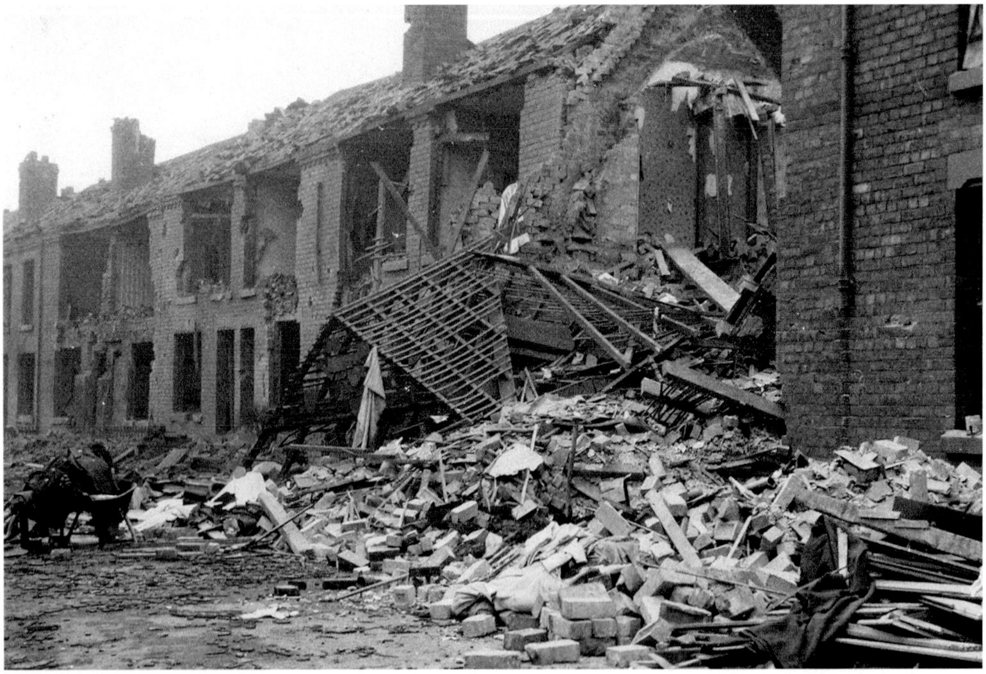

Hall O'Shaw Street, Crewe, 7 May 1941.

Introduction

The wartime police photographers of the Cheshire Constabulary took the images featured in this book. It is important to clarify that Cheshire was a much bigger county in those wartime years, and the force covered a wider area than it does now. However, some of the larger towns were served by their own police force: towns such as Congleton, Birkenhead and Macclesfield all had their own borough force and their own chief constable. The Cheshire Constabulary covered the areas not covered by a borough force. Chester, however, was a city force in its own right, even though the Cheshire Constabulary was based there. The photographers who took these photographs were from the main Cheshire Constabulary and not the borough forces, which is why some towns are not covered in the book. It was also illegal for members of the public to take photographs of the damage caused by wartime action. Accordingly, the pictures in this book are pretty rare.

The below came from a War Photography Leaflet issued by the War Office:

> Issued by the War Office on September 10th, 1939, Control of Photography Order Number 1 banned the photographing or filming of any object or subject conceivably connected with the prosecution of War. The list of prohibitions included large groupings of troops or evacuees, any form of equipment or supplies, harbours and docks, crashed aeroplanes, damaged buildings and any form of riotous or disorderly assembly. Also included were gas works, electricity plants, hospitals, ambulances and roads or railways connected with works of defense [*sic*].[1]

Cheshire was mainly a sleepy county with just a few suitable targets for the enemy, but was surrounded by areas such as Liverpool and Manchester. Crossing the county was the usual route for the bombers on their approach to their targets, and they would drop their unused bombs on the way back. Hence, we have many instances of towns and villages that have suffered from such indiscriminate bombing seen within these pages. Some locations were bombed deliberately: during the Second World War, the Luftwaffe were provided with maps of Great Britain with red-inked circled targets to bomb. These focused on locations such as Crewe with its railway works and Rolls-Royce factory, and Birkenhead with its dockyards, along with bridges, railway lines and essential buildings – all of which presented juicy targets for the enemy.

These images have not been published in a book before, but a few are on display in the Cheshire Police Museum in Warrington. One or two have been permitted for use on community pamphlets.

In compiling this book, we included some modern-day images of a few selected locations that were victims of the bombing. It is not intended to be a 'then and now' book, but rather an opportunity to see parts of relatively safe Cheshire and surrounds that were not so safe at the time due to high-explosive bombs and land mines. There are many examples of the devastating damage they caused to residential and industrial premises.

As outlined, there are many reasons why Cheshire would be targeted, but it was also a dumping ground for unused bombs, as well as one of the routes into Great Britain from Ireland. Ireland was neutral in the war, and Éamon de Valera, its president, accepted the conditions imposed on a neutral country. However, at the same time it has been reported that its towns and cities were allowed to remain lit up at night, which helped to guide the Luftwaffe across the Irish Sea to the British mainland.[2] Irish regiments fought alongside the Allies, but it is also well known that de Valera visited the German Legation in Dublin to offer his condolences on the news of Hitler's death.

1

Maps, Starfish Sites and Bombs

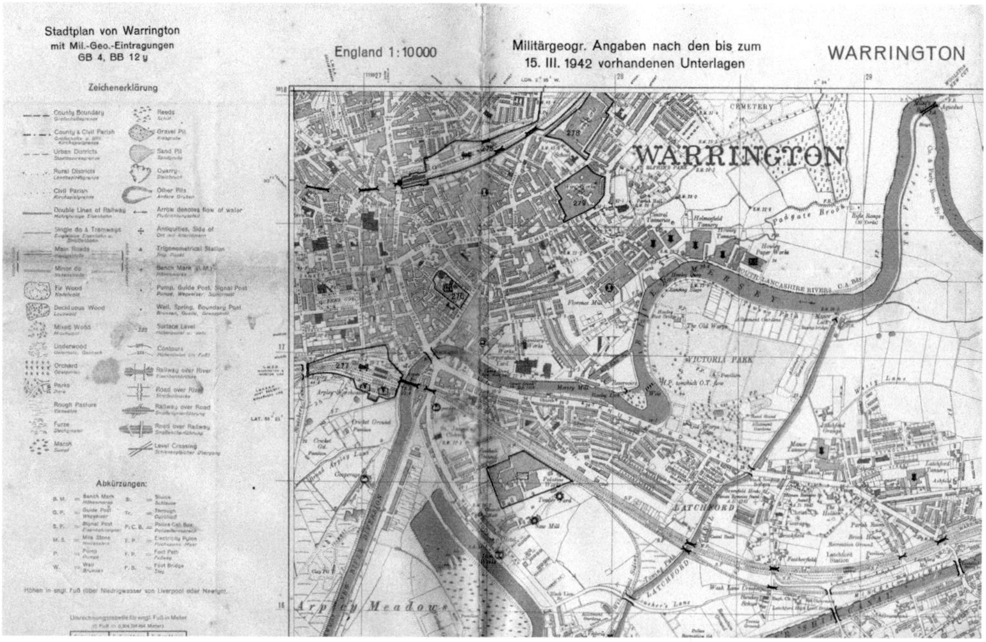

German Map of Warrington

During the First World War, the Nazis acquired street maps of Great Britain and used them to outline prospective sites to bomb. Fortunately, my RAF father acquired an original set of maps covering the North West and a book of suggested bombing sites. I do not know where he got them, but we will use snippets from them while compiling the book. To start with, here is a German image of Warrington. There are no photographs of Warrington itself as it was in Lancashire at the time, and Warrington Borough had its own borough police force (but there is one of Grappenhall). On this map are suggested locations for the bombing, including the wire factory; Central Station; Arpley Station, along with its extensive sidings; Latchford Tanner; and Palatine Works. (Authors' collection)

German Map of Birkenhead

At the time, the town of Birkenhead was within Cheshire,, although it also had its own borough police force. The targets outlined below are the docks and shipbuilders, as well as the extensive railway infrastructure. Birkenhead Docks was extremely busy building warships prior to and during the war; the most famous was probably the aircraft carrier HMS *Ark Royal*. It was laid down at Cammell Laird shipbuilders on 16 September 1935 and commissioned on 16 December 1938. At £3 million (£230 million in today's money), it would be the most expensive warship ever built for the Royal Navy, excluding battleships.

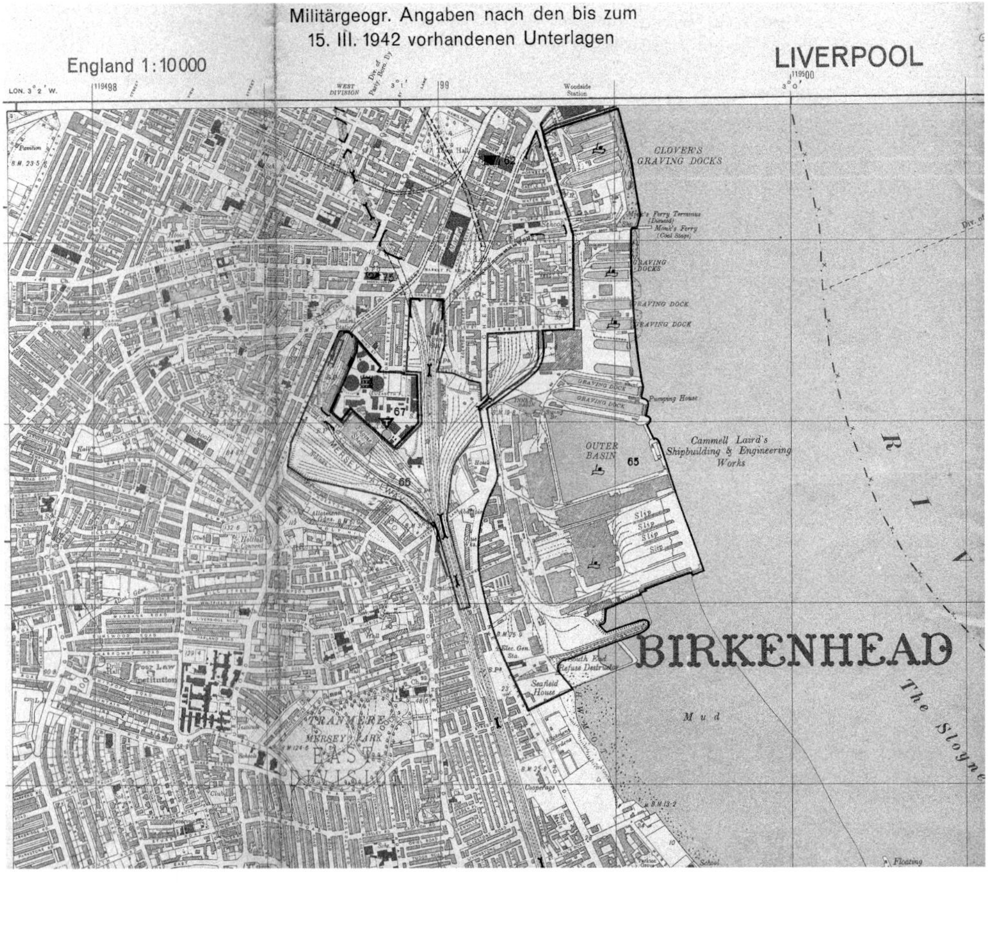

The ship had an excellent war service, with its planes disabling the German battleship *Bismarck*. The Nazis reported the sinking of *Ark Royal* on several occasions, but these were false, until finally, on 13 November 1941, the carrier was torpedoed off Gibraltar. However, only one crewman, a 44-year-old able seaman, was killed; the crew of 1,487 officers and men were rescued with no further deaths, with the ship then seen to split in two and sink. (Authors' collection)

Wartime Police Map of Cheshire

This shows police stations that had a phone and is included to show the outline of Cheshire as used in this book. (Authors' collection)

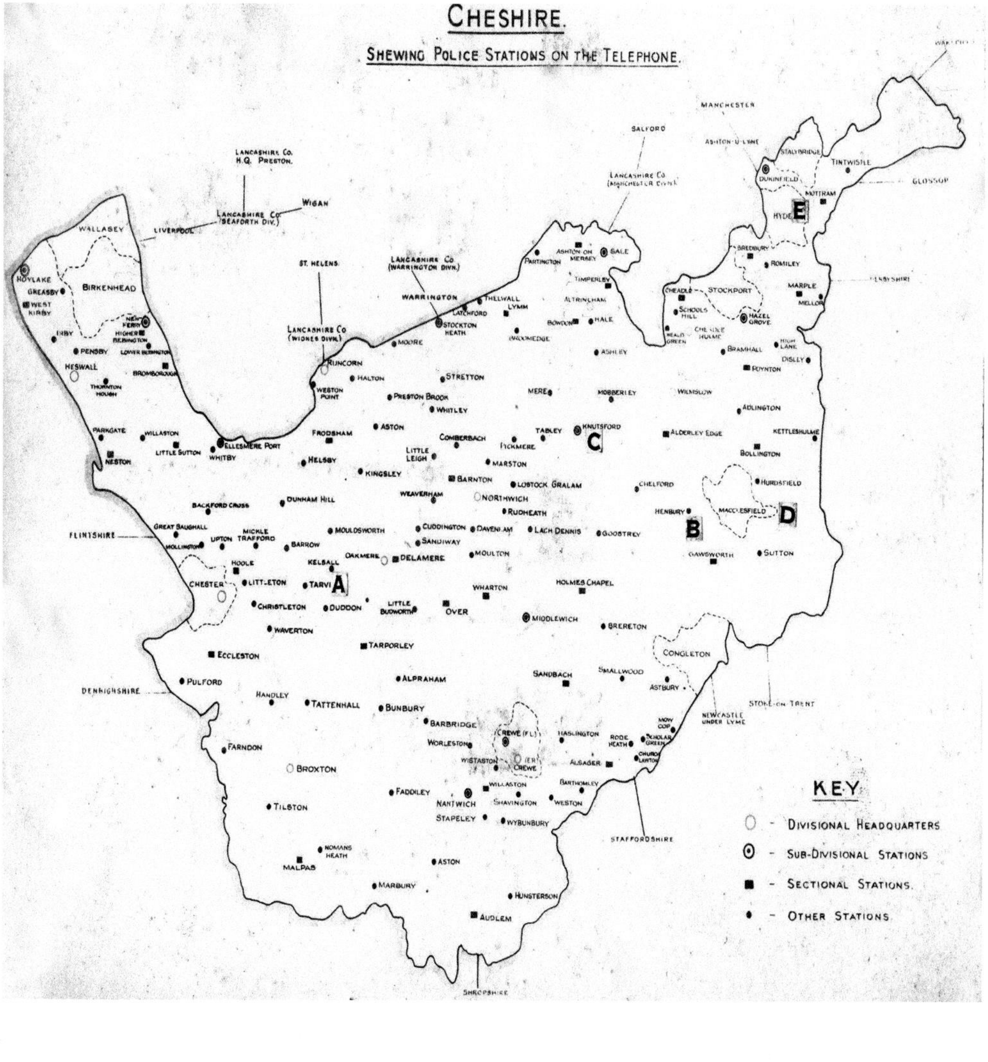

Luftwaffe Book with Photos of Suitable Targets

My father acquired this book during the war and it contains photographs of suitable targets throughout Britain. The pictures were taken both by the Luftwaffe and from Britain's tourist books and magazines; these were used to plan bombing raids on our ancient towns and beauty spots in the hopes of demoralising the British public. As they used Baedeker tourist guides, they were nicknamed Baedeker Raids, and were in response to RAF raids on Germany's historic towns. Hitler was eventually advised that this was a waste of time and bombs, and it was stopped. This was probably before Chester city became a target, as, apart from very few bombs falling on the city, only the extremities of the city, such as the aircraft factory and barracks, received attention from the Luftwaffe. (Authors' collection)

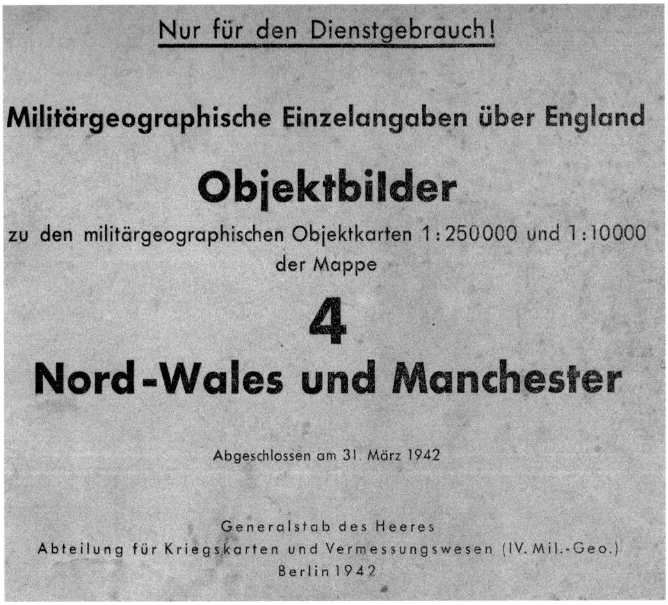
Nur für den Dienstgebrauch!

Militärgeographische Einzelangaben über England

Objektbilder

zu den militärgeographischen Objektkarten 1:250000 und 1:10000 der Mappe

4

Nord-Wales und Manchester

Abgeschlossen am 31. März 1942

Generalstab des Heeres
Abteilung für Kriegskarten und Vermessungswesen (IV. Mil.-Geo.)
Berlin 1942

Starfish Sites

Starfish sites were Second World War bombing decoy locations and there were several in the North. One at Little Budworth was built in early 1941 as a 'Permanent Starfish' site to deflect enemy bombing from the town of Northwich and the extensive ICI works there. The site was designed to be illuminated at night in open fields, in an attempt to deceive the bombers into thinking it was a built-up area. These Starfish sites were spread around the country close to essential targets such as the Crewe railway works:

> By late 1941, a 'QL' decoy was incorporated into the site as part of the 'C-series' of civil decoys to protect the Imperial Chemical Industries plant in Northwich. The 'Starfish' decoy operated by lighting a series of controlled fires during an air raid to

replicate from above an urban area targeted by bombs. The 'Q' decoy sites displayed simulated railway marshalling yard lights, locomotive glows, factory lighting, and furnace glows to reconstruct the chemical plant. The site is referenced as being in use until 1943.[3]

Aerial photography from 1960 showed the site had subsequently been converted to agricultural use, and no features of the decoy remained. There was another Starfish site for Northwich at Bostock. By the end of the war, there were 237 Starfish sites protecting 81 locations across Britain.

Another attempt at deceiving the bombers involved burning oil in barrels, a tactic used particularly by the British Petroleum Warfare Department to create black smoke and conceal the location of factories and other strategic sites from aerial reconnaissance. This was used to hide the Rolls-Royce works in Crewe, which will be covered later. This 'smoke curtain' aimed to prevent enemy bombers from locating and destroying key targets. The Petroleum Warfare Department also developed various flame warfare weapons.

Bombs Mentioned in this Book

110lb Bomb

This was the most common high-explosive bomb designed for general demolition. It was 43in long and 8in in diameter, with an explosive charge of 50lb.

Incendiary Bomb

A small but lethal bomb that consisted of a magnesium alloy body with a three-finned tail that was filled with thermite, which is an incendiary compound. They did not explode on impact, but the needle in the igniter was driven into a small percussion cap, which in turn ignited the thermite filling and produced enough heat to melt steel. The bombs were 13.6in long and 2in in diameter.

560lb HE Delayed-Action Bomb

Delayed-action bombs were used by both the Germans and the Allies. They were timed to explode sometime after impact, with the fuses set to go off any time from a very brief interval to several weeks, and could be used to hinder bringing airfields back into use after they had been bombed. The bombs were able to enter a building through the roof and penetrate through several floors to the ground floor to explode inside the building, rather than just causing damage to the exterior. Likewise, when bombing a warship, the bomb passed through the decking and superstructure. A short delay would enable an aircraft to drop the bomb without being caught in the explosion during a low-level attack. Longer delays were intended to disrupt rescue and repair workers and spread terror in the neighbourhood. Bomb disposal workers were also fair game.

Parachute Mine

The Germans initially dropped these powerful weapons into the water to attack shipping. The Luftmine A was 5ft 8in tall and weighed 1,100lb, while the larger Luftmine B was 8ft 8in tall and weighed 2,200lb. The mine would descend at 40mph and, when released over land, would detonate twenty-five seconds after impact. These were heavy and powerful weapons that caused severe damage. They were first used as land targets on 16 September 1940, and from the following month they were dropped on British cities such as Birmingham, Liverpool, Manchester and Coventry.

V-1 Flying Bomb

The V-1, officially the Fieseler Fi 103, was the first cruise missile, and work on developing it started in 1939. It later became known as Hitler's Vengeance Weapon, nicknamed 'Hellhound' by the Germans and known to the Allies as the 'buzz bomb' or 'doodlebug'. The first ones were launched against London on 13 June 1944, and thousands were later launched along the French and Dutch coasts, sometimes from specially upgraded Heinkel He 111 aircraft. They were not guided, except via a compass, but the distance flown was determined by the amount of fuel in the tank: when it ran out of fuel, it dropped to the ground. Allied fighter planes were sometimes able to catch the V-1, tip its rudimentary wings and knock it off course. The V-1 was an effective idea, and if it had been available earlier in the war it would have made a significant difference. Its use resulted in 22,892 deaths, compared with 92,566 in the Blitz overall.

The Fi 103R, code-named 'Reichenberg', was a manned version of the V-1 for suicide attacks, although it was not used in action. A more sophisticated weapon, the V-2 guided missile, came too late in the war to make a difference; most failed on the launch pad or missed the target. Werner von Braun, the designer, was soon taken to the USA after the war to work on its further development and this ultimately led to the US space programme.

2

South Cheshire

Crewe

Crewe was both a railway junction, where six lines converged to connect the north, south, east and west of the country, and the home of the Crewe Works, which supplied some of the most powerful locomotives nationally at the time. Crewe was also chosen as the location for the manufacturing of Rolls-Royce Merlin aero-engines to be used for the Hurricane and Spitfire aircraft employed in the Battle of Britain after Rolls-Royce began to outgrow their Derby factory. Naturally, such a target was welcomed by the German bombers; we have already seen that books were published with many other examples of suitable targets.

Part of the gable ends of the Rolls-Royce works were painted to look like a row of houses. Crewe suffered greatly during the Blitz and received numerous visits from the Luftwaffe, which possibly targeted the Rolls-Royce factory and the railway works. Crewe Hall was a prisoner-of-war camp housing over 2,000 German officers.[4]

Air Raid Damage at Crewe, 18 September 1940

We begin with images of the bomb damage caused to Crewe Works.

Crewe was at the forefront of introducing railways to Britain, and it is only to be expected that it would be one of the most important rail centres from the very early days. The station was opened in 1837 and is one of the most significant in the world. It was initially suggested to build it at Winsford, but an earlier proposal to do this was declined; the same applied to Nantwich due to objections from local landowners. So, the small village of Church Coppenhall was chosen – a village that would later be incorporated into the new railway town of Crewe.

As time went on, Crewe Works became one of the most extensive railway engineering facilities in the world, spanning more than 2 miles and employing over 20,000 people at its peak. Hence, it was a significant target for the Nazis, and they certainly gave it some attention.[5]

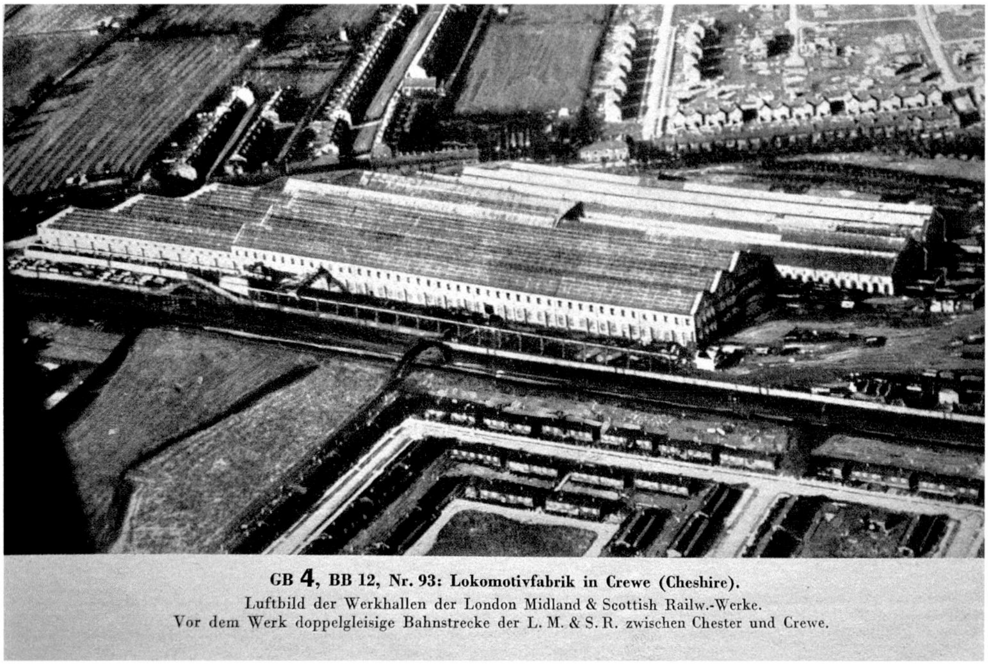

Above: An original German photo of the works prior to bombing.

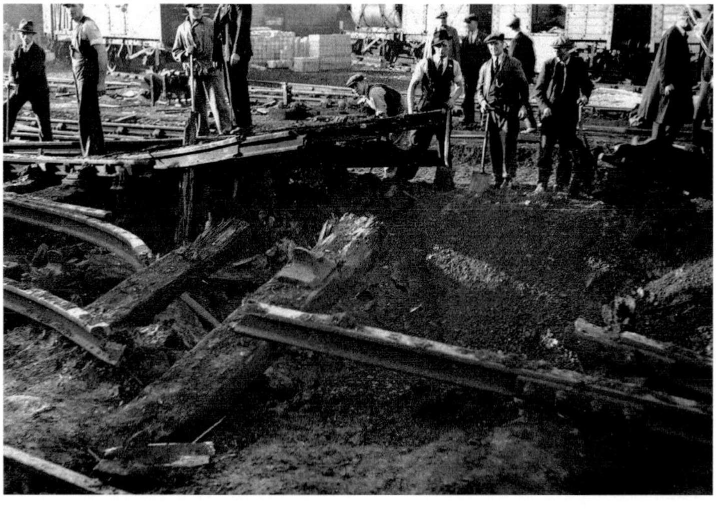

Air raid damage at Crewe Works.

Air Raid Damage at Crewe, 3 October 1940

Photographs showing damage to Crewe Works and British locomotive Black Five 4-6-0 No. 5425. The loco was taken to Crewe Works, where it was repaired and put back into service. It was not withdrawn until February 1968, by which time it had been numbered 45420.

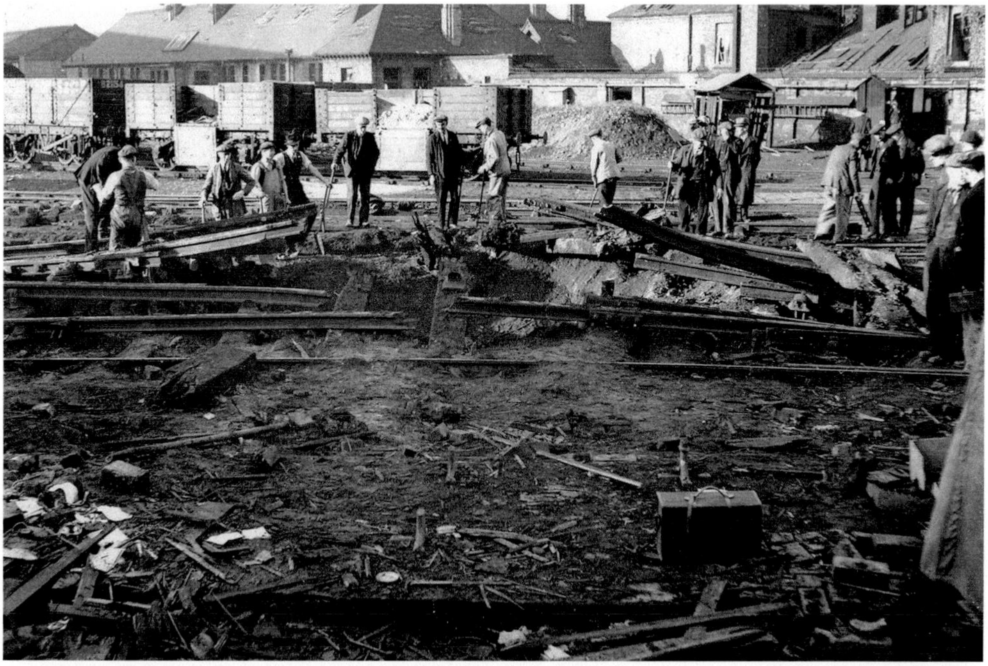

Above: Air raid damage to Crewe Works.

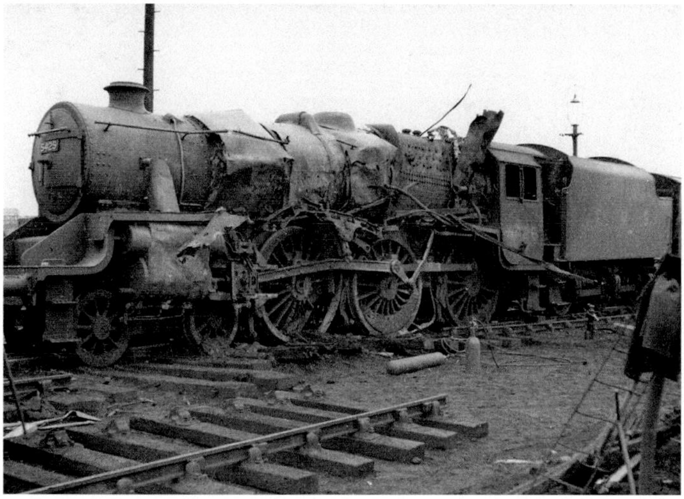

The bombed railway engine.

Air Raid Damage at Shavington cum Gresty, Crewe

On 28 October 1940, a bomb damaged the wall of the Cheshire Cheese pub at Shavington and destroyed the surrounding premises. Here are photos of a cottage and its wall opposite the pub; the parked car was damaged as it was just 7 yards from the bomb crater. Although bomb damage was caused around the pub, it survived relatively intact.

In the 1990s, the pub owner, Greenall Whitley, sold its entire estate, and the Cheshire Cheese became part of Pubco. For a while, the pub was known as the Koconut Grove, and it served real ale and Indian food. Today it is known as the Hickory Smokehouse.

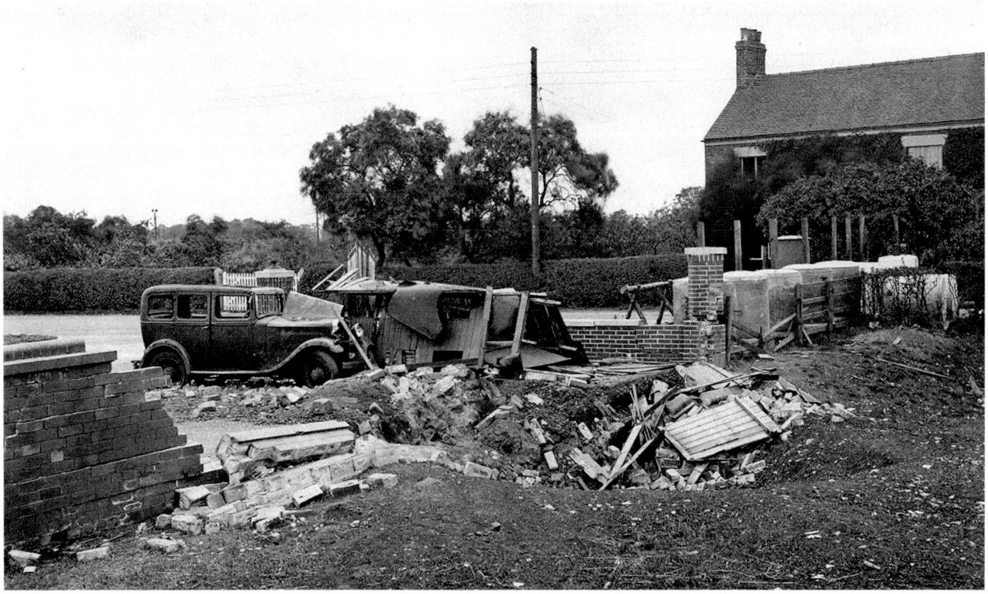

A bomb crater and a damaged car.

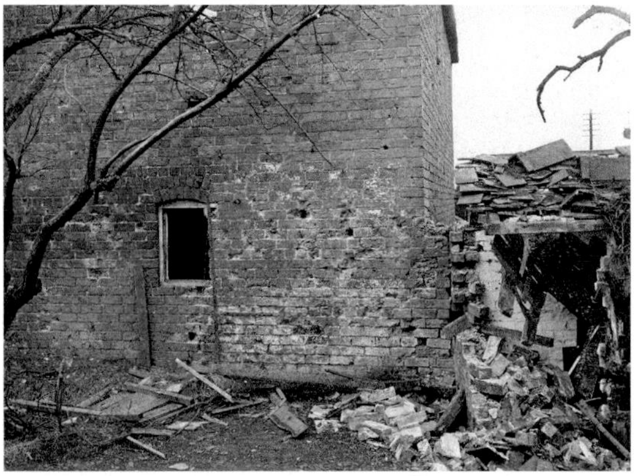

Damage to the wall of a cottage opposite the Cheshire Cheese.

A German Parachute Mine

This mine fell at Marbury, Crewe Division, on 28 November 1940.

The parachute mine had an approximate height of 5ft 10in and a diameter of 2ft. The parachute was made up of forty-eight sections, had a circumference of 48 yards and was attached to the mine by twenty-eight ropes, each ½in thick.

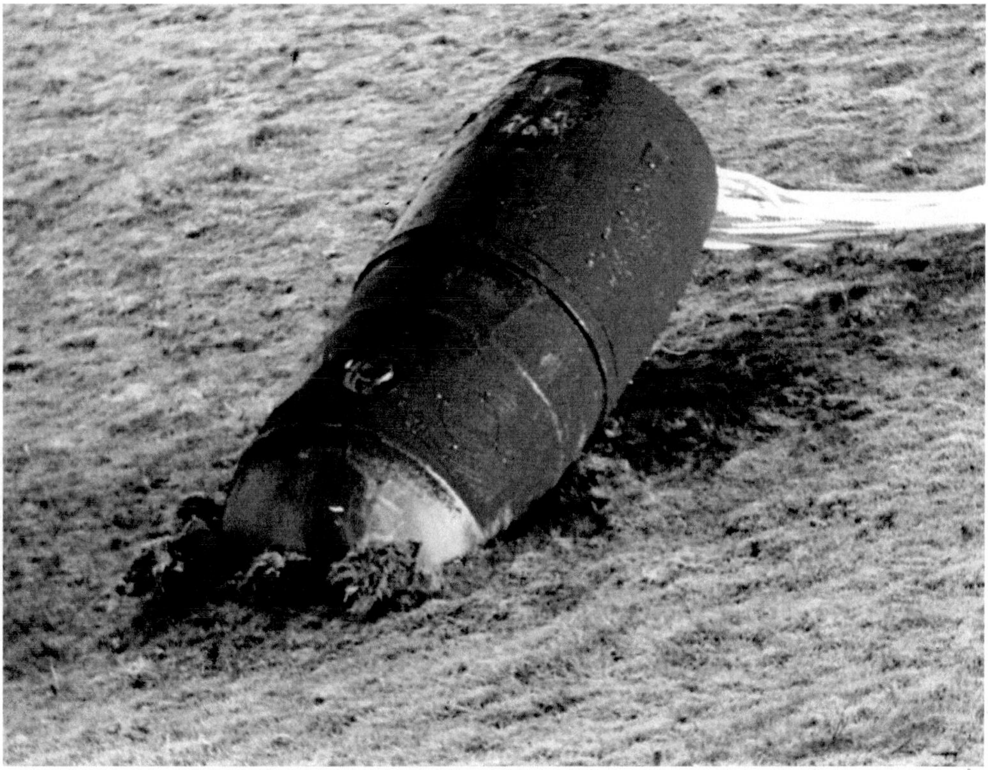

Unexploded parachute mine in a field at Marbury on the Cheshire border.

Air Raid Damage at Bedford Street and St Andrews Avenue, Crewe

Bedford Street was heavily bombed on 29 August 1940 when it was hit by five high-explosive bombs. One of the buildings damaged was Bedford Street School, which was built in 1901 by the London and North Western Railway and designed by F.W. Webb, the company's Chief Mechanical Engineer. The school would be partly rebuilt, allowing the children to return. When the air raid siren went off, they put on their gas masks and continued their lessons in the air raid shelter. The school closed in 1979.

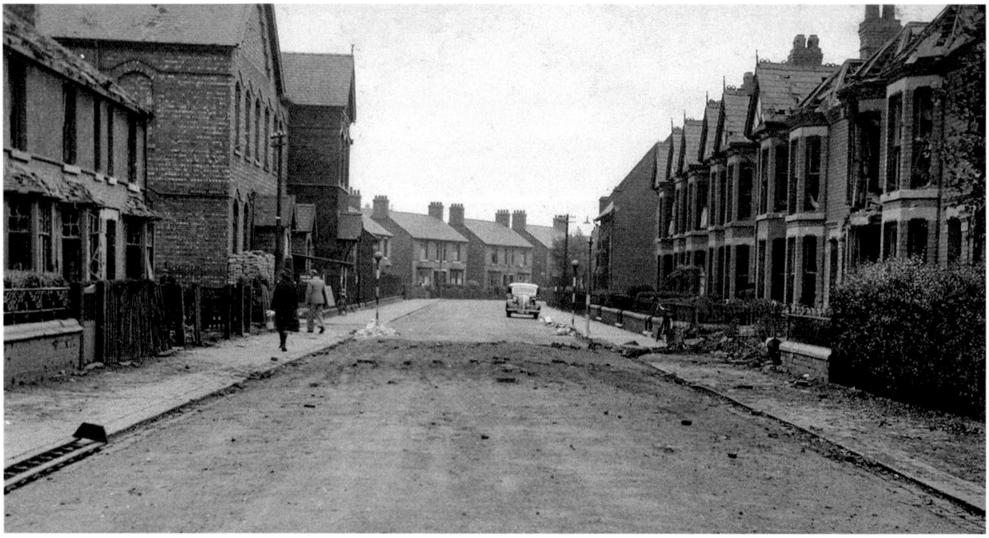

Bedford Street, Crewe.

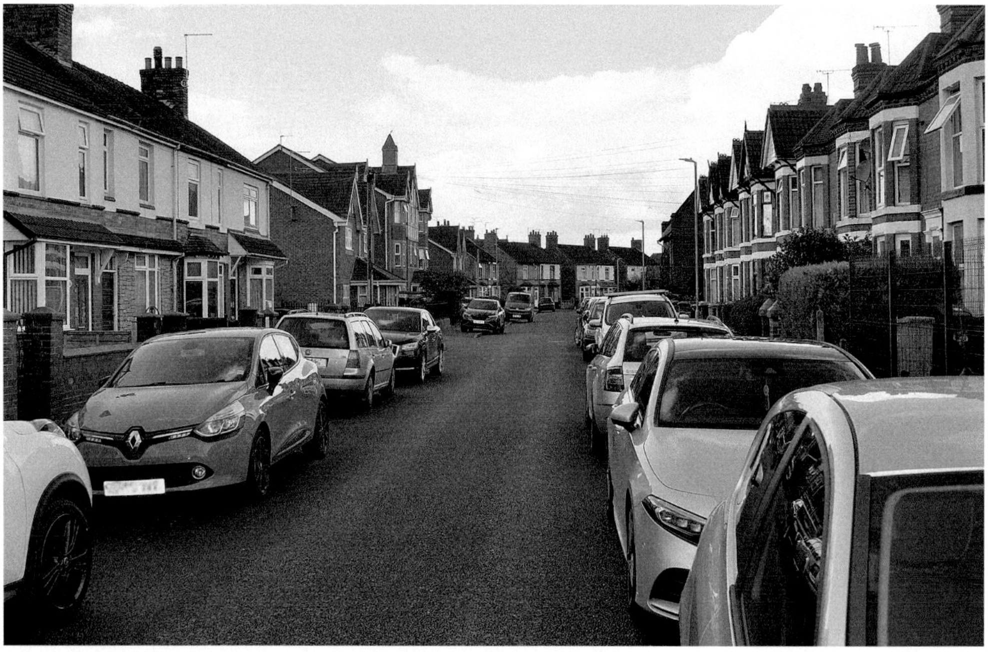

Bedford Street in the present day. (Authors' collection)

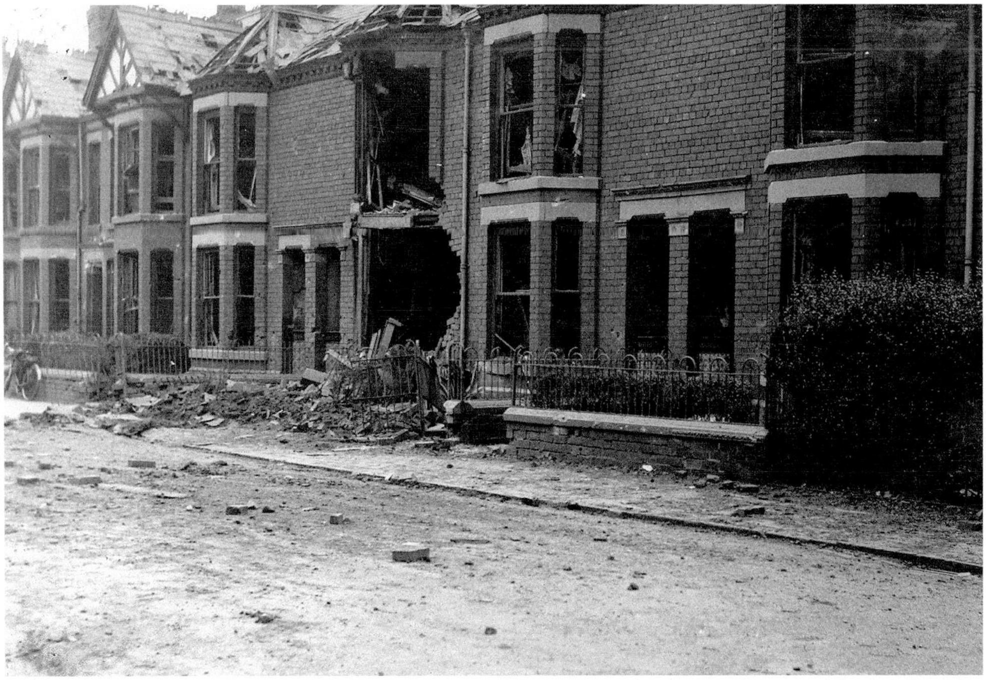

Bedford Street houses.

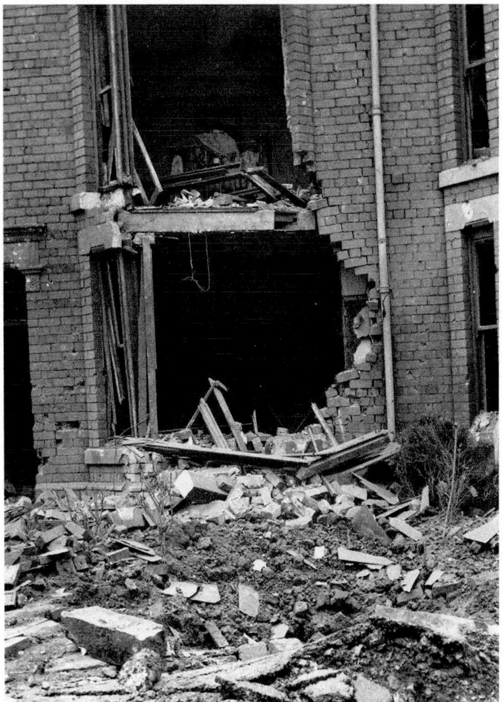

A close-up of one of the damaged houses on Bedford Street.

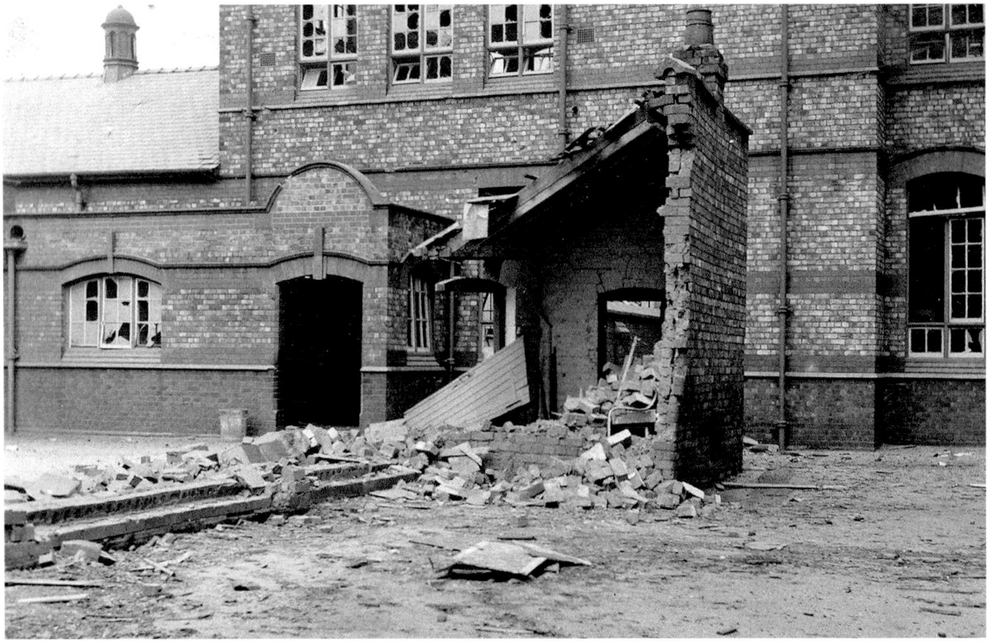

Bedford Street School.

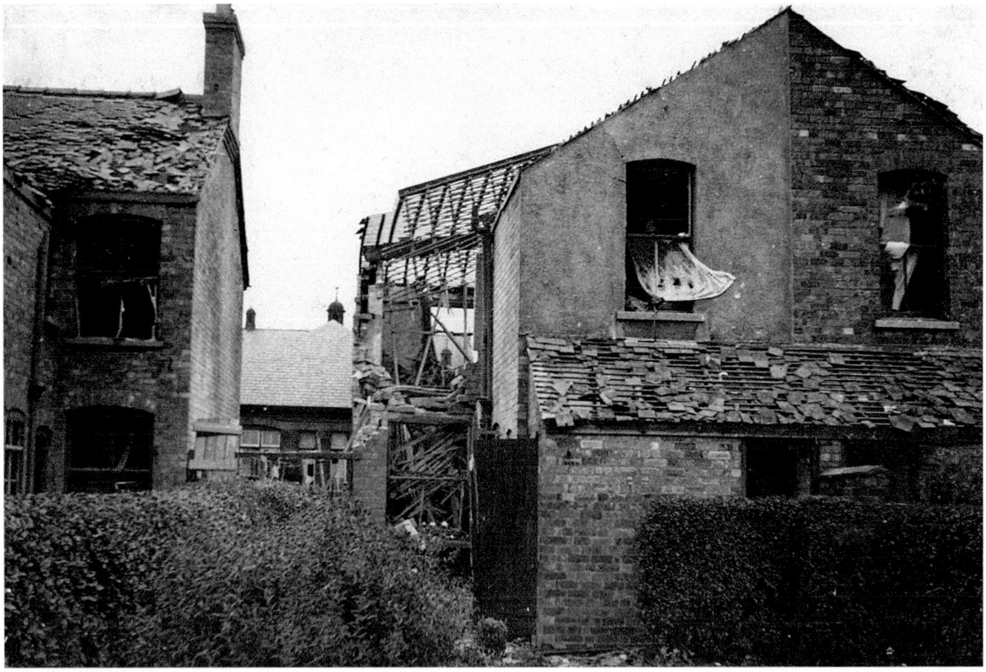

St Andrews Avenue.

Air Raid Damage at Ruskin Road, Crewe

On 26 September 1940, a bomb struck the Ruskin Park dairy, which was an end-terrace house at the junction of Ruskin Road and Lunt Avenue. The premises have been totally rebuilt and are now homes.

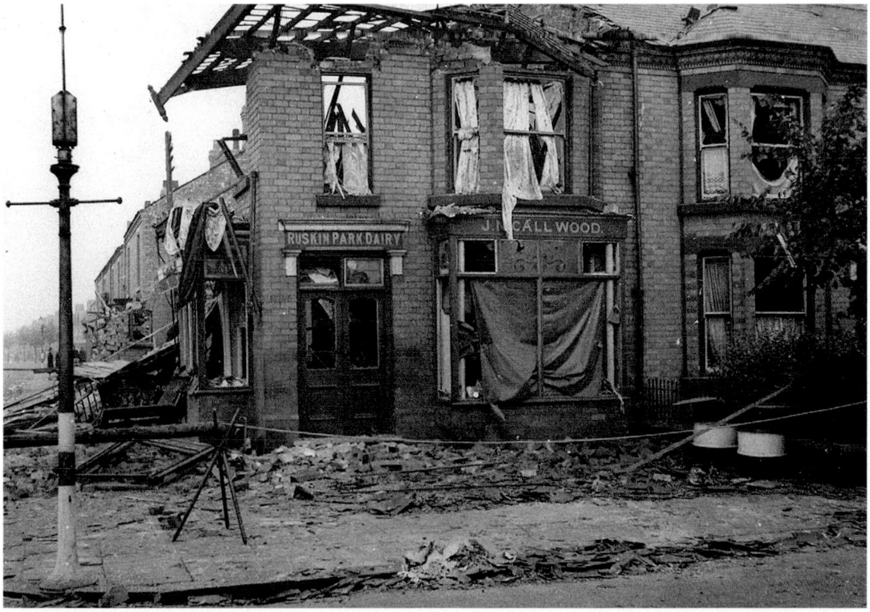

The front of Ruskin Park Dairy after being struck.

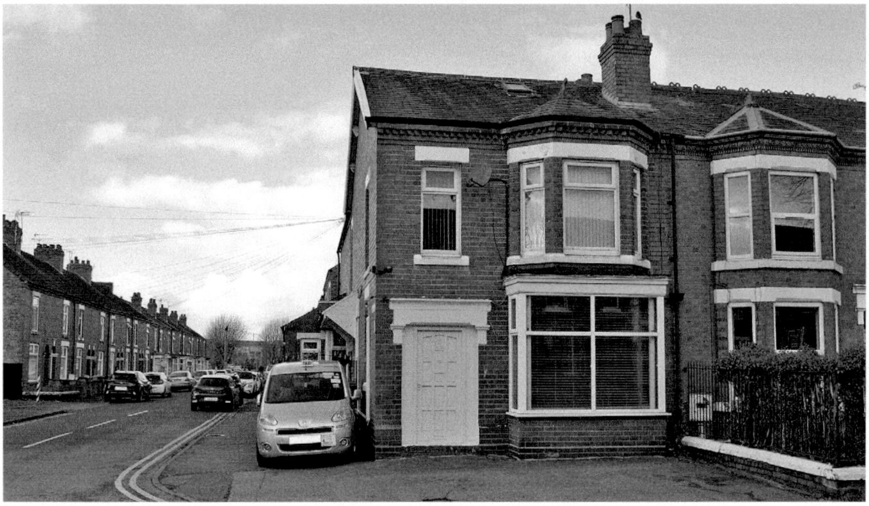

The dairy frontage in the present day. (Authors' collection)

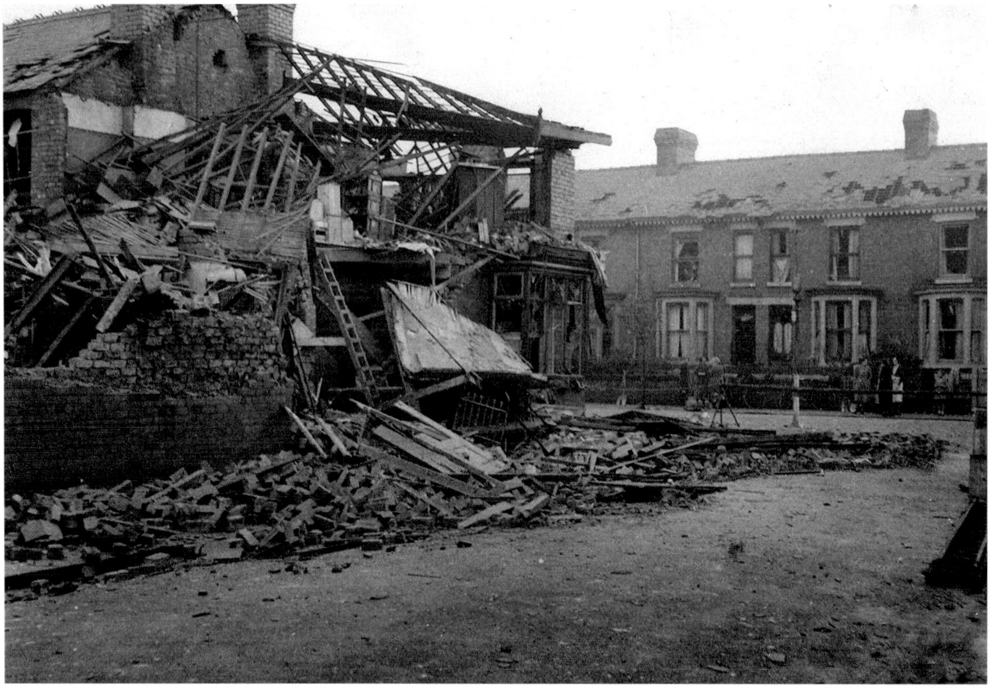

Side of the dairy in wartime.

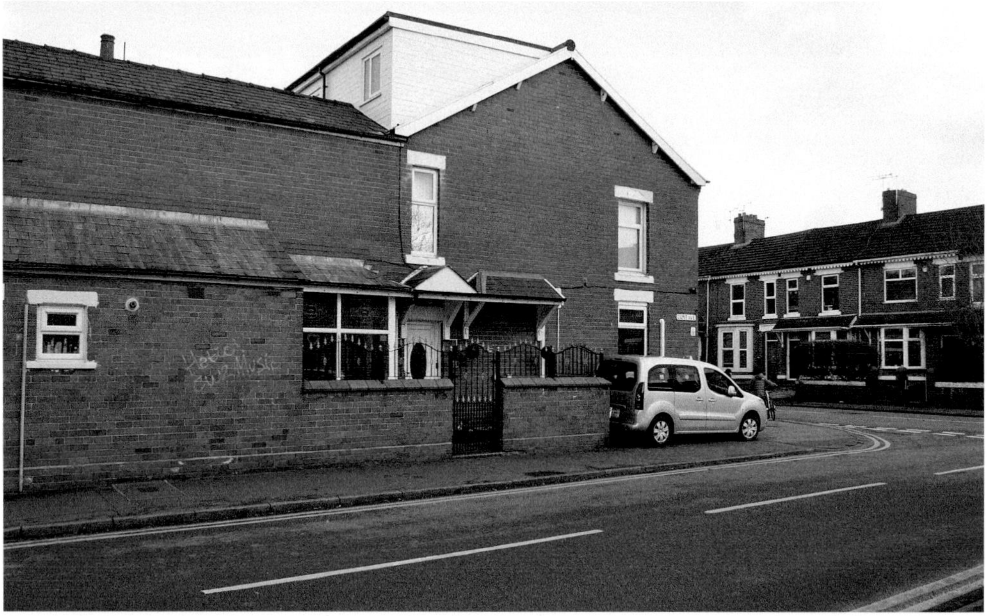

The dairy side in the present day. (Authors' collection)

Air Raid Damage at Bradfield Green, Crewe, 26 September 1940

Just one photograph here of the damage caused to Bradfield Green Farm by an incendiary bomb. The site has since been renamed Church Farm, as it is opposite St Peter's church in Minshull Vernon. The photo was taken from the rear of the barn, looking towards the road.

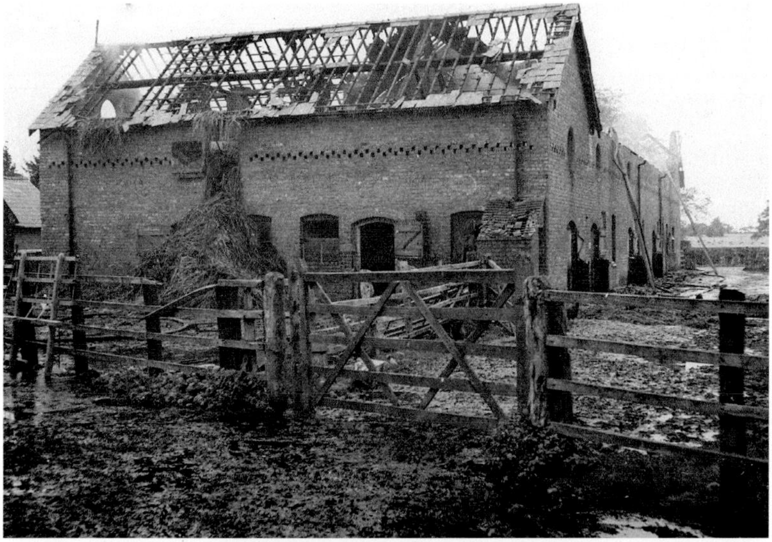

Bradfield Green Farm with bomb damage.

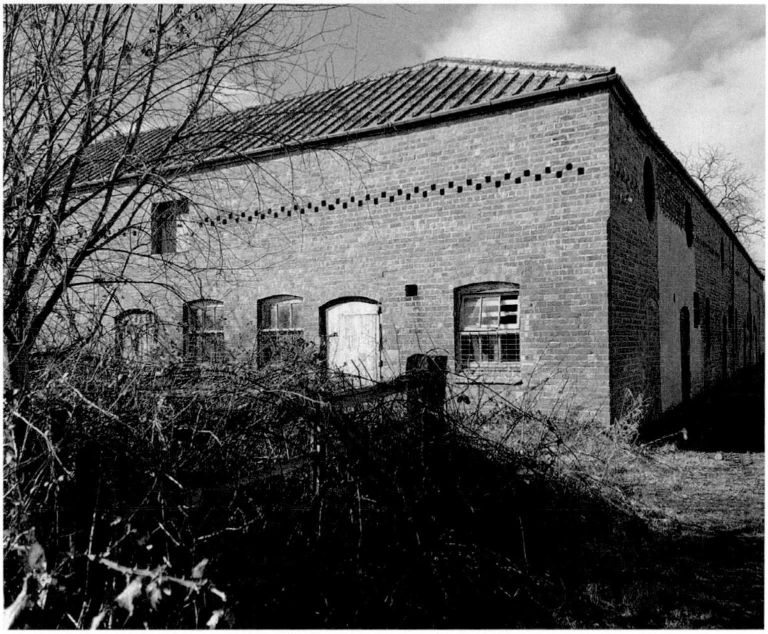

Bradfield Green Farm, now Church Farm. (Authors' collection)

Air Raid Damage at Middlewich Street, Crewe, 26 September 1940

Middlewich Street is long with terraced houses on each side. It was bombed severely during the war, as can be seen here. The actual address for these buildings was challenging to find, so this is a difficult location to obtain modern images.

A parachute mine is shown as an example as it was one of these weapons that caused the damage here. The unexploded mine pictured was dropped at Marthall near Knutsford. The two naval officers are unknown.

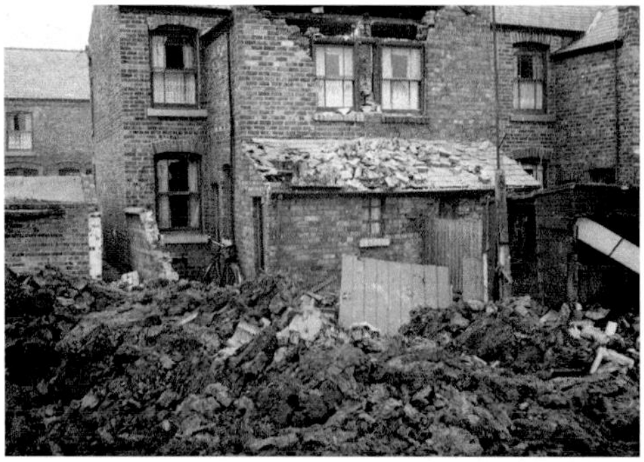

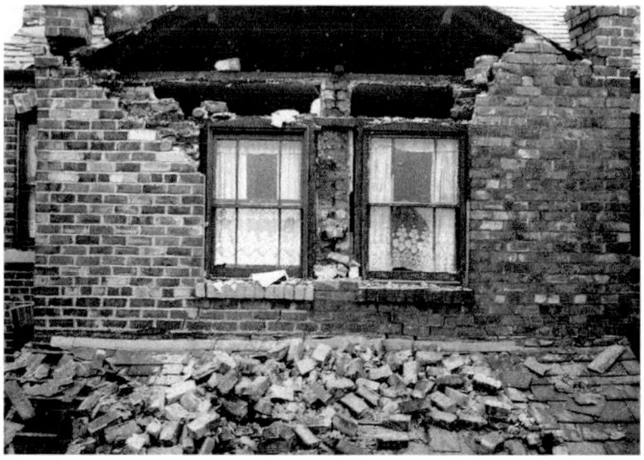

The damage a parachute mine did to Middlewich Street.

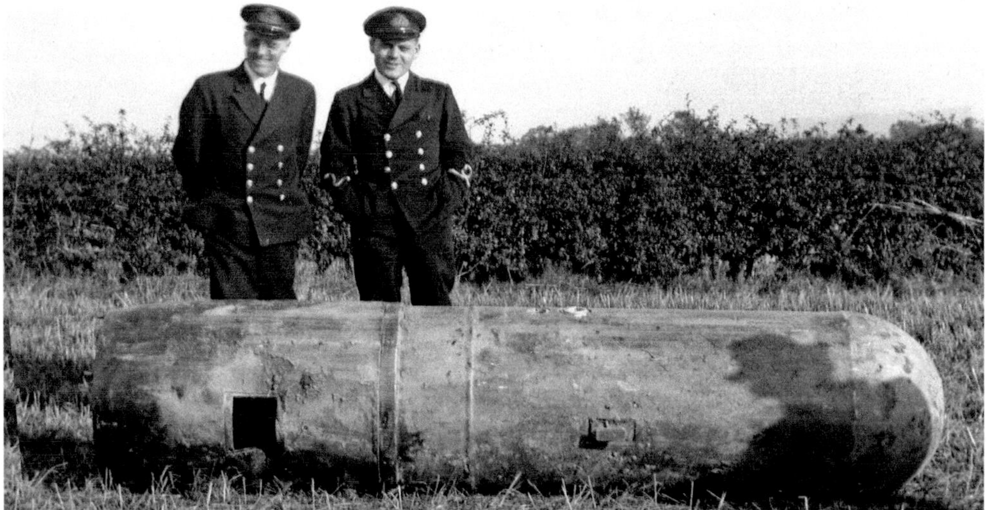

An unexploded parachute mine.

Air Raid Damage at Alton Street, Crewe

Alton Street received significant bomb damage on 26 September 1940, as can be seen in the photographs below. There are actually two shelters in the top photograph: one was fitted with additional longitudinal wooden struts, which protected it, while the other one was not, and so was totally destroyed. A woman was sheltering in the first shelter and was uninjured; no one was in the other shelter.

Alton Street.

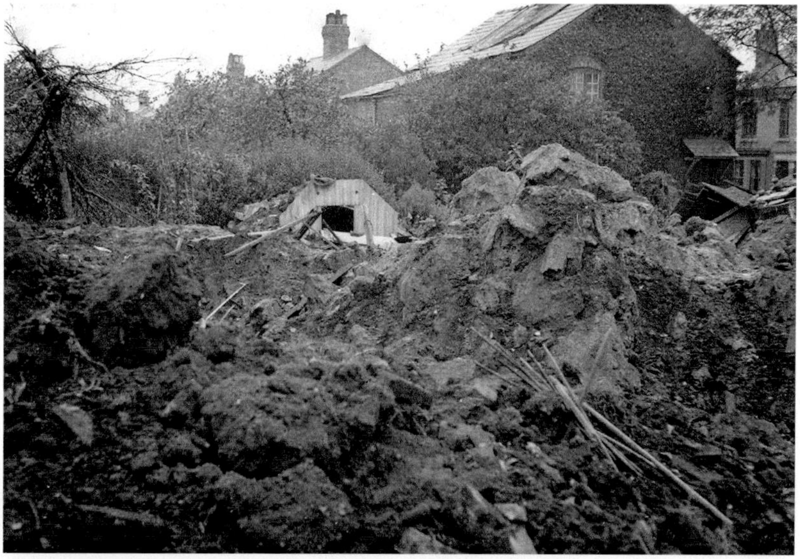

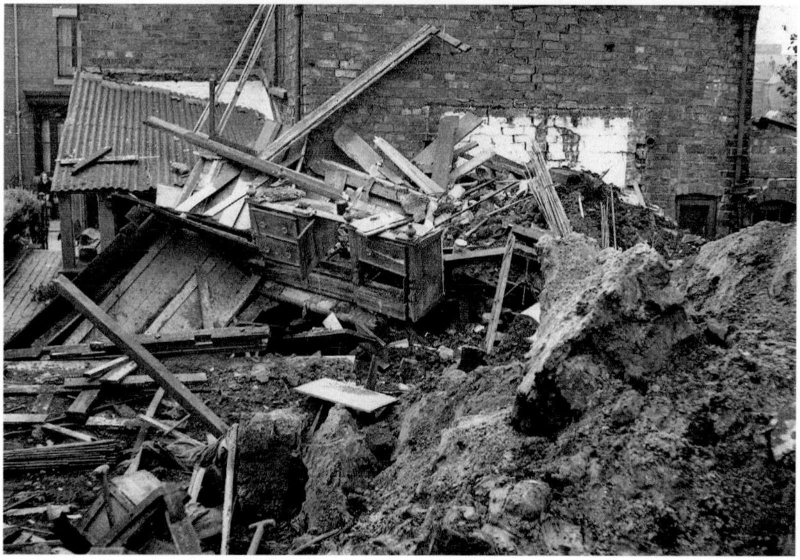

A bomb crater close to the house in Alton Street.

Air Raid Damage at Earle Street, Crewe

Earle Street was bombed on the evening of 7–8 April 1941 in one of Crewe's worst bombing incidents. Three civilians were killed at 105 Earle Street on 8 April: air raid warden Samuel Barnett, 70 years old; his wife Esther Ann, 66; and their daughter Hilda, 24. Other residents of Earle Street took refuge in St Peter's church at the end of the street.

Many people from Crewe were killed in this bombing raid, including 24-year-old Police Constable Frank Marshall and 18-year-old ARP warden Arthur Condliffe.

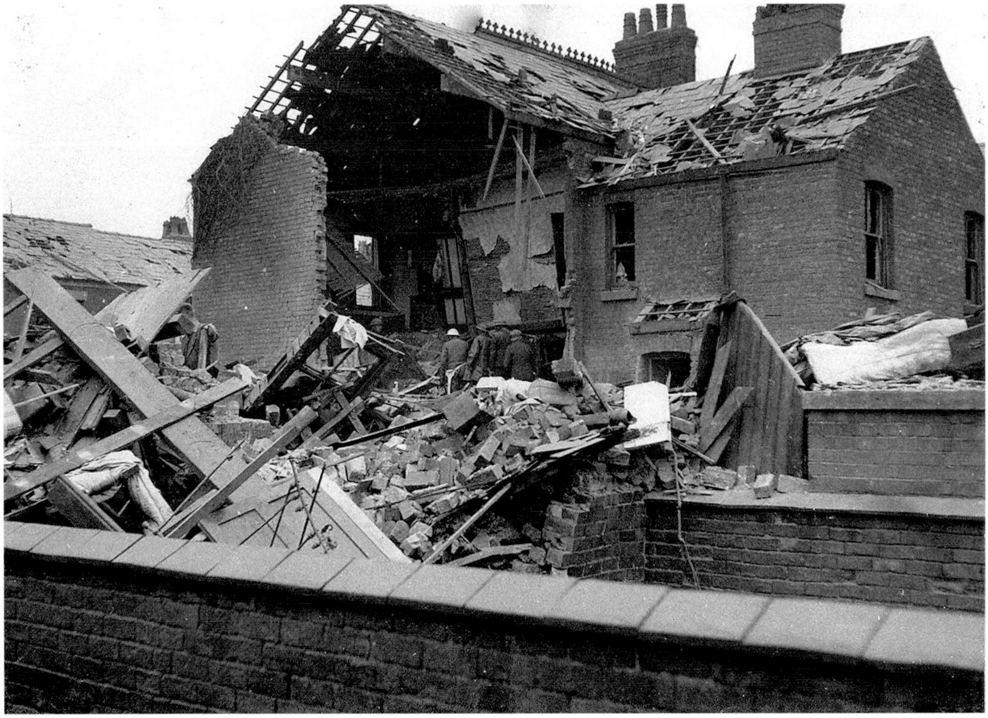

5, 6, 7 and 8 Earle Street, Crewe.

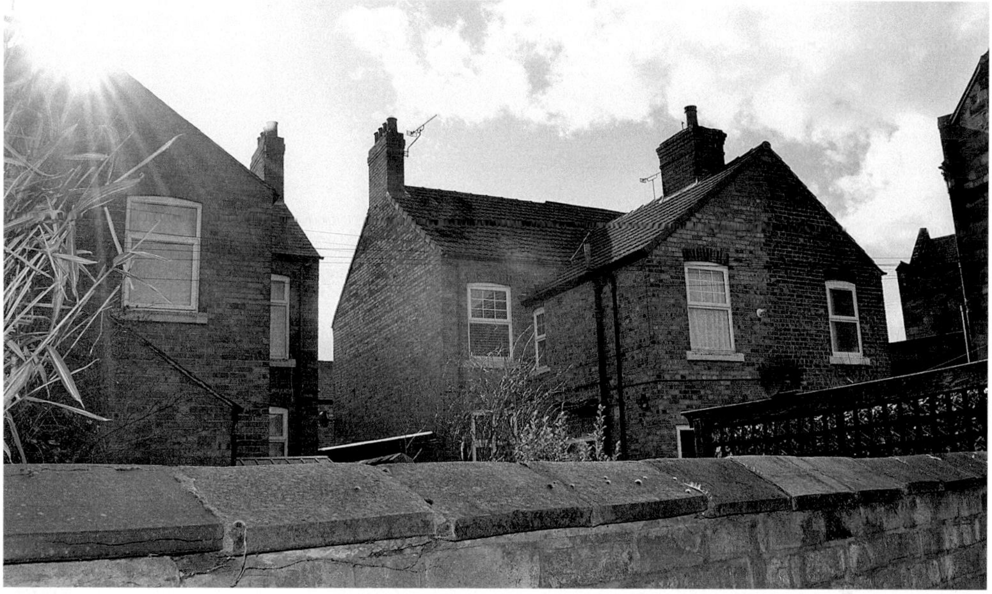

Earle Street in the present day. (Authors' collection)

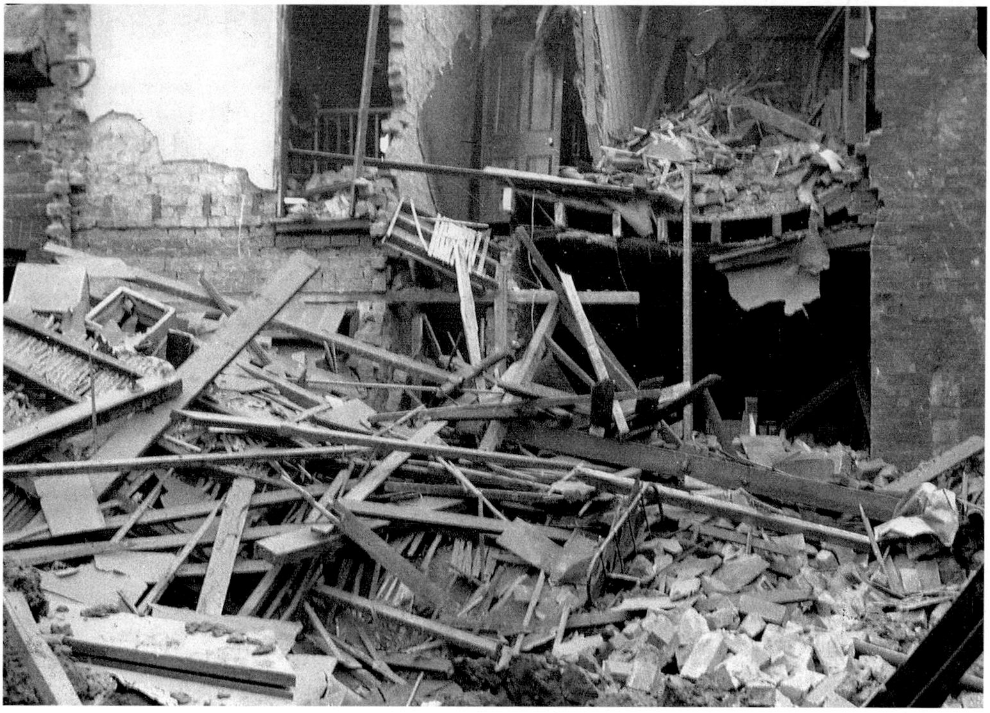

Earle Street.

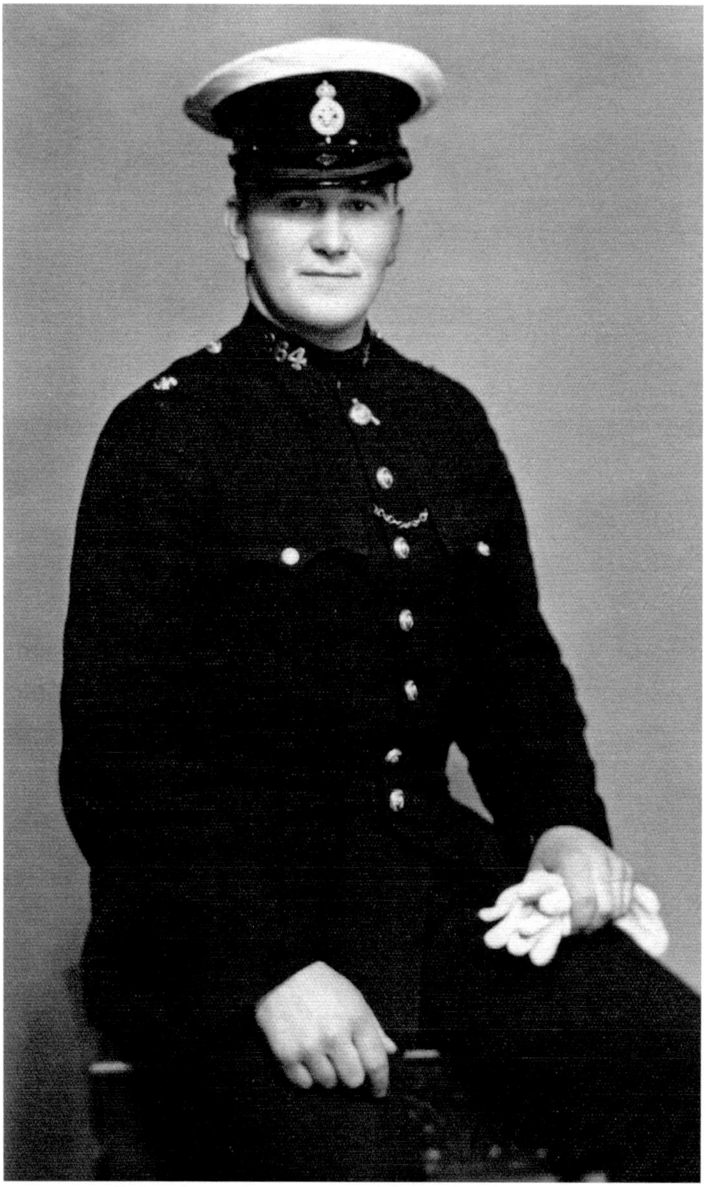
PC 264 Frank Marshall, who died in the raids of 7–8 April 1941.

Air Raid Damage at Crewe Rolls-Royce Works, 29 December 1940

In the war, the aero-engine wing of the Rolls-Royce company stepped up to meet the needs of the RAF, providing engines, especially the Merlin, for the many types of fighters and bombers.

In the 1930s, Rolls-Royce had grown out of its Derby premises and needed to improve its facilities to produce high-class motor cars. It was decided that a new factory was needed, and one was built in Crewe on what was previously farmland. Building work was completed in 1938, but by then the government was looking for a suitable location in which to build Rolls-Royce aero-engines and it decided on Crewe. Merlin engines began to roll off the production line just five months later. More than 24,000 Merlin engines would be produced there, reaching a peak in 1943, and 10,000 workers were employed. However, Crewe was a critical railway junction, with several important factories, so it was a natural target for German aircraft.

During the war, oil drums filled with waste oil were placed around the factory and would be lit during air raid warnings, giving off black smoke that went some way to concealing the buildings. Despite the camouflage, at 15:09 hours on Sunday, 29 December 1940, a German Junkers Ju 88 bomber targeted the factory. The bomb was dropped without any air raid warning. Sixteen workers were killed instantly, with another casualty dying in hospital a few days later.

After the war, a memorial consisting of a propeller containing the names of the workers who died was placed on the factory wall: William Duncan Lascelles, 29; Kathleen Minnie Lafford, 21; Muriel Fanny Higgins, 24; John Brooks Hatton, 19; Charles Harrop, 37; Ellis Brough, 43; Elsie Potts; Irene Snelson; John Abel; Gilbert Davies; Henry Frail; Reginald Lee; William Naylor; Samuel Dudley; William Williams; John Nicklin; and Cyril Nunnerley.

Post-war, aero-engine production remained at Derby and progressed from piston engines to jets, while Rolls-Royce and Bentley car production moved to the aero-engine factory at Crewe, which was its original intended purpose, More recently, Rolls-Royce manufacturing moved after a company de-merger and sale, and the Crewe factory subsequently focused on Bentleys, meaning the memorial to Rolls-Royce workers now resides in a Bentley factory.[6]

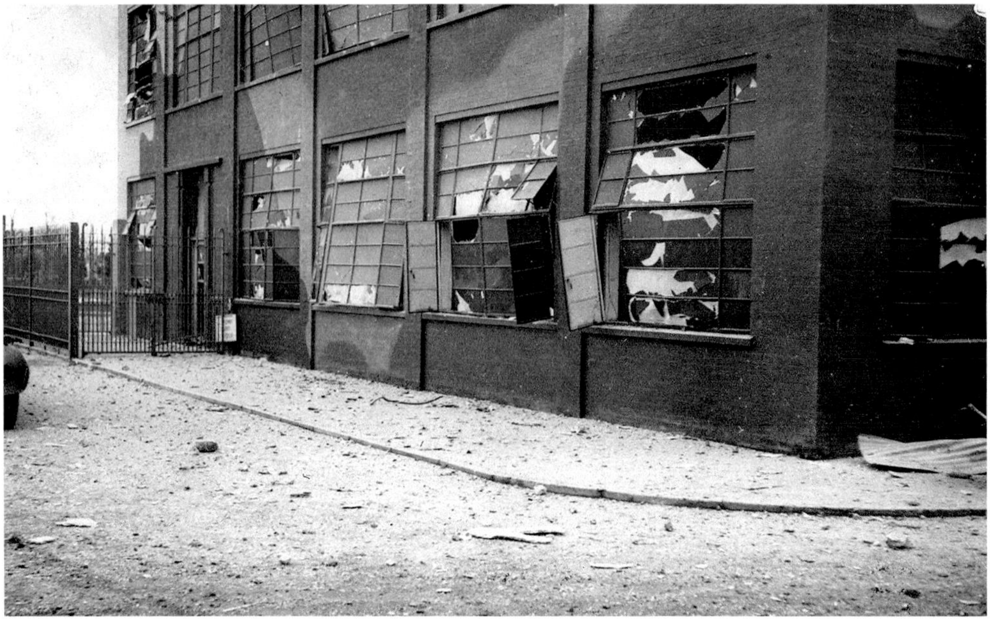

The Rolls-Royce offices.

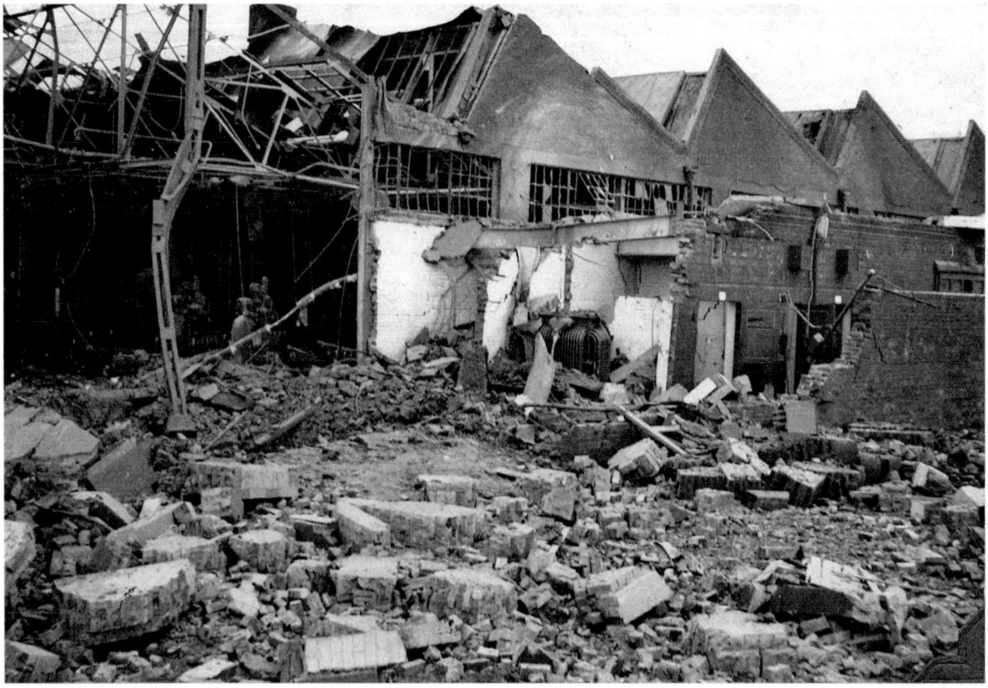

The Rolls-Royce works.

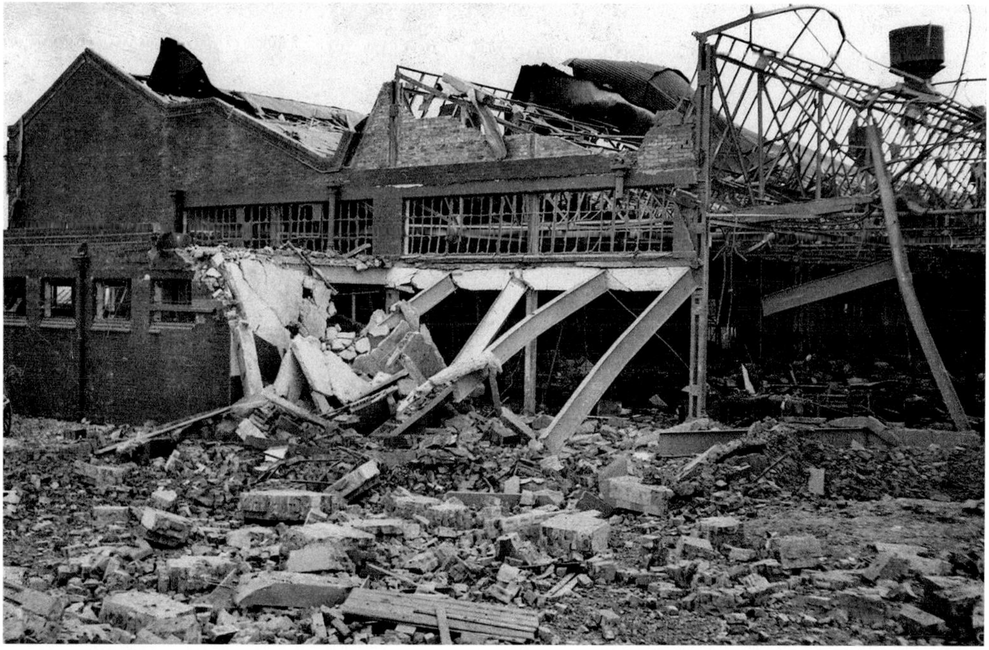

Rolls-Royce aircraft engine factory.

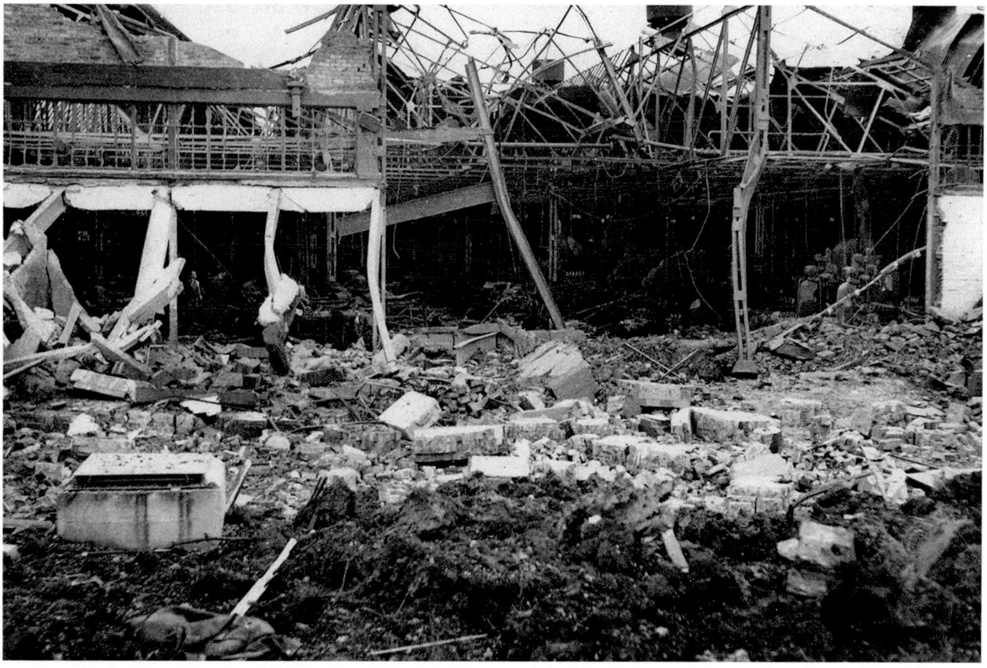

Destruction caused by a 1,000lb HE bomb.

Air Raid Damage at Brindley, Crewe

Damage was caused to Smith's Farm, Brindley, by a parachute mine on 28 November 1940. The area of damage caused by this most destructive of weapons is visible here.

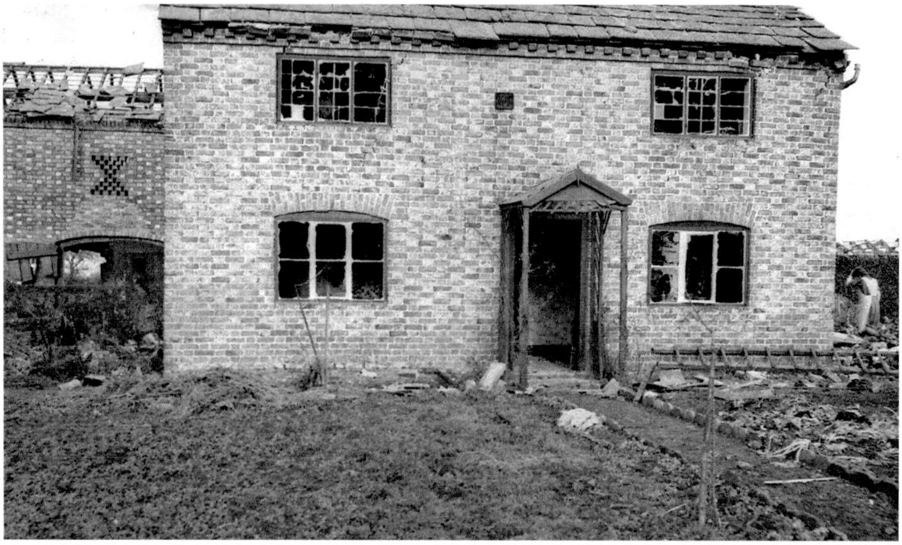

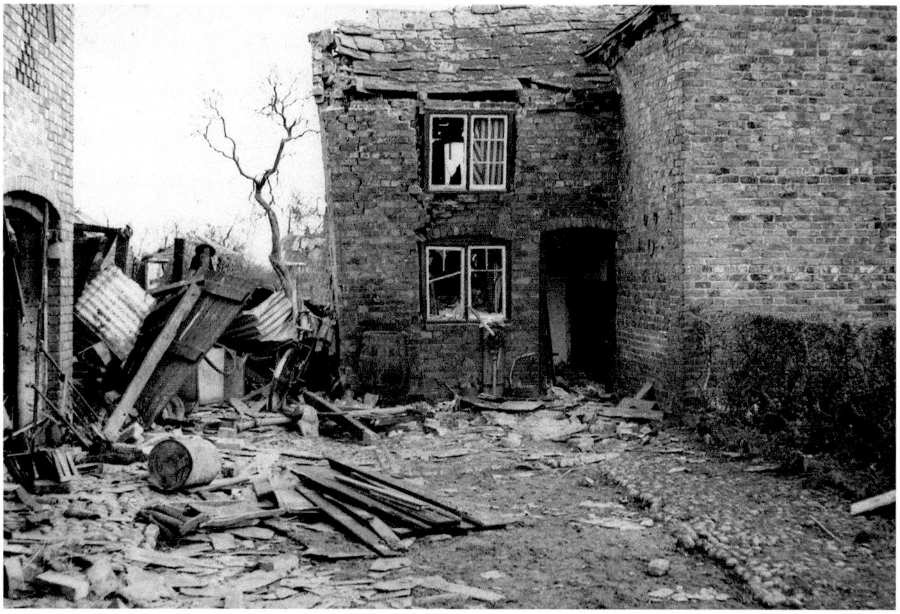

Smith's Farm, Brindley.

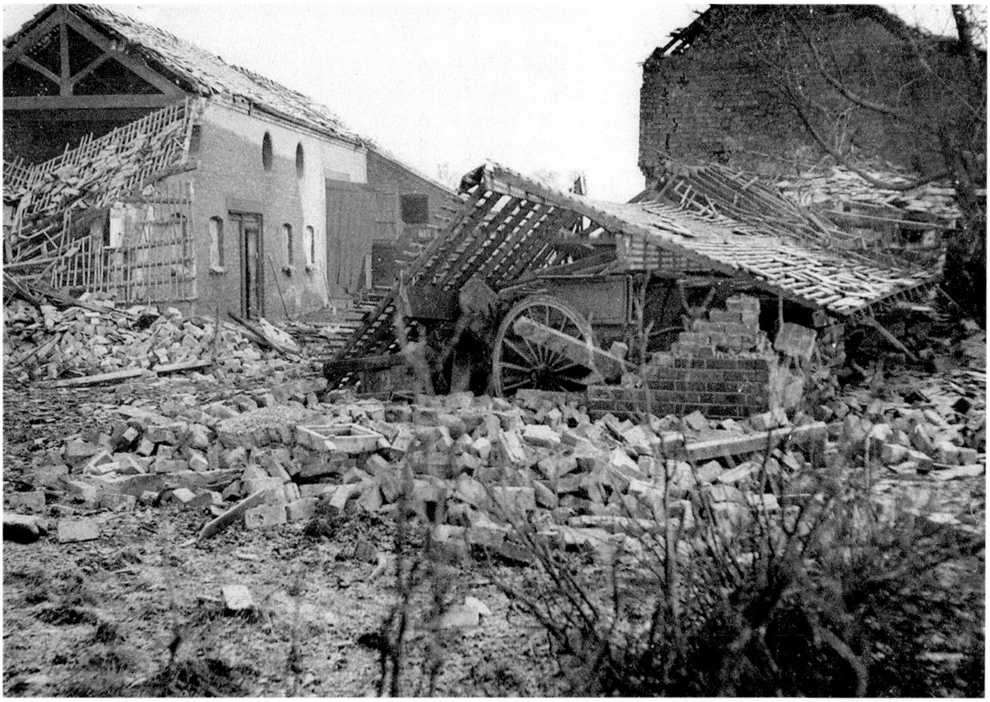

Yew Tree Farm, Wybunbury.

Air Raid Damage at Wybunbury, Crewe, 1 January 1941

Damage to farm buildings at Yew Tree Farm, Wybunbury. A bomb at this location can only have been the result of a dropped leftover bomb, as the farm was not a primary target, but the damage was considerable.

Air Raid Damage at Nantwich Road, Crewe, 3 August 1940

Two photographs showing a 110lb bomb and the hole that had to be dug to deactivate and recover it. The hole was 23ft deep, with a 3ft tunnel at the bottom. This gives a good example of just how deep a bomb can penetrate underground, depending, of course, on the consistency of the ground it penetrates. Fortunately, the bomb didn't explode, but such efforts were not always successful.

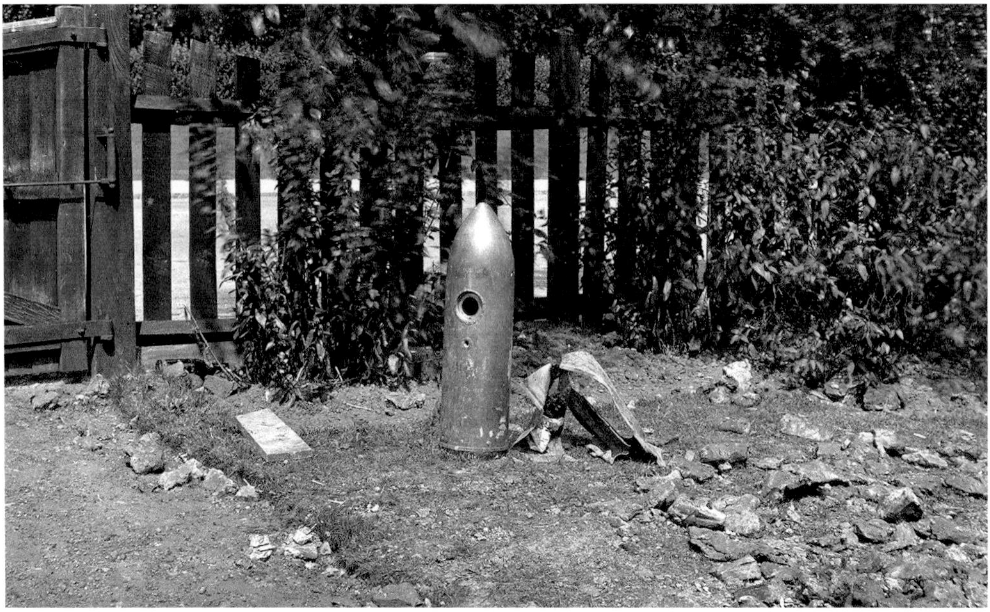

The unexploded bomb.

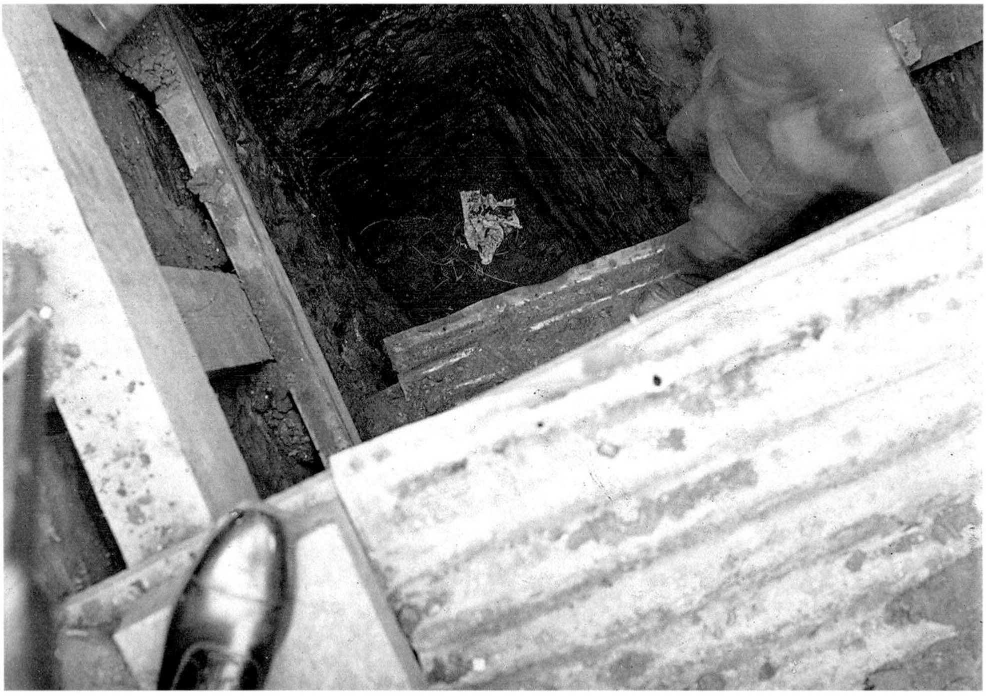

The depth of hole required to remove the bomb.

It is time to give a mention to the brave men responsible for deactivating unexploded bombs, which obviously was a hazardous occupation. Two weeks later, on 17 August 1940, they were not so lucky:

> Six brave men from the Royal Engineers Bomb Disposal team sadly lost their lives trying to defuse a bomb in the fields around Nantwich in Cheshire. The location was near Alvaston Hall. Initially it was thought that the bomb that killed the men was one of five German bombs that were dropped on the same night, in the area around Nantwich, from what was believed to be one single German Bomber, most likely a Heinkel He III, returning from a bombing raid in Liverpool.[7]

There is also evidence to suggest that these bombs could have fallen from separate raids over a number of nights: one fell in a field at Mile House Farm in Worleston; another at Windy Arbour in Nantwich; one at Brook Farm, Alvaston; one behind 8 Birchin Lane in Nantwich; and one behind Dairy House Farm, Colleys Lane, Willaston.

As previously mentioned, certain bombs could be set to detonate by a timer between landing and around seven days later. Hence, the time delay was built in with the intention of killing the disposal team and civilians unaware of the bomb. The six men from the Royal Engineers bomb disposal unit were sent out to attempt to disarm four German bombs that had not detonated on impact. It was initially thought that these were dropped in an attack on Crewe Works, but it transpired that they came from a bomber on its way back from a raid on Liverpool, and the pilot had decided to jettison its bombs over Nantwich.

The men – Sergeant Edward Greengrass, Sapper Harold Thompson, Sapper Michael Lambert, Sapper Albert Edward Fearon, Sapper George Lucas and Sapper John Percival – defused three bombs. However, when they tried to defuse another, it exploded, and at least four of the men died instantly. In the next two days, John Percival and Edward Greengrass also died.

Due to concerns over security and morale, the incident remained secret during the war, and the men's names were not included on war memorials in Crewe or Nantwich. More recently, the Crewe branch of the Royal Engineers decided that a memorial should be erected, and this was unveiled on Sunday, 7 October 2012.[8] The memorial stone is located in the gardens of Alvaston Hall, which was chosen as it is the nearest suitable site to the original incident.

Air Raid Damage at Wheelock, 26 April 1941

Wheelock is a small village near Sandbach that was severely damaged on the night of 26 April 1941. The bombers may have been aiming for the Crewe Works, approximately 3–4 miles away.

A parachute mine landed close to Crewe Road, Wheelock, which damaged many buildings, including the Wheelock Methodist church opposite Chapel Street as it joins Crewe Road. Wheelock Methodist church, now part of Unity Methodist church, has a history dating back to 1874. The building was designed by George B. Ford of Burslem and built in 1872. In the 1873 returns of accommodation, it was listed as seating 232; however, by the time of the 1940 statistical returns, it could accommodate 430.

Two of the photographs feature the church on Crewe Road. After the damage shown in the first photo, it was completely restored and is open to this day, as seen in the second.

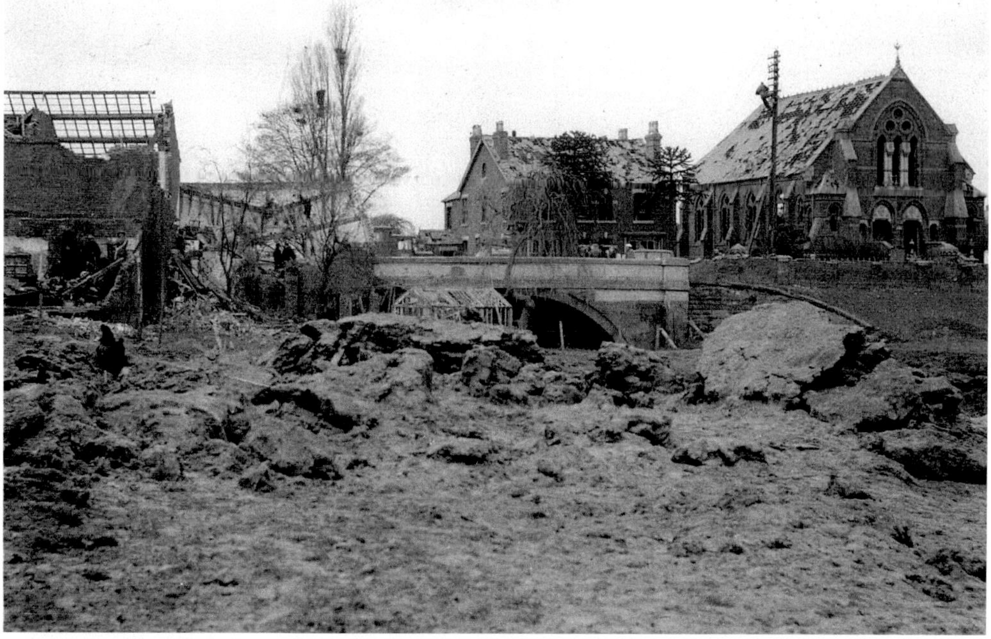

Wheelock after being hit by a parachute mine; the Methodist church is on the right.

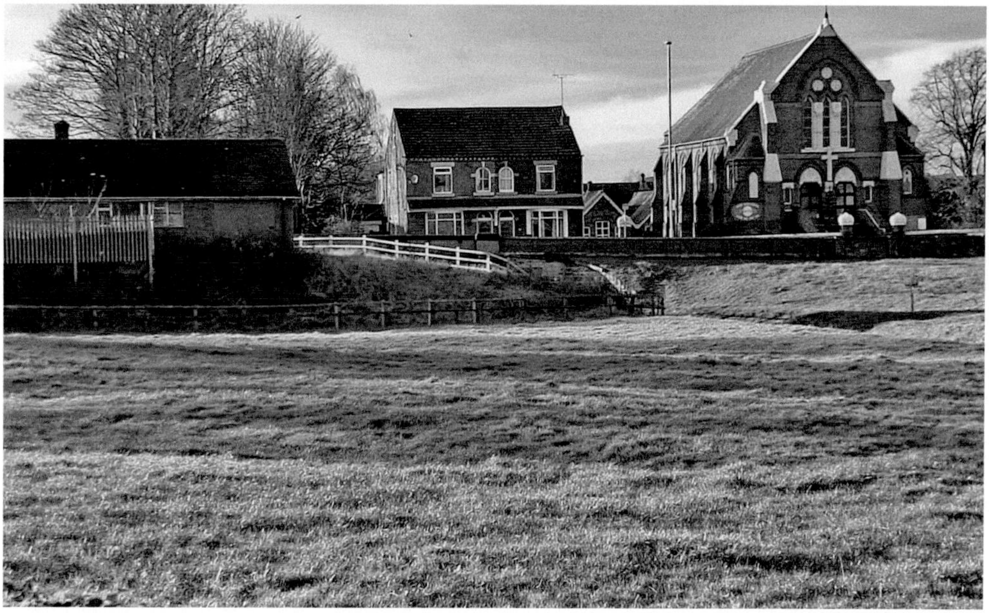

Wheelock in the present day. (Authors' collection)

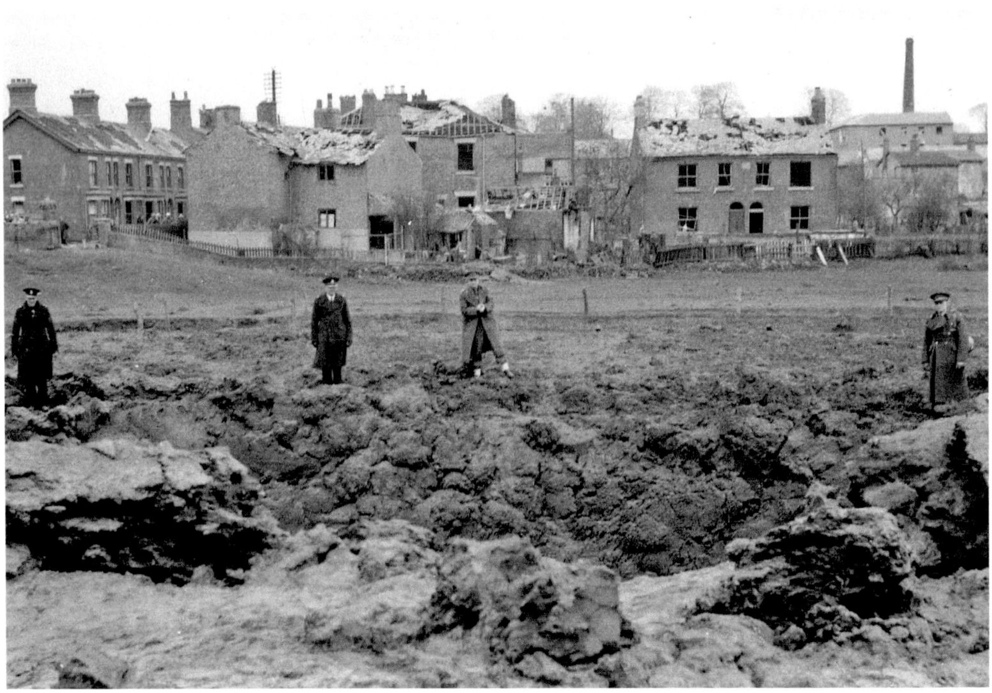

Wheelock.

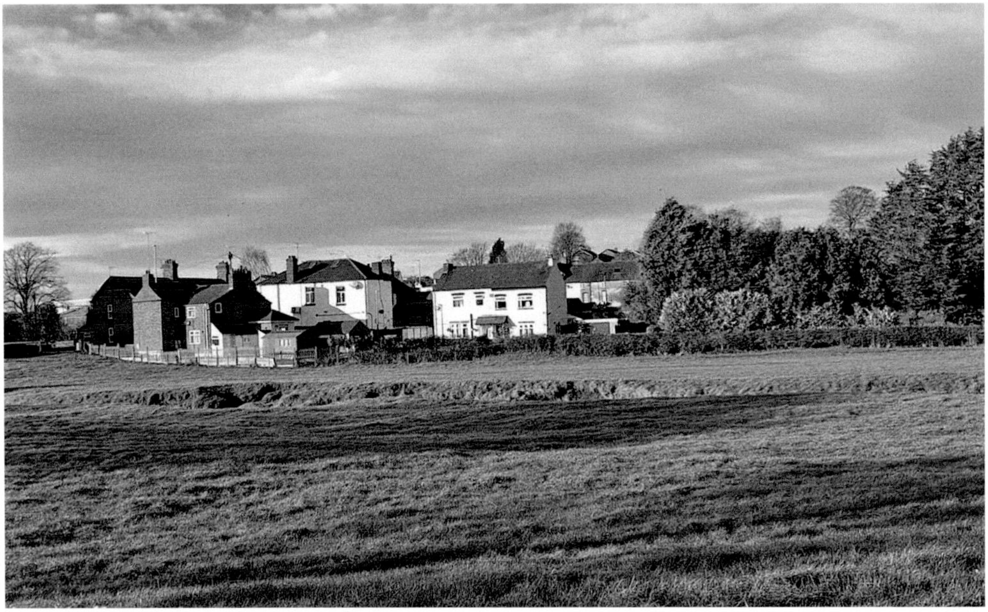

Wheelock in the present day. (Authors' collection)

3

Mid Cheshire

Air Raid Damage at Bunbury, 28 November 1940

The site of St Boniface in the picturesque village of Bunbury has had a church on it since the eighth century. The original Anglo-Saxon wooden church was replaced by a stone Norman church in 1135; this was rebuilt in 1320, before undergoing further rebuilding in the late 1300s under Sir Hugh Calveley. Much of the current church dates from this period. On 28 November 1940, a German aircraft returning from a night raid on Liverpool jettisoned several bombs over the village, damaging the church and surrounding village. The bombs caused the destruction of Church Row, which has now been rebuilt. The damage to the church was fortunately slight compared with other targets and has since been rectified.

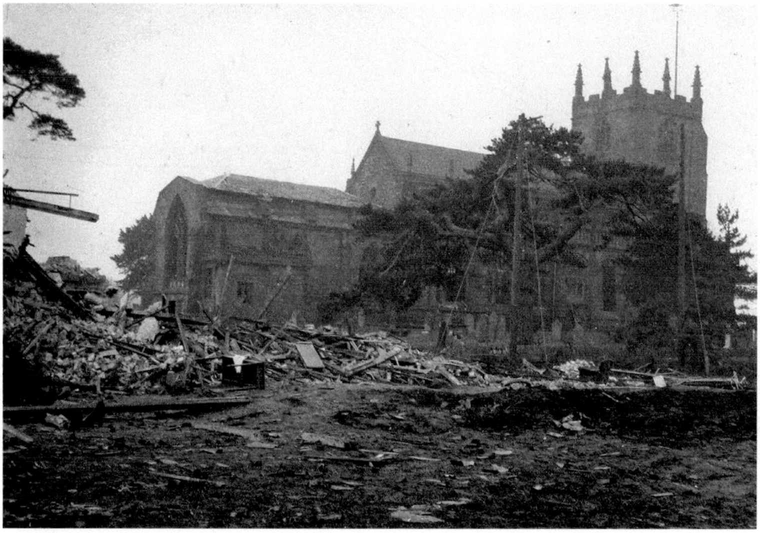

Damage caused by a HE bomb at Bunbury.

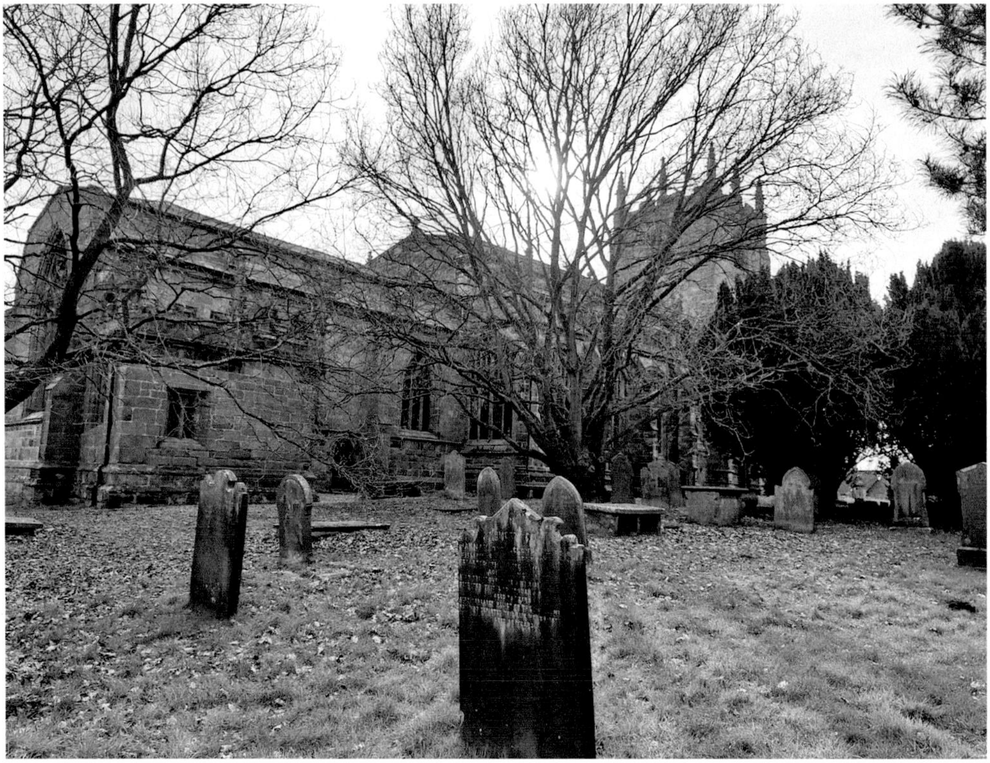

The same view in the present day. (Authors' collection)

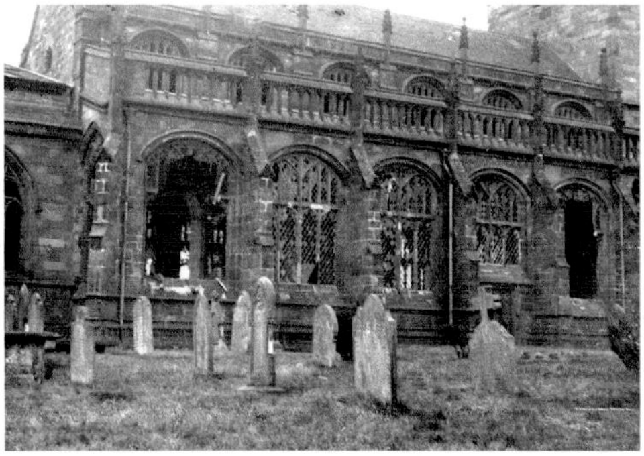

More damage caused by a HE bomb at Bunbury.

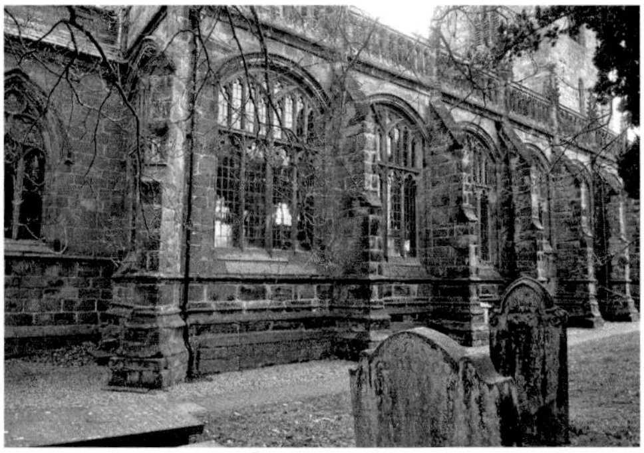

The same view in the present day. (Authors' collection)

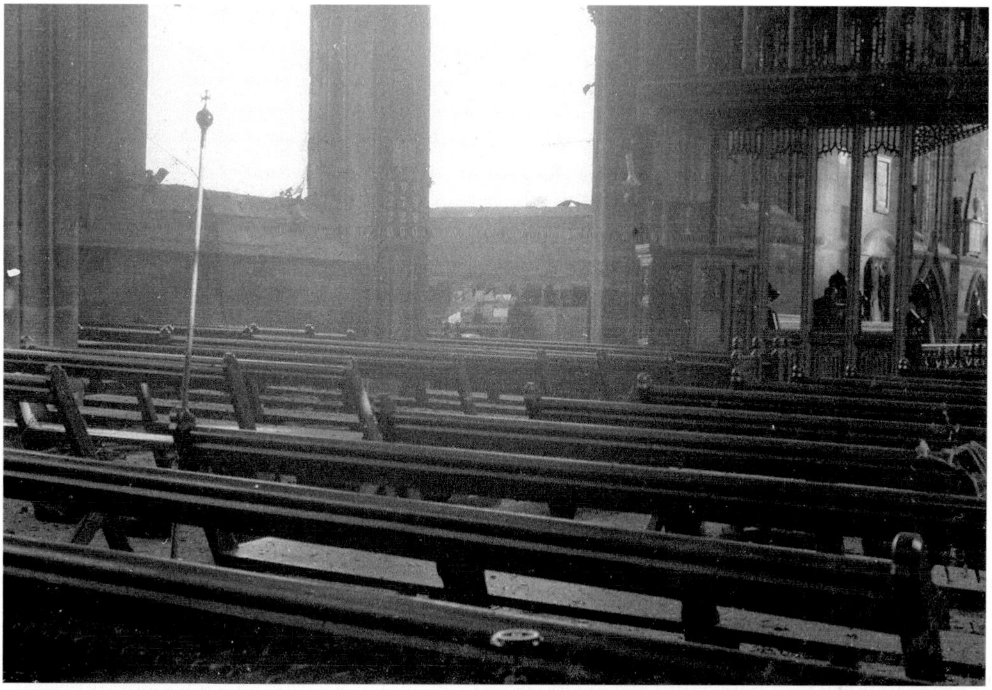

Interior damage to St Boniface's, caused by a HE bomb.

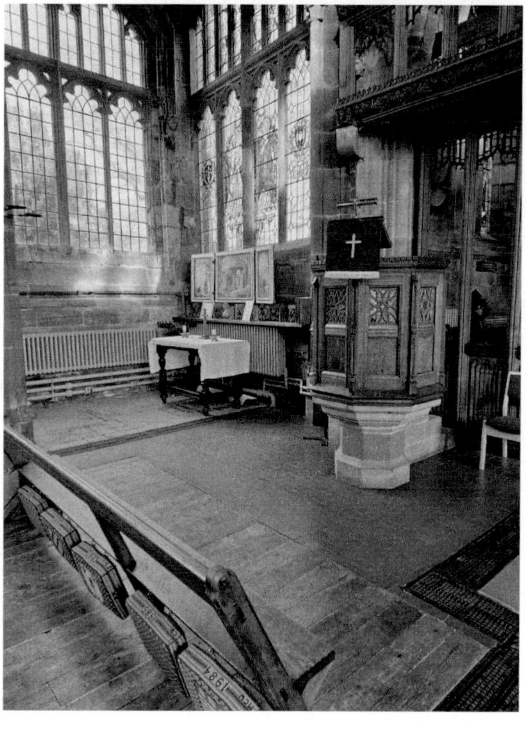

The same view today. (Authors' collection)

Air Raid Damage at Northwich, 25 October 1941

The damage to Messrs Bates Works in Northwich was caused by a parachute mine, which dropped approximately 200 yards away at the edge of a flash of water on wasteland at the rear of Witton Foundry, Station Road, at 21:05 hours. It damaged over 250 houses and shops but there were no casualties.

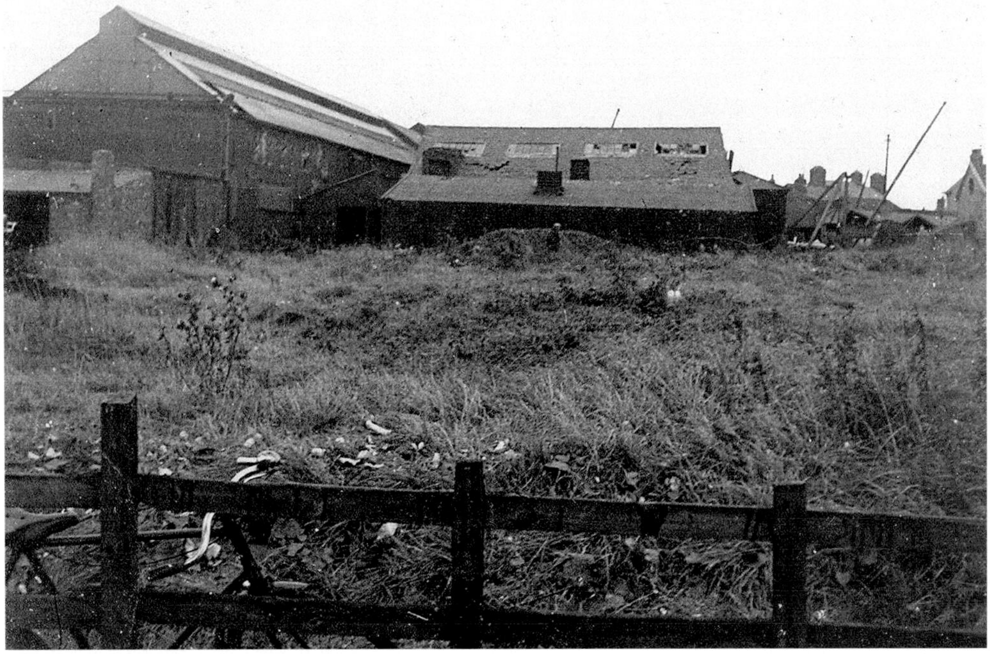

Damage to Messrs Bates Works, Northwich.

Air Raid Damage at Weaverham, 28 November 1940

Two photographs showing damage caused by a parachute mine to a farmhouse and buildings at Nook Farm, Weaverham.

Nook Farmhouse was one of the prettiest in the area and was situated at the junction of Grange Lane and West Road (now part of the roundabout on the new bypass). On Thursday, 28 November 1940, there were six people in the house when a 500lb bomb landed in one of the nearby fields. Some glass was broken in the windows, but the people in the house remained inside. They were still there, sitting around the fire, when the house received an almost direct hit from a parachute mine that landed about 20 yards from the house. These mines contained 1,000lb of high explosives and were designed to cause maximum damage – in this instance, a cottage at the top of Forest

Street had the gable end blown off, and the buildings on West Road were severely damaged. Meanwhile, all six at the farm were injured, some of them seriously. Had it not been for the big oak beams that held up the roof, everyone would have died.

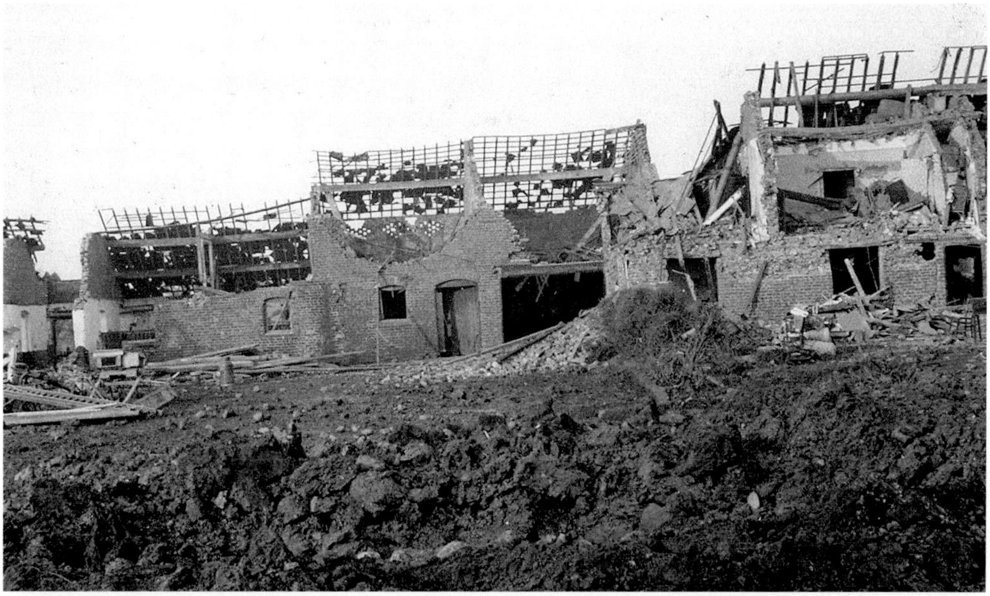

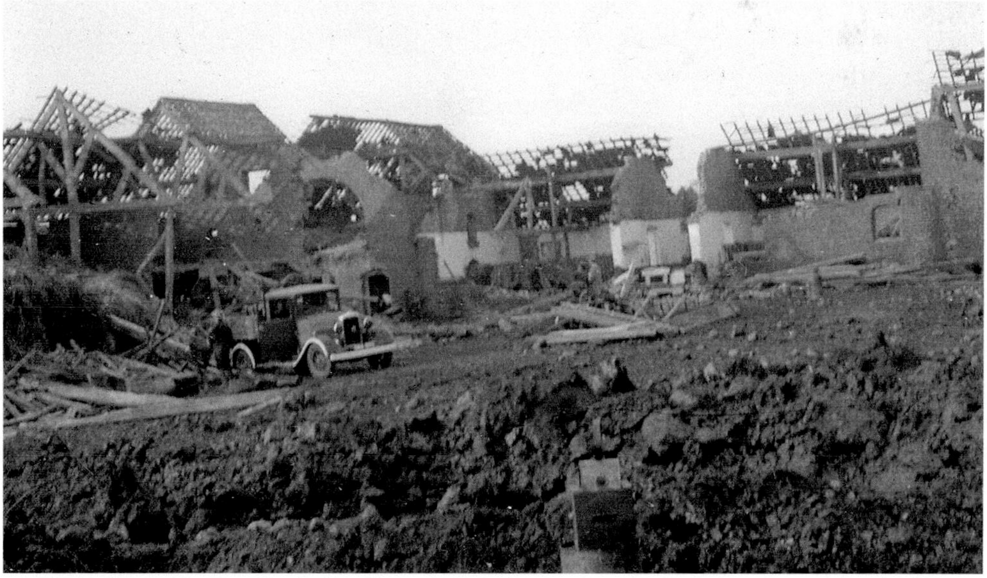

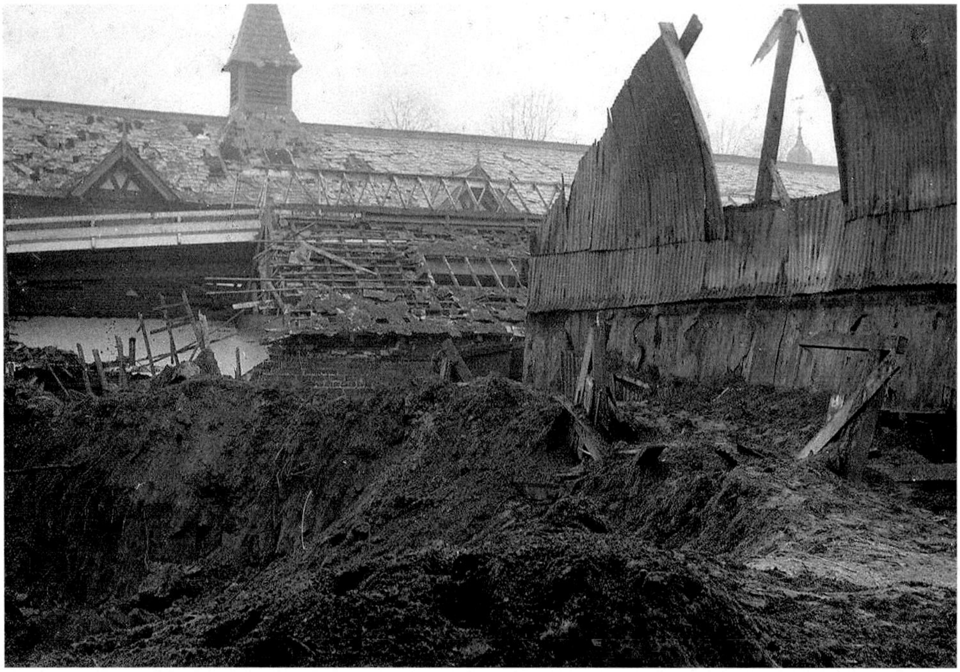

Damage caused by a HE bomb to farm buildings at Bostock Hall.

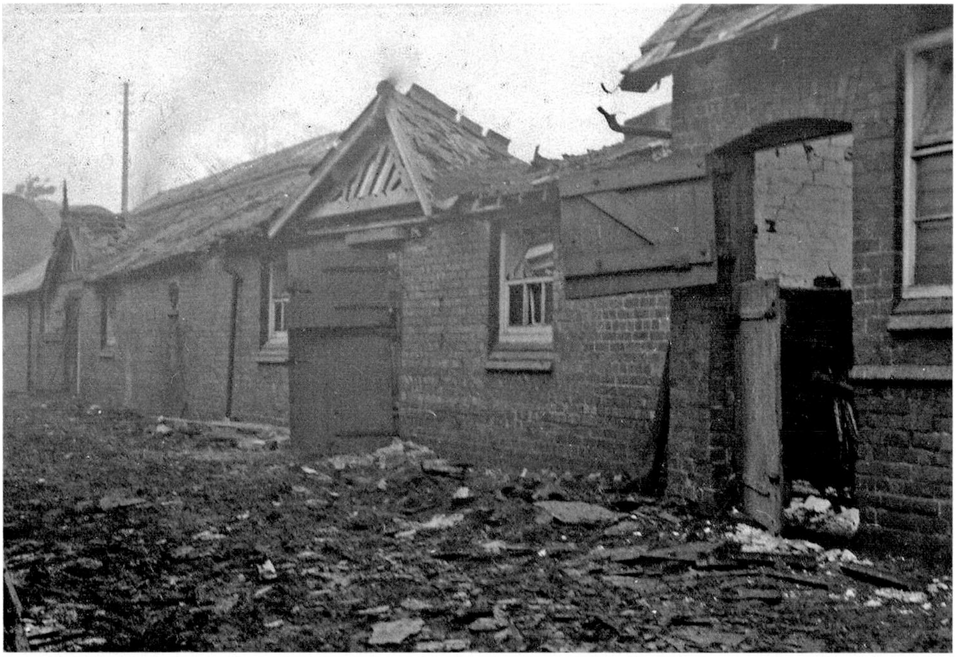

Bomb damage to farm buildings at Bostock.

Air Raid Damage at Bostock Hall, Middlewich, 28 November 1940

Three photographs showing damage caused by a HE bomb to farm buildings at Bostock Hall, Middlewich, a former Georgian house. The original build date is lost to time, but it was rebuilt in 1775 for Edward Tomkinson, and further alterations and additions were carried out around 1875. Fortunately, although the outbuildings were damaged, the hall itself sustained only minor damage. The building is now divided into apartments.

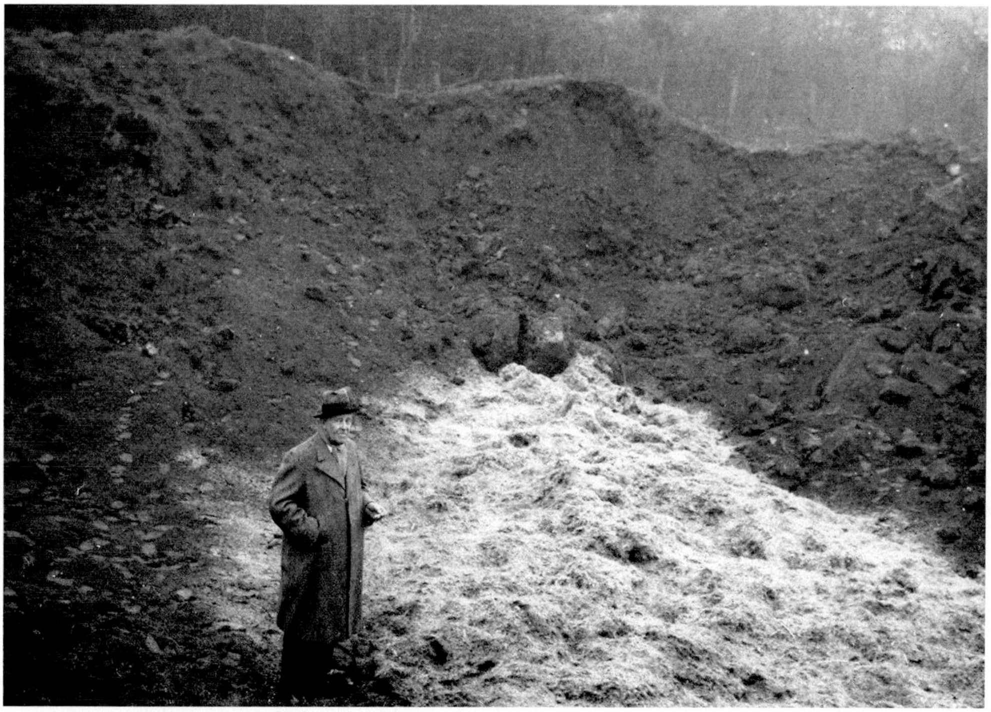

Bomb crater at Bostock Hall.

Damage at Little Budworth, 28 November 1940

Two photographs showing damage caused by a HE bomb to a house named Hawkswood, a large, high-class house sitting among the shrubbery of Little Budworth Common. It was very unfortunate to be hit by a German bomb at that location – one possible reason could be that the American Army had a camp on the common and on the grounds of nearby Oulton Hall and the Luftwaffe had targeted this camp. The house has now been completely restored and extended.

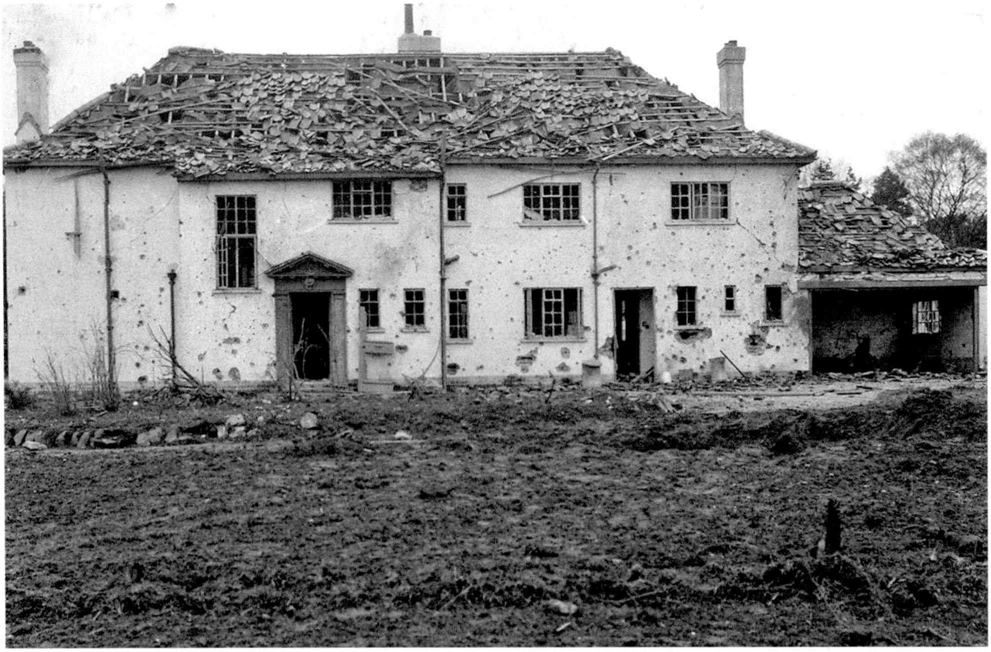

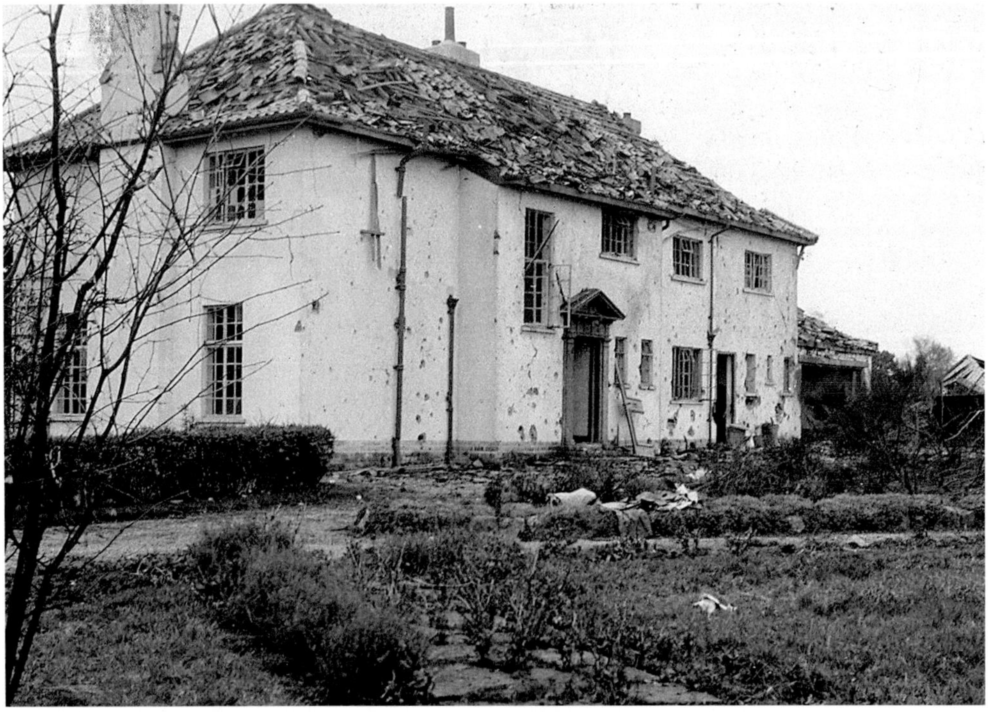

Damage caused by a HE bomb to Hawkswood, Little Budworth.

Bomb Dropped at Winsford at 01:15 Hours on 5 May 1941
When Winsford became the target for the Luftwaffe, an unexploded 500lb bomb failed to go off after landing in a field belonging to Woodford Hall Farm.

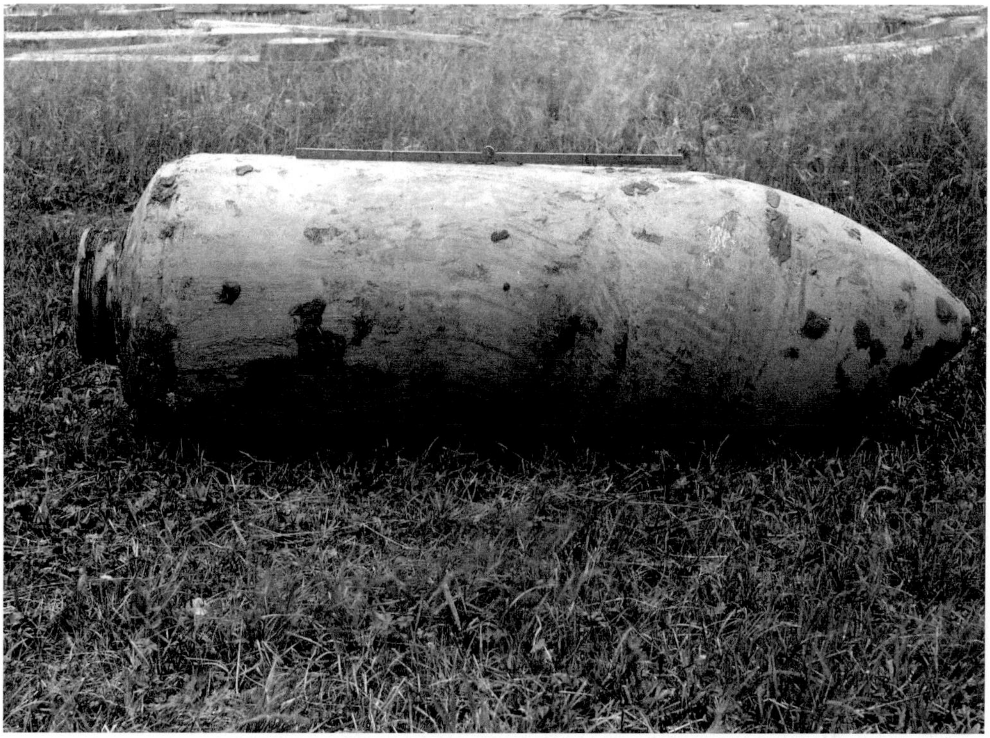

Air Raid Damage at Delamere, 28 November 1940
The first photo overleaf shows the damage that was caused to a house at Abbey Wood Estate, an area within Delamere, Cheshire. The bomb fell some 500 yards from the house and buildings at Abbey Wood, at a location known as Old Pale. This meant that the damage at Abbey Wood was relatively minor, consisting of broken windows and a damaged roof. The Abbey Wood Estate is situated near the Vale Royal Abbey Arms pub, off the main road between Chester and Manchester, and is now open to the public as a venue for weddings and other events.

Grange Cottages, close to the nearby Fishpool Inn, Delamere, also suffered relatively minor damage.

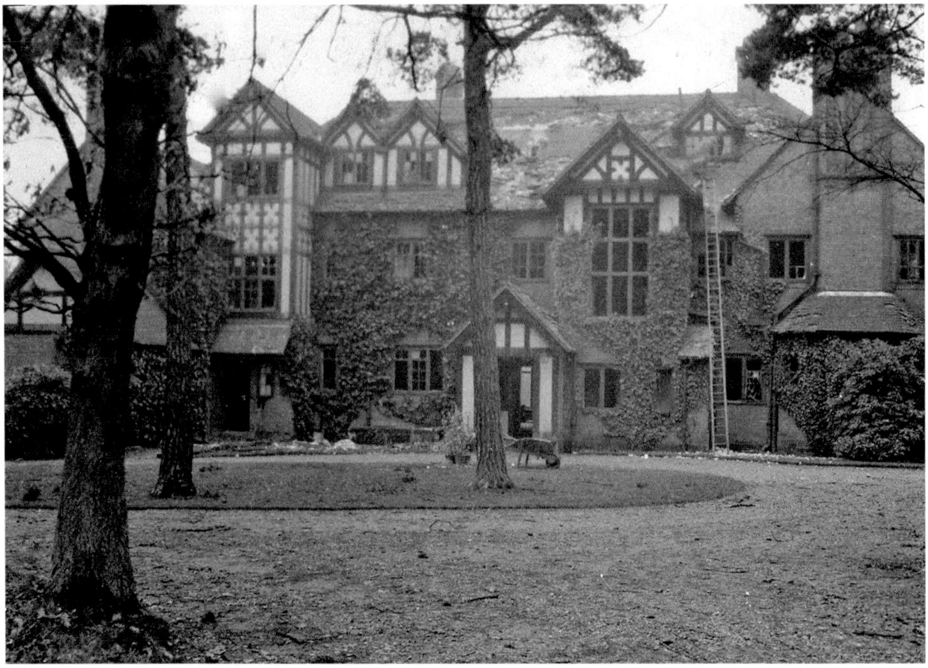

Damage to the house and buildings at Abbey Wood, Delamere, caused by a HE bomb.

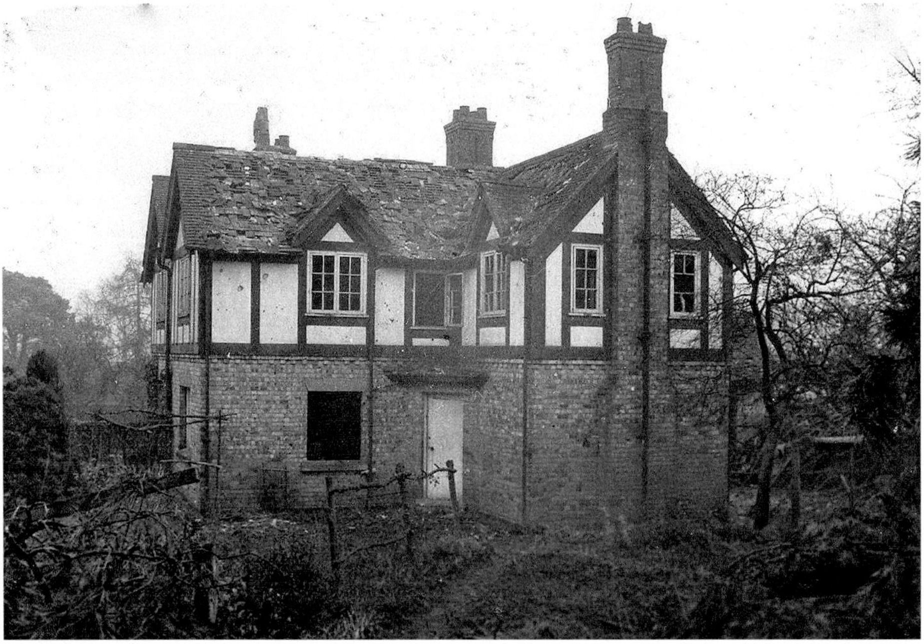

Damage at Grange Cottage, Delamere.

Air Raid Damage at Cotebrook, 28 November 1940

A lorry that ran into a bomb crater on the Tarporley Road at Cotebrook. It was carrying what looks like tree cuttings, showing us that, even in those early days of the war, life carried on – but with drawbacks such as big holes in the road.

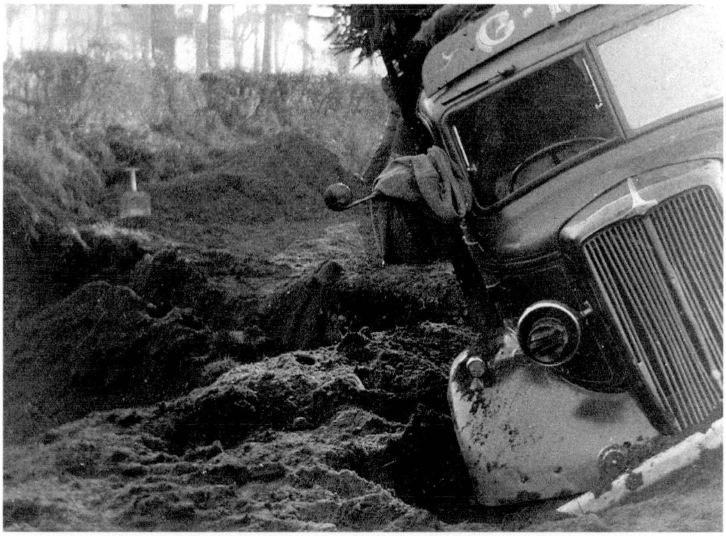

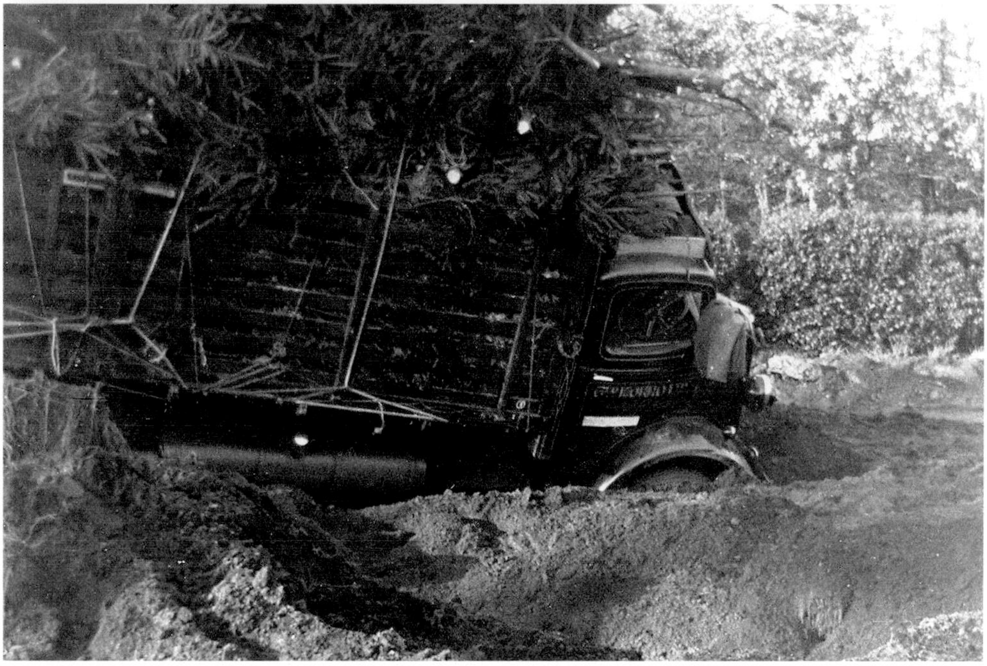

Air Raid Damage at Winsford, 8 October 1940

Photographs showing the damage caused to the Salt Union Wagon Repair Depot in Winsford by high-explosive bomb splinters. In the late 1800s, numerous salt workings existed in mid Cheshire; as a result, sixty-six salt operators from the area, led by a salt magnate, formed the Salt Union to manage the mines and stabilise prices throughout the industry. In 1892, problems persisted as the Northwich mines competed with the primary Winsford mine, resulting in overcapacity. As a result, Winsford's mine at Meadow Bank was closed. However, salt mining in Northwich was not particularly successful: it caused significant damage to the land above the mines, resulting in substantial subsidence that would ultimately lead to the closure of the last mine in 1928. The Winsford mine would then reopen, and remains open to this day, providing most of the country's salt for road use and other purposes. To transport the salt and coal for the furnaces, the ICI, as it was then, built its own railway linked to the main lines, both at the West Coast Main Line and the Chester–Manchester, Cheshire Lines Railway. The workshop was bombed on 8 October 1940.[9]

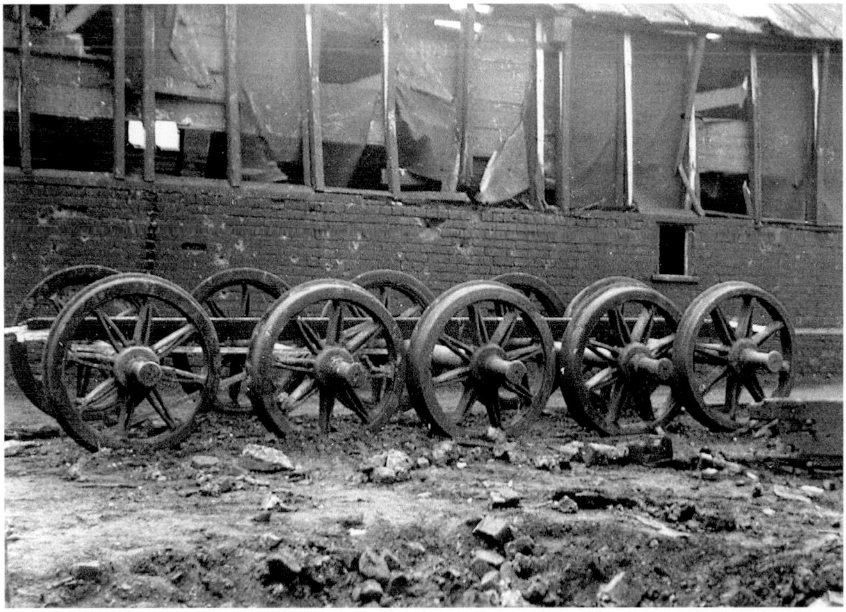

Building and wagon wheels.

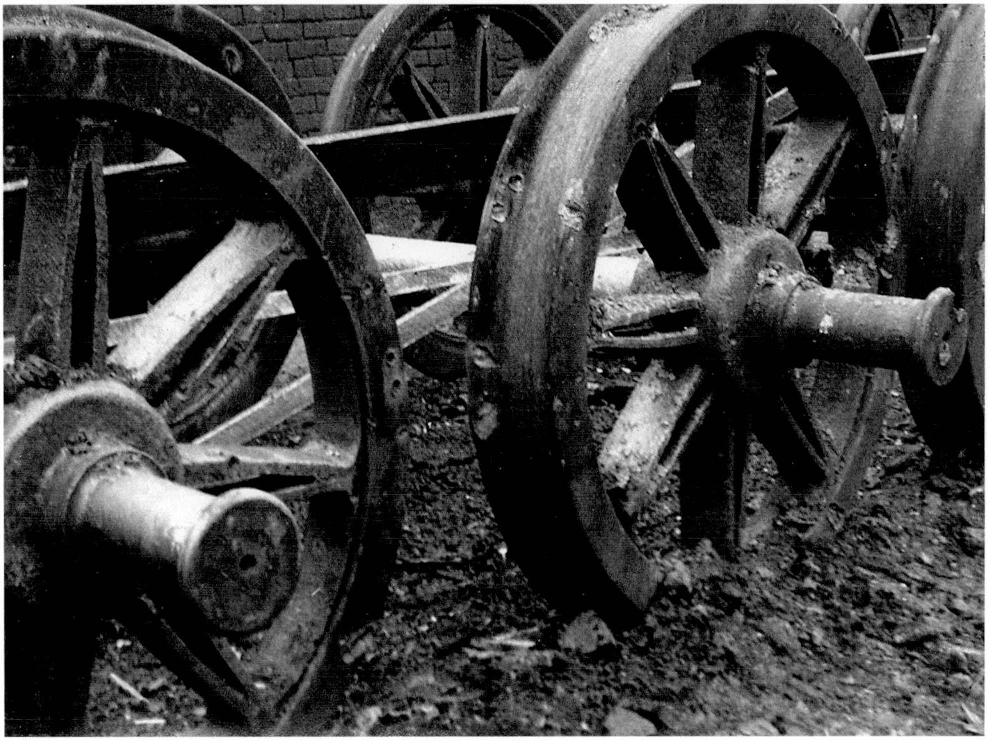

Wagon wheels showing shrapnel marks in the heavy steel.

Air Raid Damage at the Canal Lock, Tiverton, 25 October 1941
Three photographs showing damage to property caused by a parachute mine. Luckily, there was no one in the house when the mine dropped. At this time, the lock would have been busy with canal traffic working for the war effort.

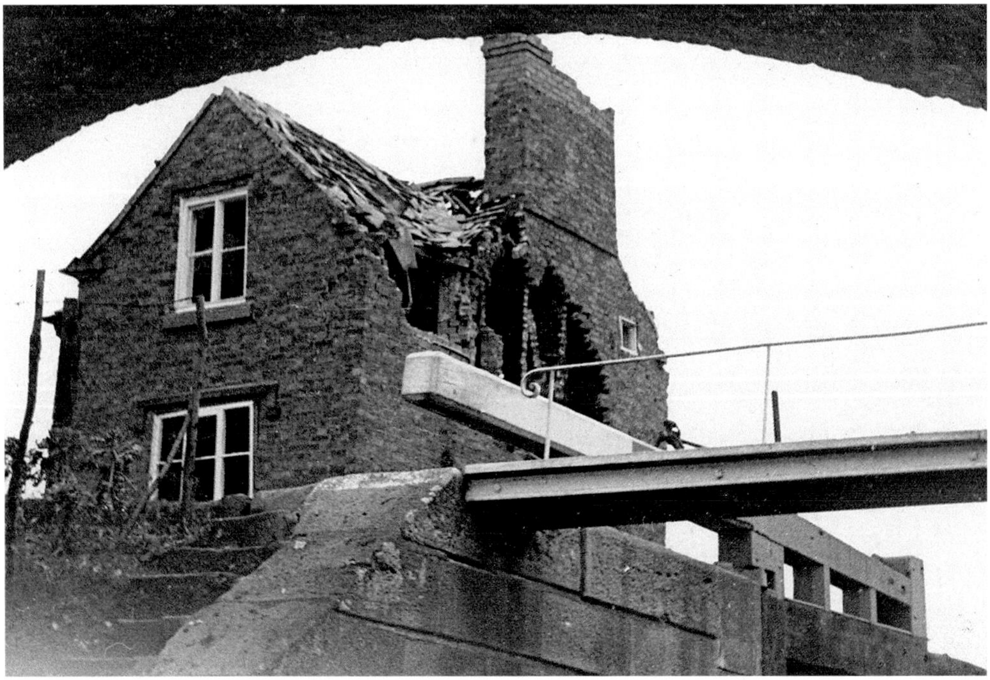

A view from the lock.

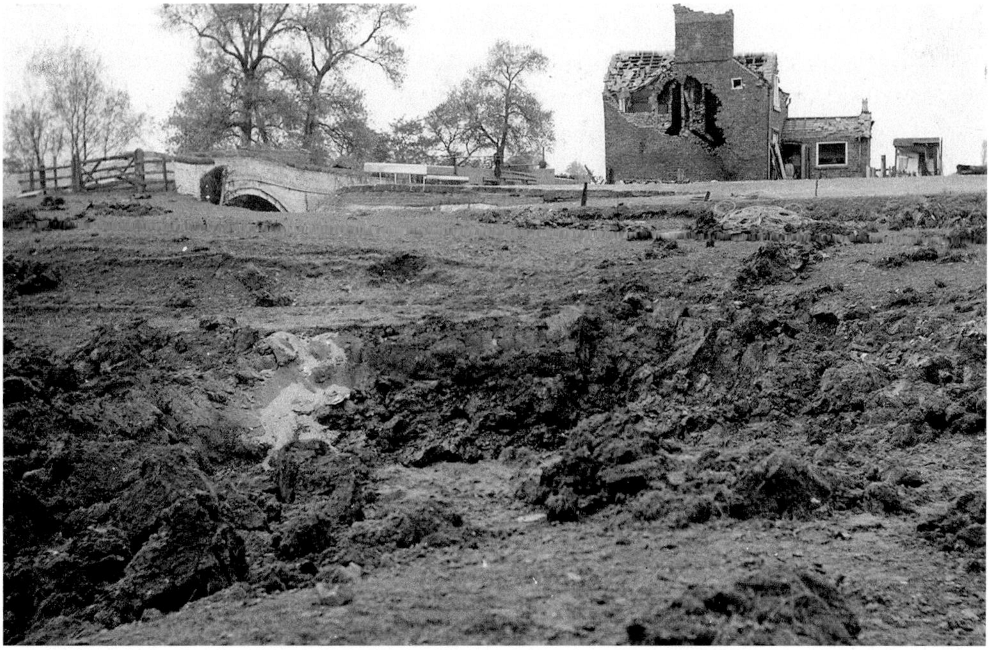

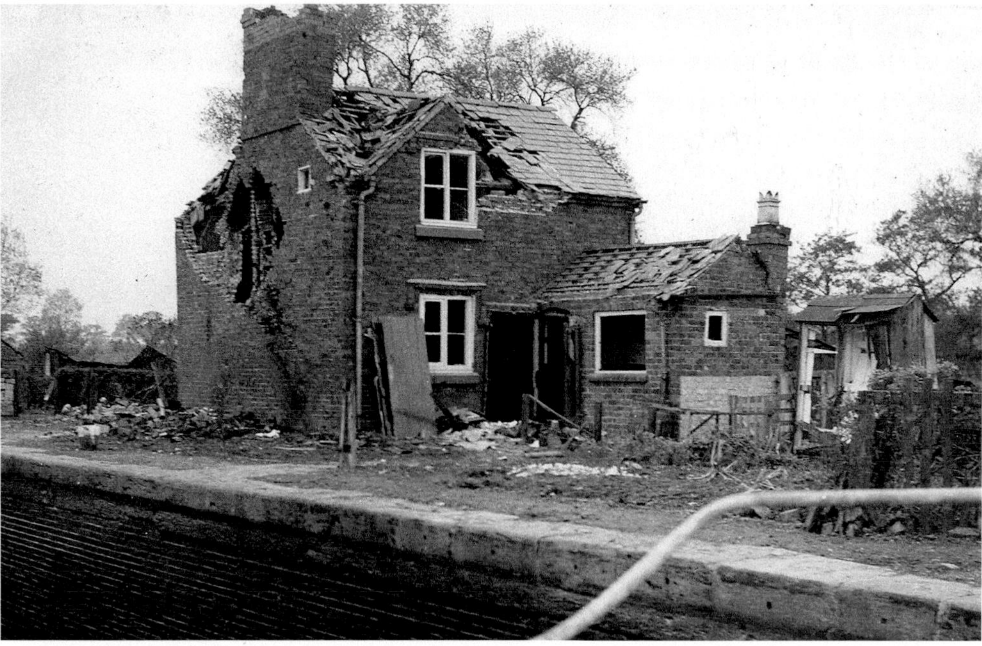

Tiverton Lock House.

Air Raid Damage at Barbridge, 8 October 1940

Damage to property at Barbridge, at the junction of two canals. Like at Tiverton, the bombs would have hit at a busy time.

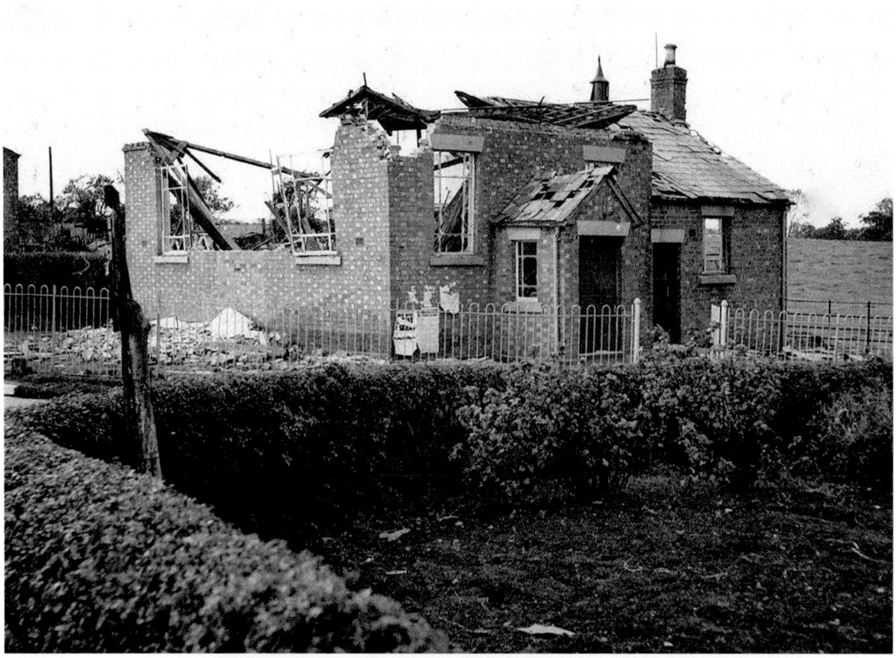

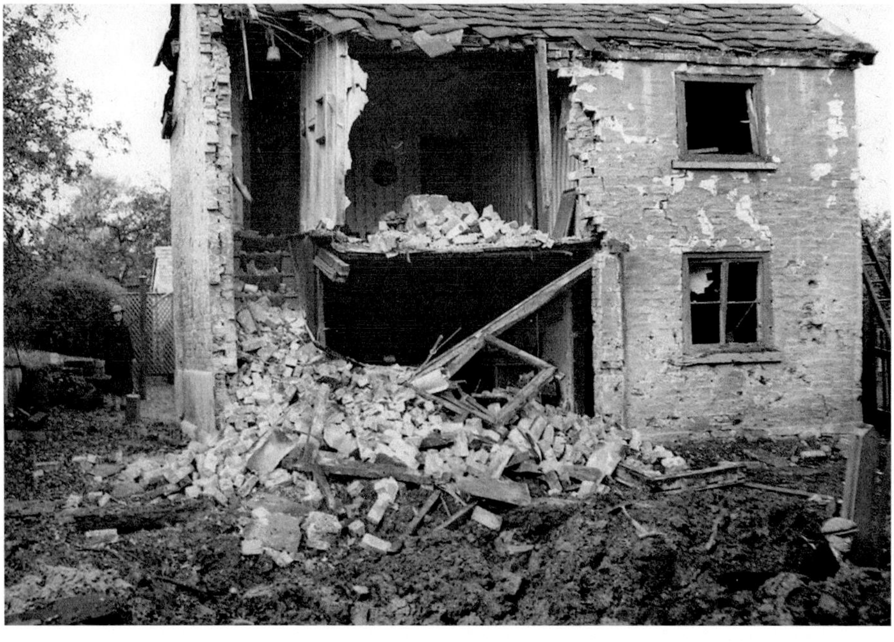

4

North Cheshire and South Manchester

Air Raid Damage at Bramhall, Dukinfield Division, 23 December 1940
Some of the bombs damaged a church near the railway, while the signal box and other nearby buildings were also casualties. Several houses on Holland Road, Bramhall, were damaged, as shown in the photos.

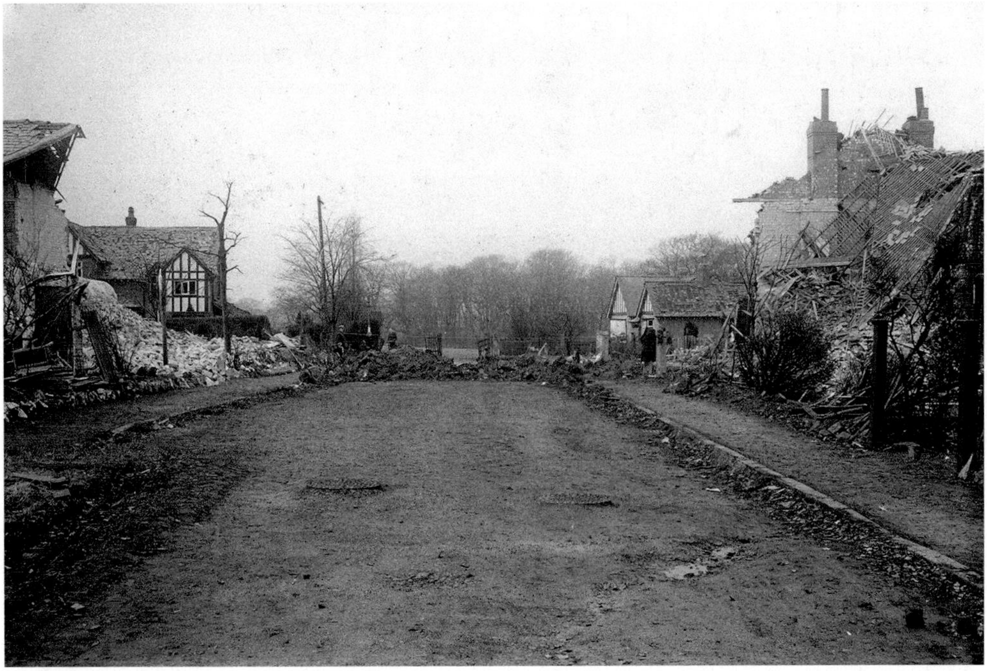

Damage to a house at Holland Road, which was caused by a parachute mine.

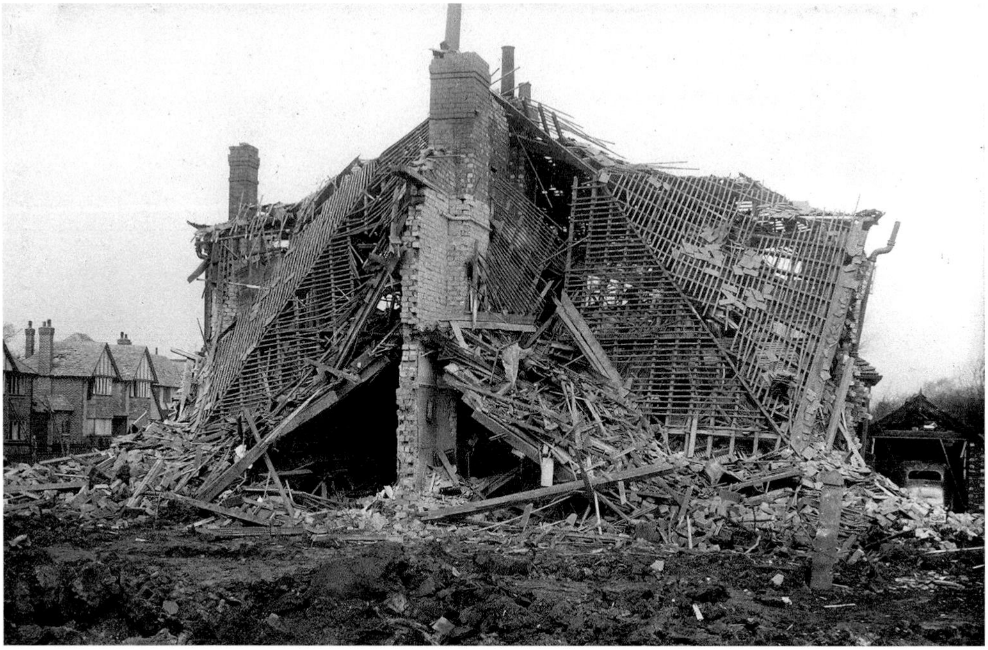

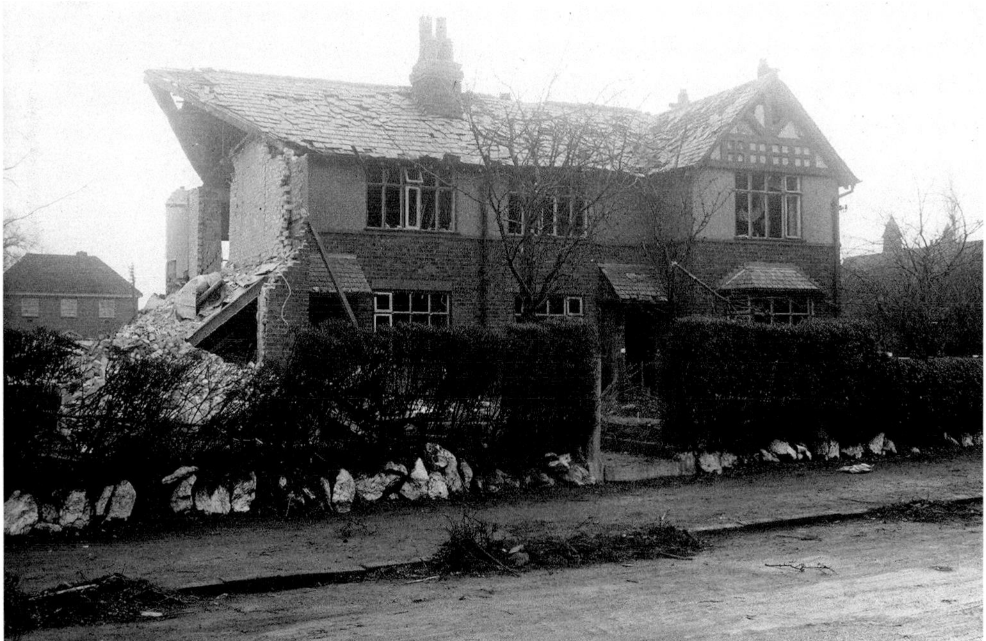

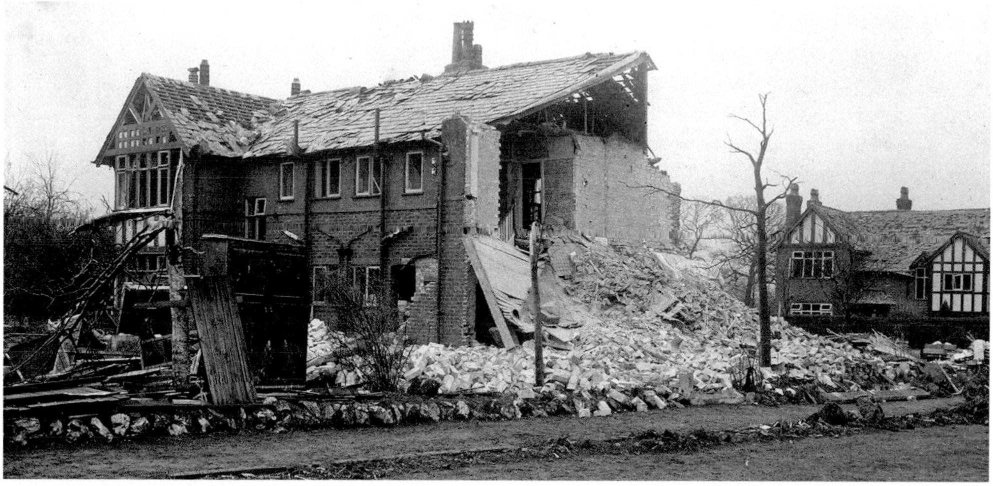

Holland Road, Bramhall.

Air Raid Damage at Oulton Avenue, Sale, 18 November 1940

On 18 November 1940, several properties in Oulton Avenue, Sale (now within Greater Manchester), were damaged, as can be seen in these photographs. A woman was sheltering in the Anderson shelter in the photograph below and received a fractured arm from a bomb splinter.

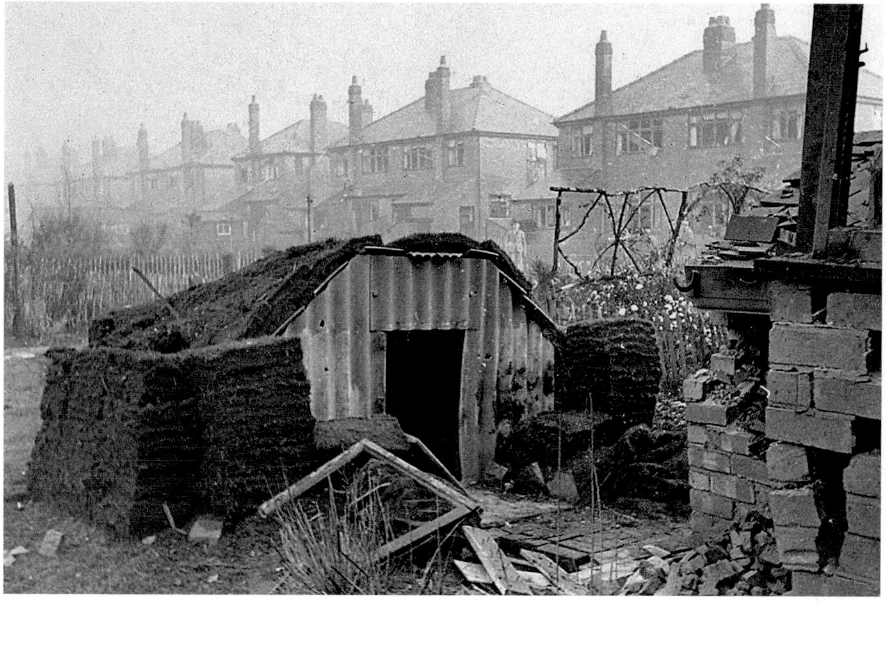

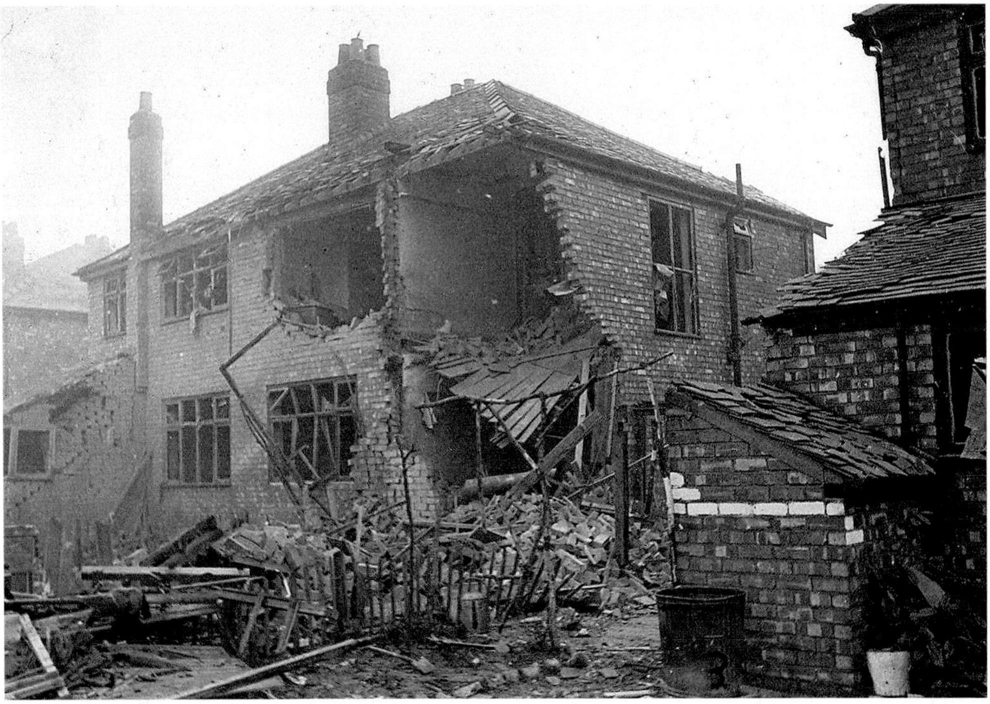

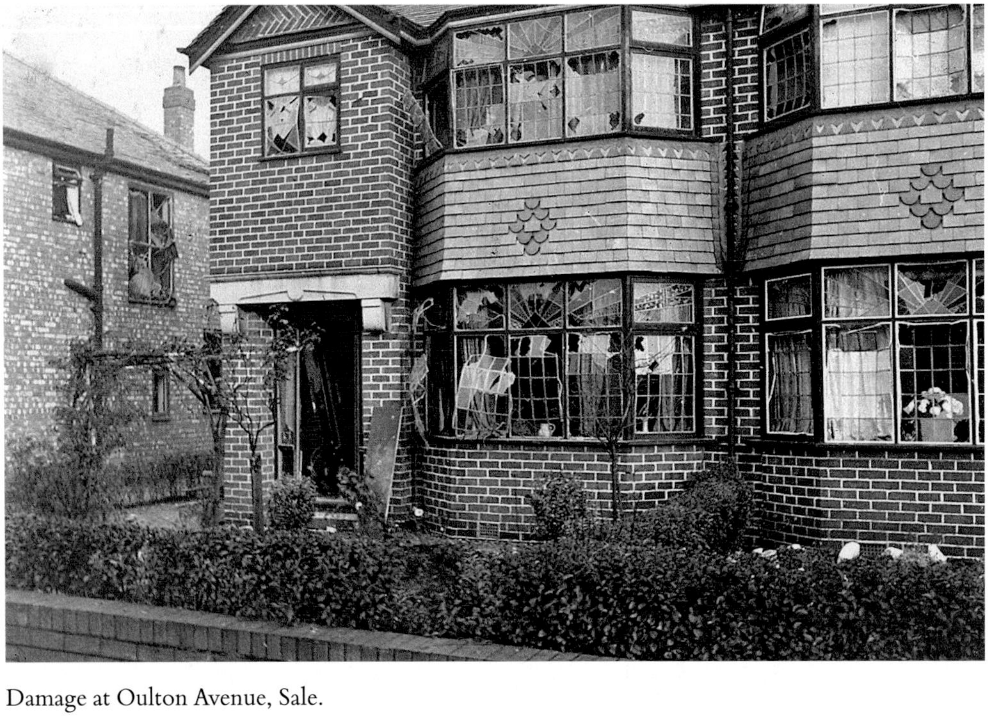

Damage at Oulton Avenue, Sale.

Air Raid Damage in Bredbury and Cheadle, 23 December 1940

There was only one fatality in this air raid on Bredbury: a man named Mr Woods was standing on his doorstep in Woodley when a small bomb landed nearby, the blast killing him.

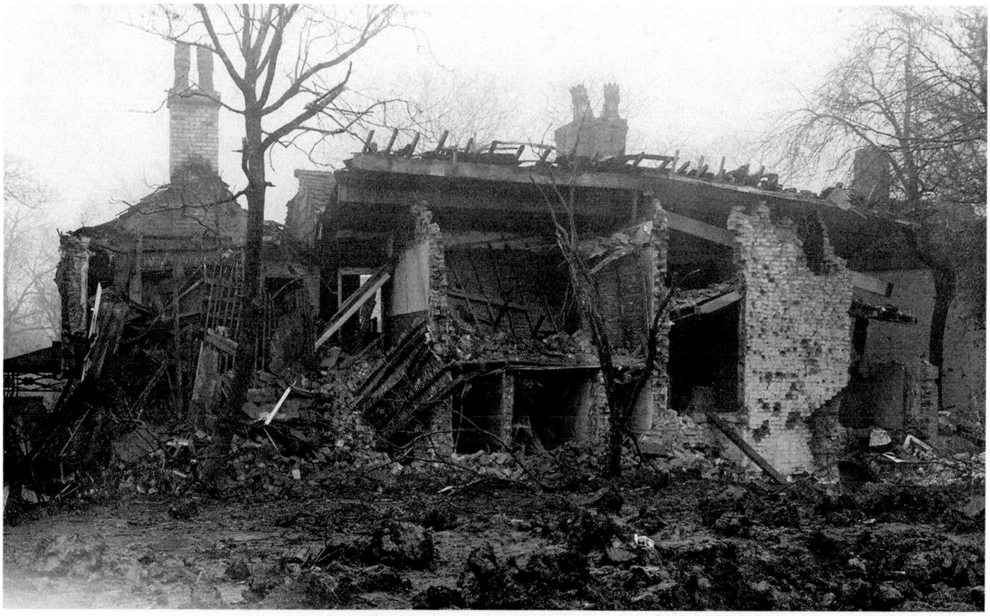

Destruction of a house at High Lane, Woodley.

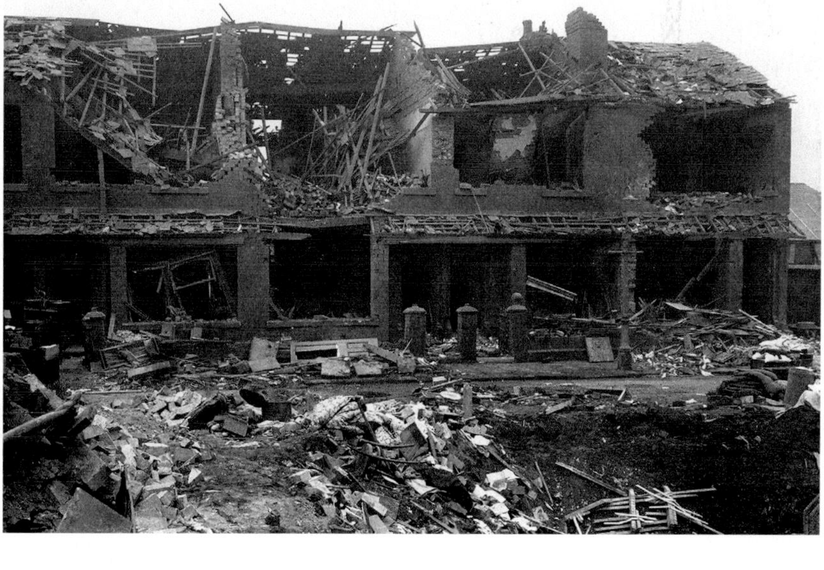

Air Raid Damage at Cheadle, 12 October 1940

Three photographs were taken at the rear of the George and Dragon Hotel, Cheadle. A high-explosive bomb caused the crater shown in photograph two. The aviary shown on the left of the second photograph was 44ft from the centre of the crater, and the greenhouse shown on the right of the photograph was 62ft from the centre of the crater. The greenhouse was only slightly damaged, as shown in the pictures, and none of the birds were hurt.

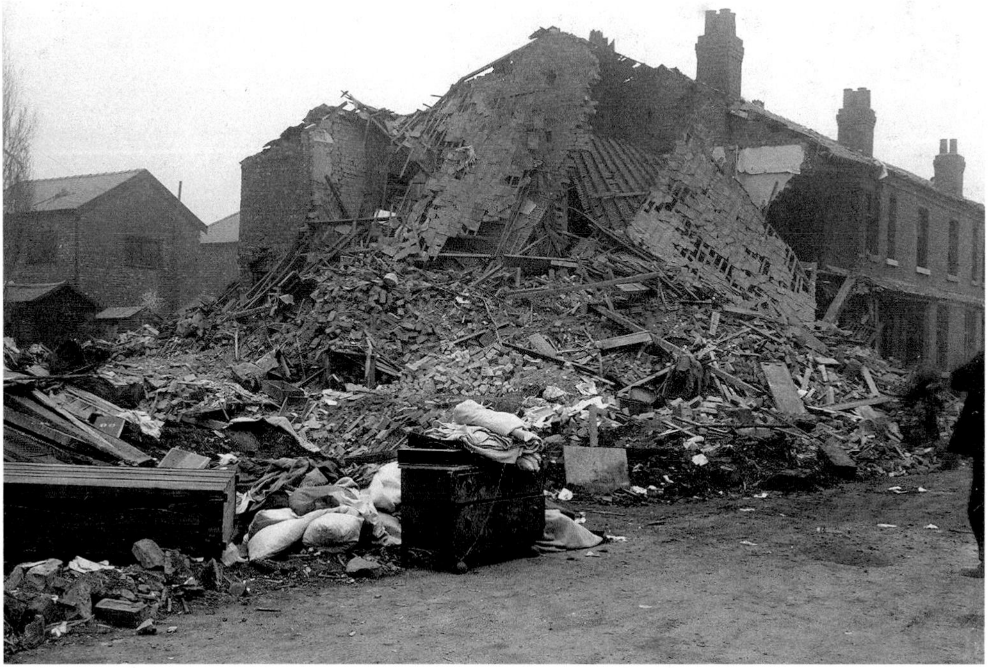

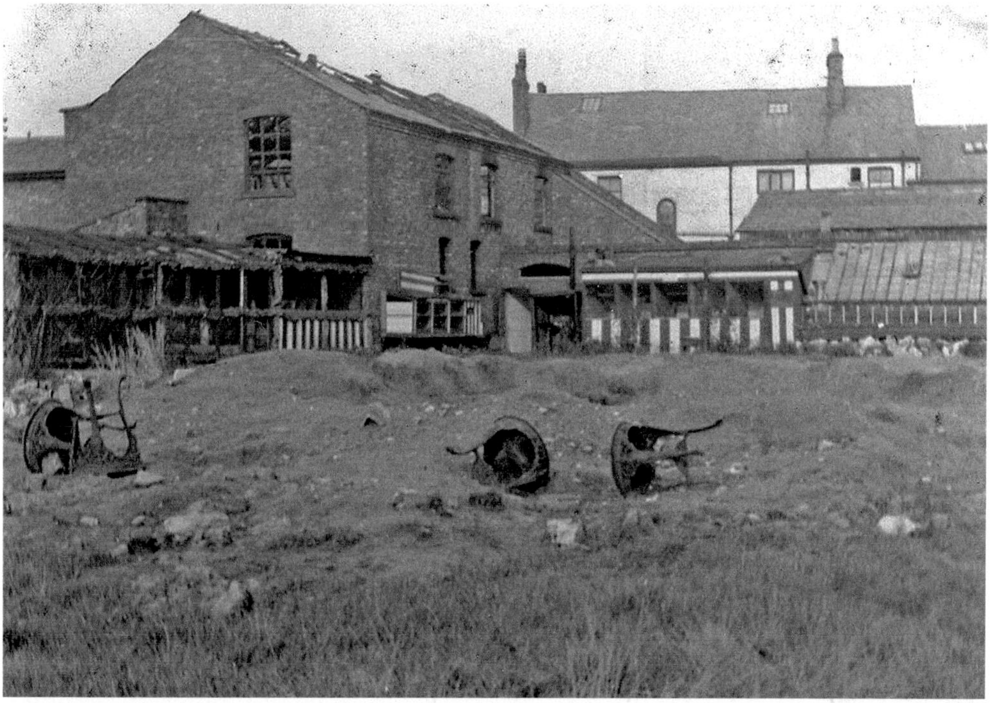

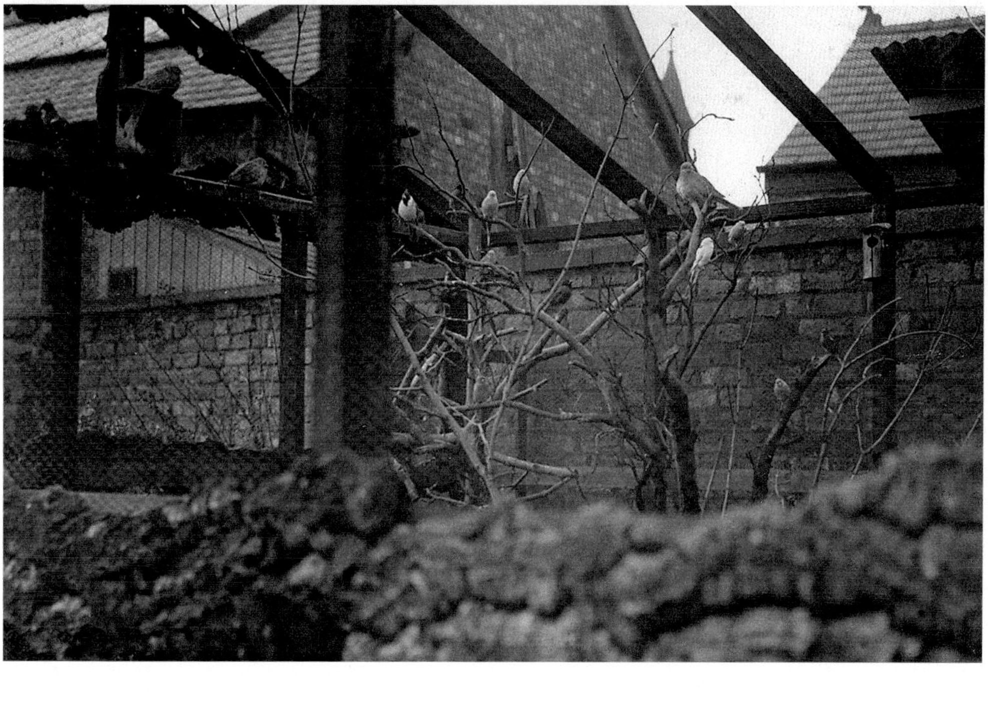

Air Raid Damage at Altrincham, 23 December 1940

Altrincham was bombed heavily during the 'Manchester Blitz'. At 2 a.m. on 23 December, a high-explosive bomb landed at the entrance of Stamford Park by Charter Road and Mayors Road. There were many tragedies during these two days of bombing in this area of Altrincham, including the deaths of two children aged just 5 and 2 and their mother from the Hough family; their father was spared as he had signed up for the forces just two weeks prior. In nearby Moss Lane, six houses were destroyed, which resulted in twelve deaths, including the Sanders family at No. 43: a father, mother and 2-year-old child. The family dog was found alive in the child's pram. A memorial garden on Oakfield Road marks the tragic events of this period.

The bombing of Charter Road caused enormous damage to a corner shop and houses opposite, where the Jenyon family lived. The father (an air raid warden), his wife, their daughter and their 11-year-old granddaughter were staying together for Christmas. As a result of the damage caused to their house, a neighbour, Annie, offered them shelter in her home nearby, but this was not to end well:

> Tragically, Annie's house was hit in the evening bombing, and Edwin, his daughter and grand-daughter all died. Edwin was serving as an Air Raid Warden when he died; his wife Maud, having survived both explosions, eventually died in 1970 aged 85.[10]

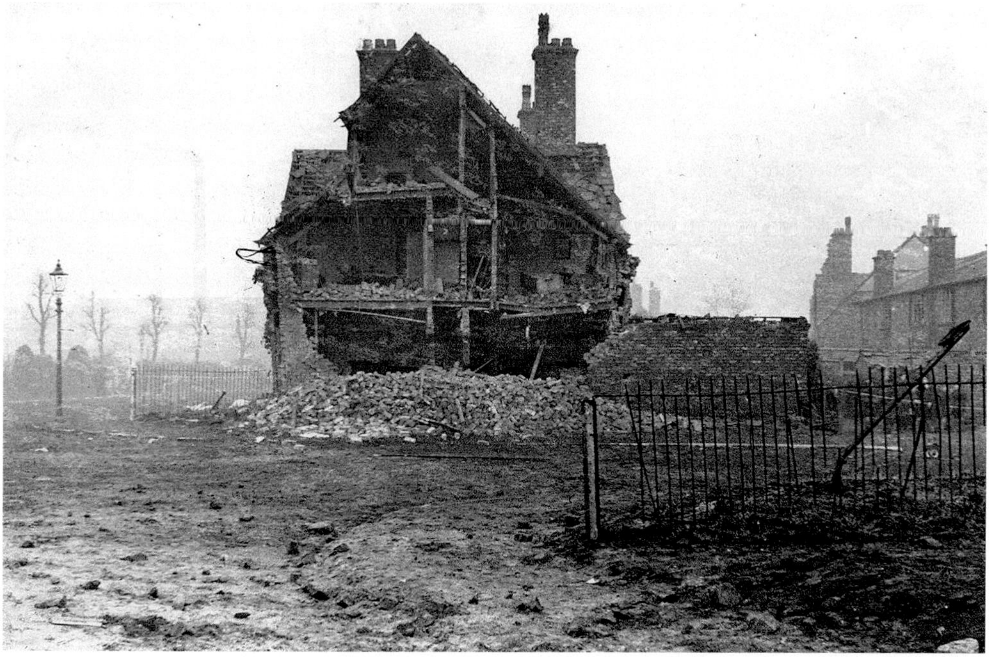

Damage to a house on Lawrence Road, Altrincham.

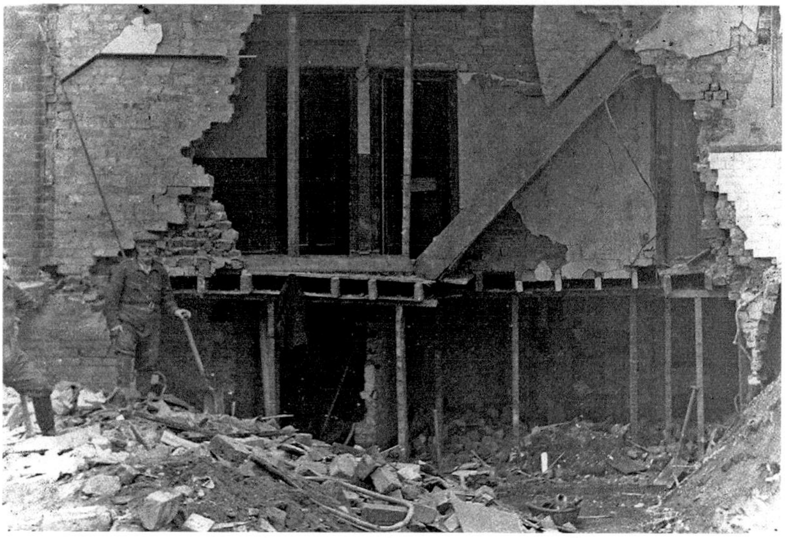

The cellars of a house in Charter Road, Altrincham.

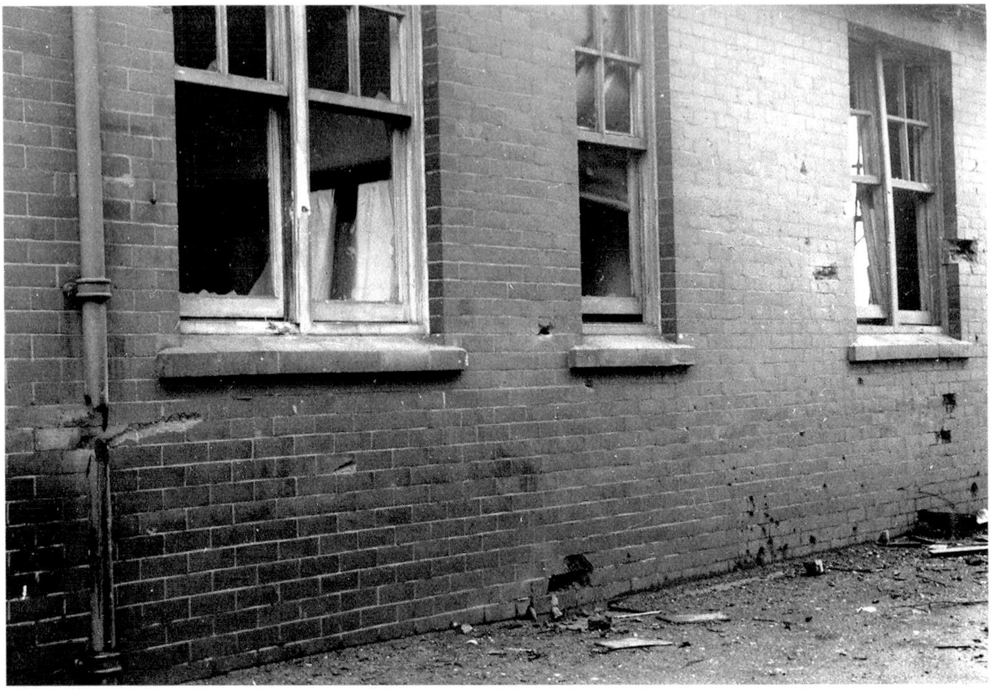

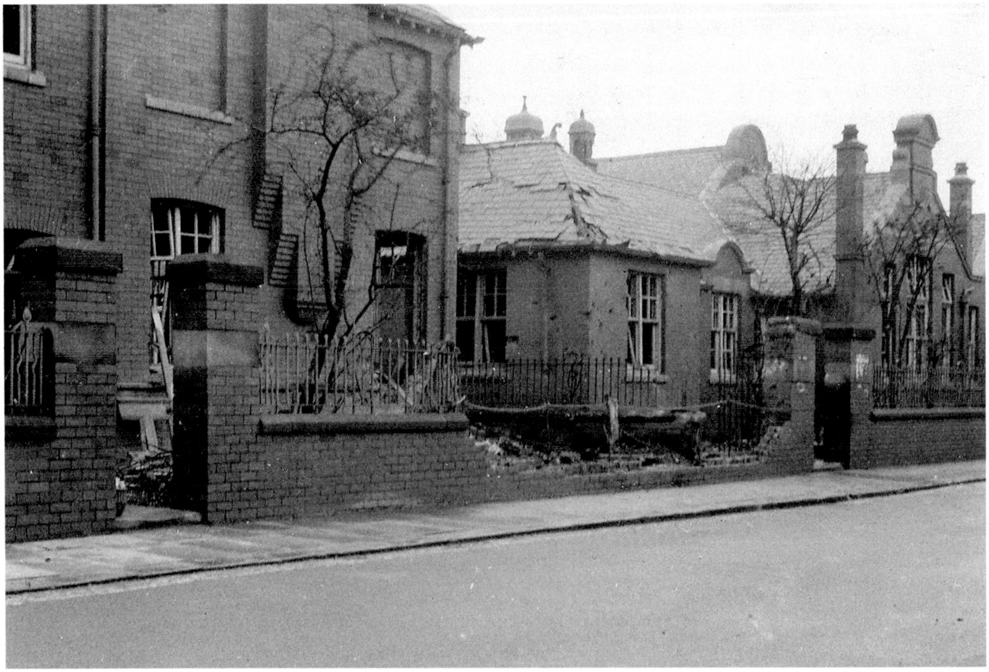

Damage to Worthington Road School caused by a HE bomb.

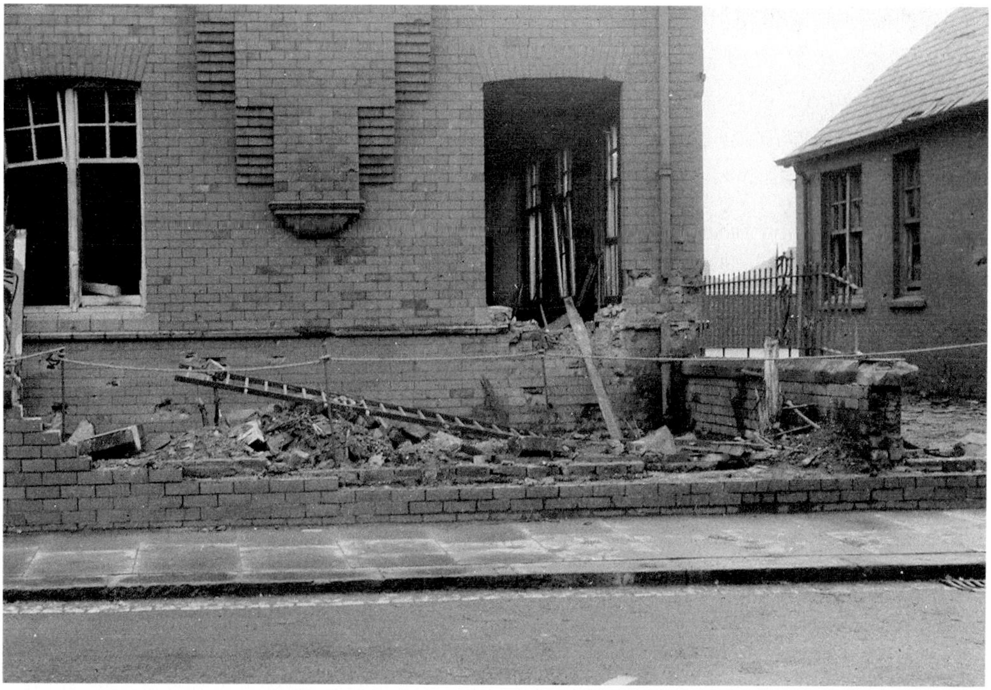

Air Raid Damage at Worthington Road School, Sale, 18 November 1940

On 18 November 1940, German aircraft dropped an 'unused' bomb after a Manchester raid as part of a jettison of six high-explosive bombs over Sale Moor. The bomb landed on the boundary wall of Worthington Road School and caused considerable damage; the wall was at the front of the school, near the caretaker's house, and the bomb blast damaged windows, walls and the roof. Fortunately, the children were safe in the four shelters that had been erected just after the beginning of the war.

The school building was repaired within three months, enabling the school to resume full use.

Air Raid Damage at Bowdon, Altrincham, 23 December 1940

These two photographs showing damage caused by a parachute mine that fell on one of the lodges at an entrance to Dunham Hall, once the residence of Roger Grey, the 10th and last Earl of Stamford. Due to boundary changes, the hall now stands in Trafford near Altrincham in Greater Manchester, but during the Second World War, it was located in the parish of Bowdon, Cheshire. During the First World War, it served as Stamford Military Hospital; during the Second World War, it was used as a US Army camp and later as a prisoner-of-war camp. It was designated a Grade 1 listed building in 1959 and was given to the National Trust upon the earl's death in 1976; the house and its expansive grounds are now known as Dunham Massey and are open to the public.

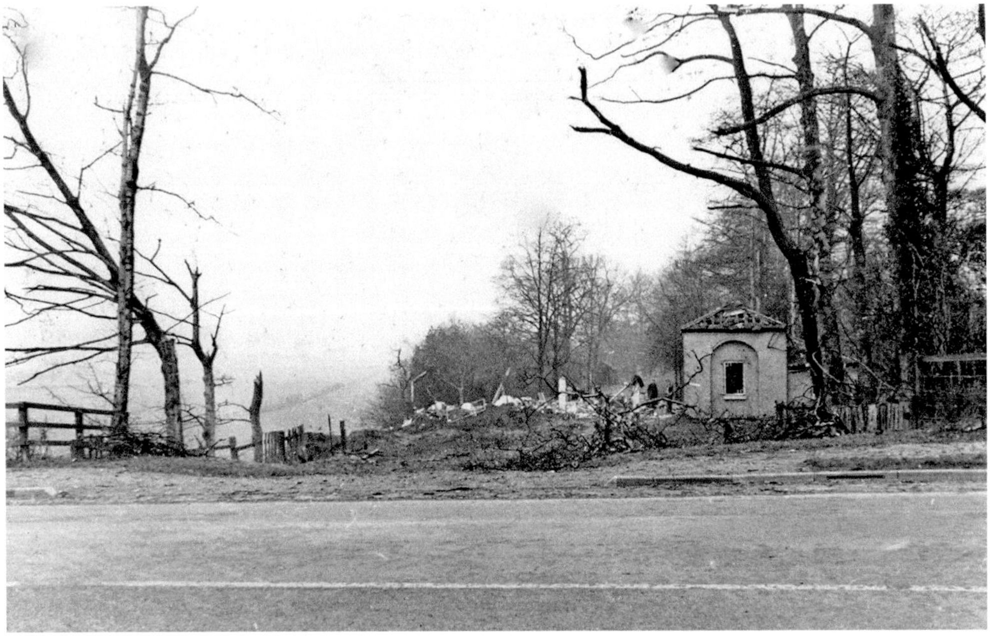

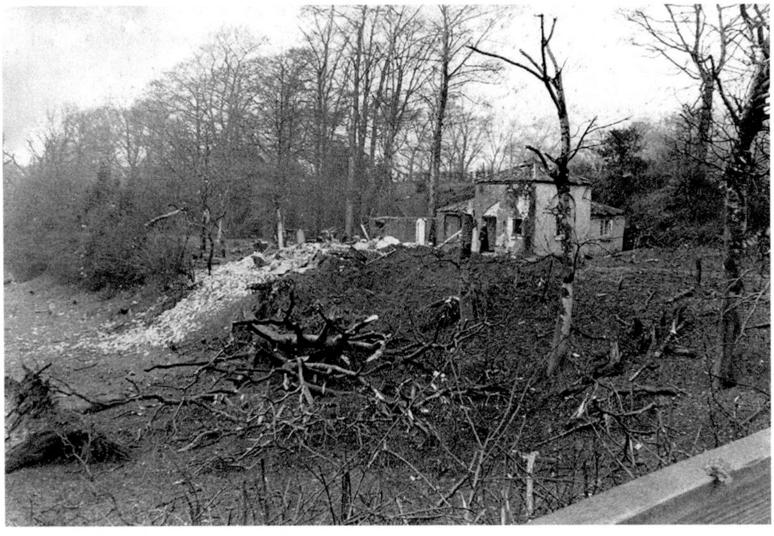

Damage caused by a parachute mine that fell on one of the two lodges at Dunham Hall.

Air Raid Damage, 23 December 1940, Thelwall, Timperley

Damage was caused to a car at Thelwall Grange and to a house at Westwood Grove in Timperley.

In 2018, a suspected Second World War bomb was found on Thelwall Lane in Warrington and was safely detonated by the army.

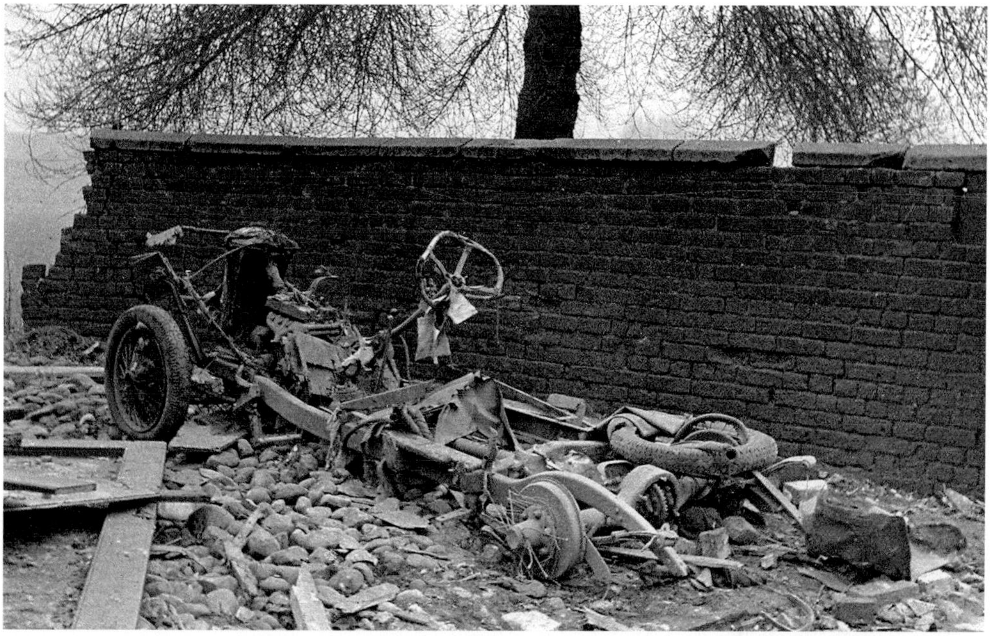

Damage caused to a car at Thelwall Grange.

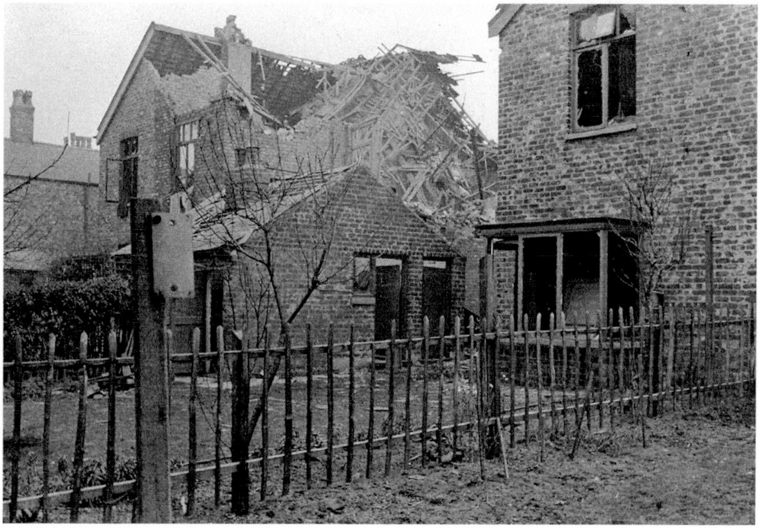

Damage to a house at Westwood Grove.

Air Raid Damage at Sale

Five photographs showing damage caused by high-explosive bombs at Penrhyn Avenue, Sale, on 23 December 1940.

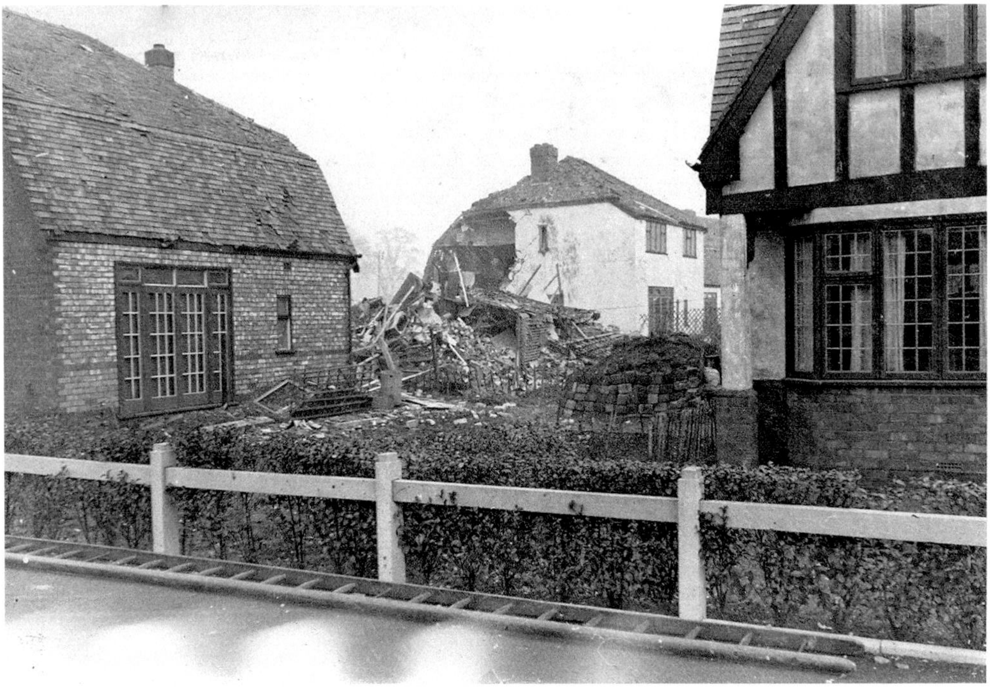

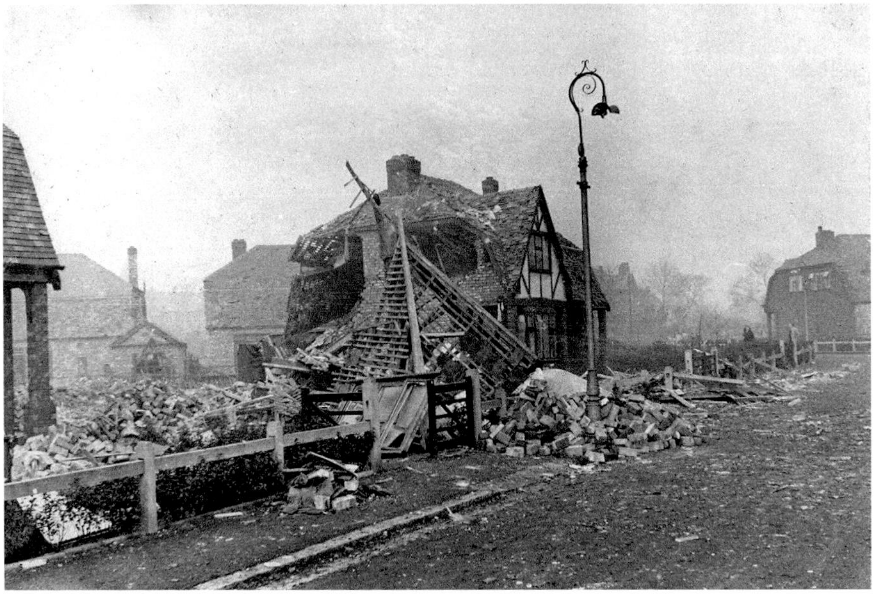

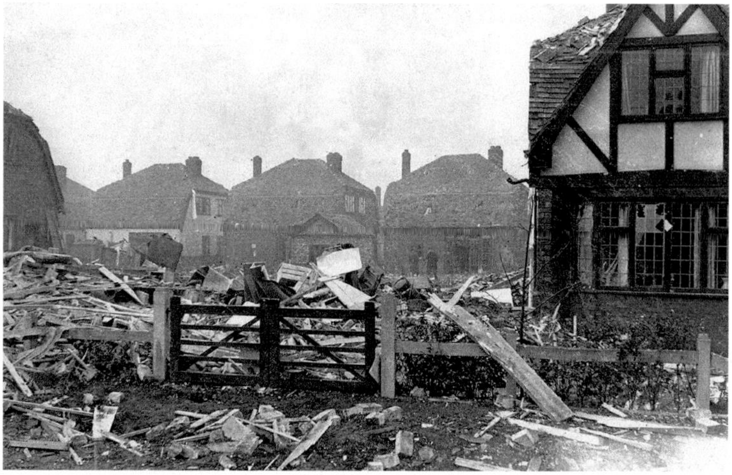

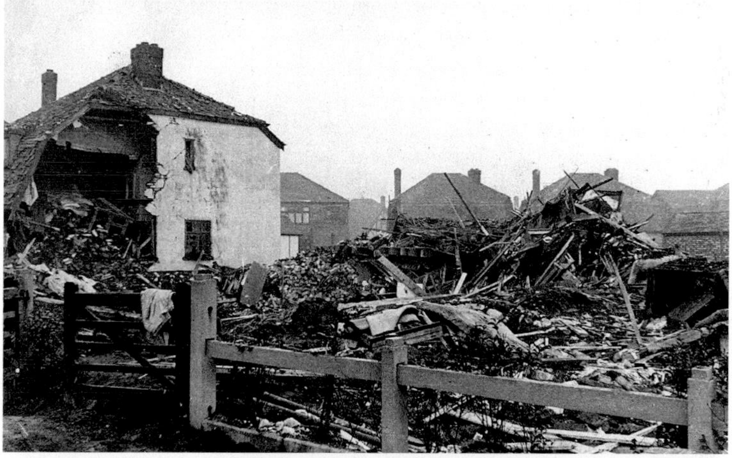

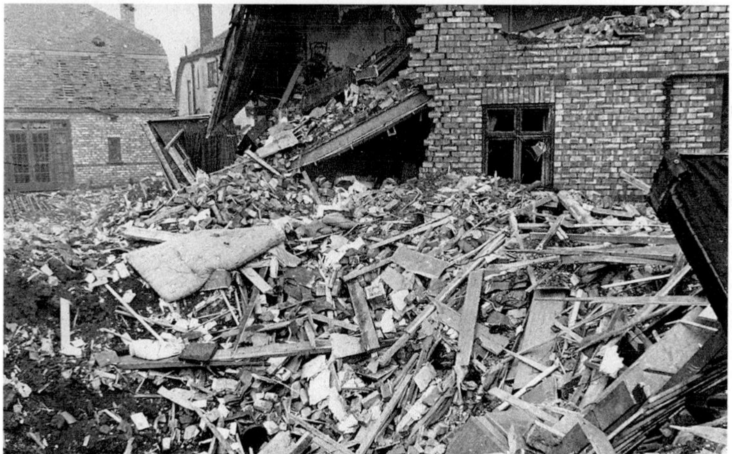

Air Raid Damage at Derbyshire Road, Sale

Three photographs that show damage caused by a high-explosive bomb to a house named 'The Croft' in Derbyshire Road, Sale.

Christmas 1940 was not a time of peace and goodwill for Sale as the residents had to cope with the deluge of Blitz bombings. During two nights of bombing on 22 and 23 December, many of the town's significant buildings were severely damaged, including St Paul's church on Springfield Road; the Woolworths store on School Road; the Healthwear Clothing factory on Hayfield Street; and the town hall, which was set aflame by incendiary bombs.

On Derbyshire Road, a direct hit destroyed the front of 'The Croft', injuring two people, and the blast damaged other properties nearby, as can be seen in the photos.

No one was killed in the raids on Sale, but at least 800 people died across Manchester and its surrounds. Sale's Ashfield Road Savoy Cinema was used as a temporary mortuary over this dreadful Christmas. The Savoy Cinema closed in 1977 and was demolished in 1985; a block of flats now occupies its former site.

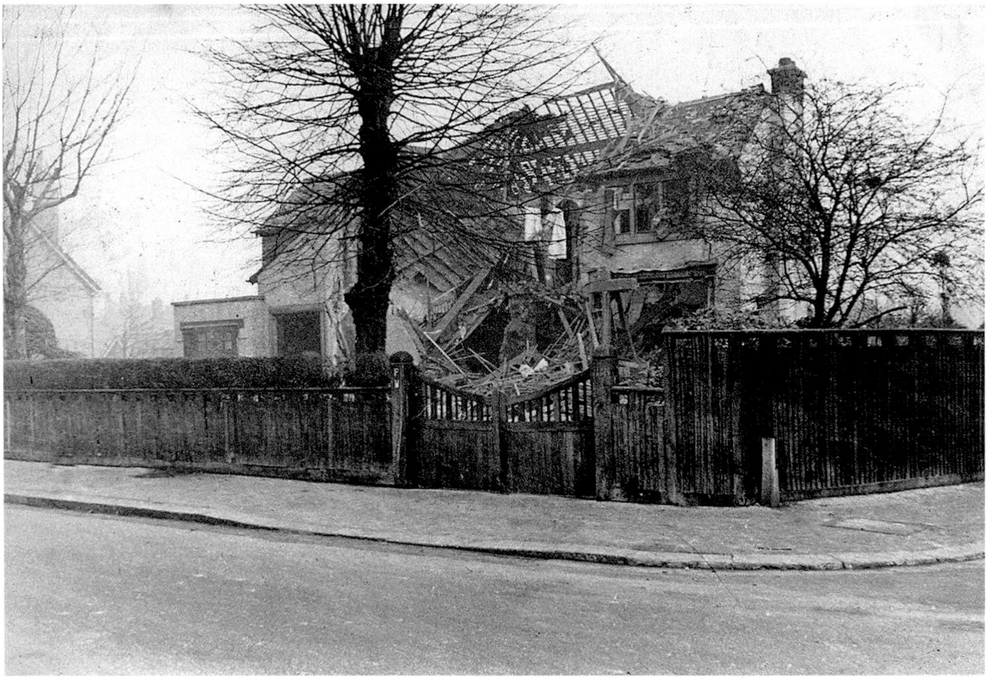

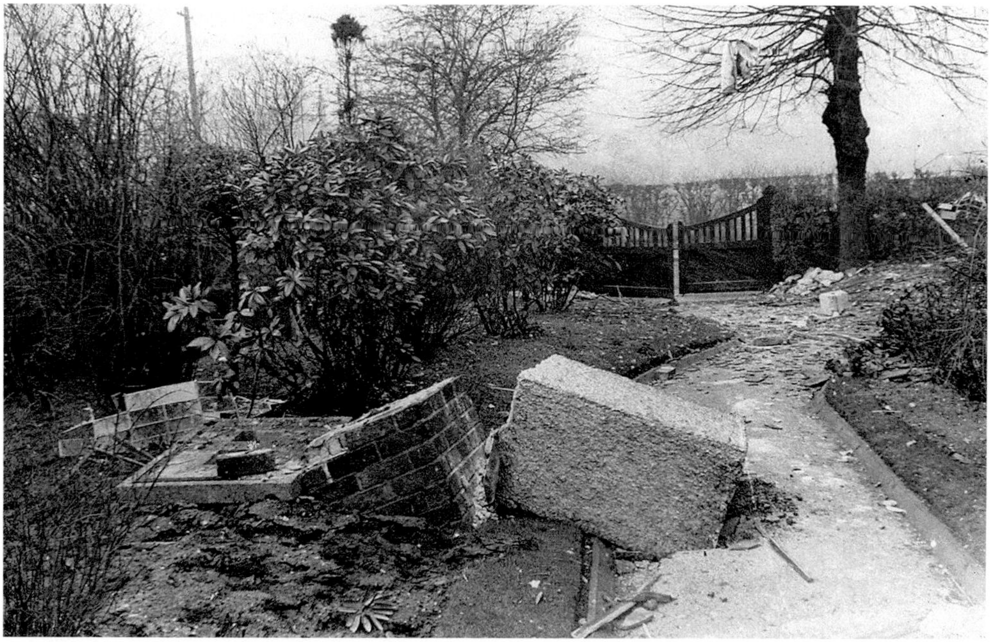

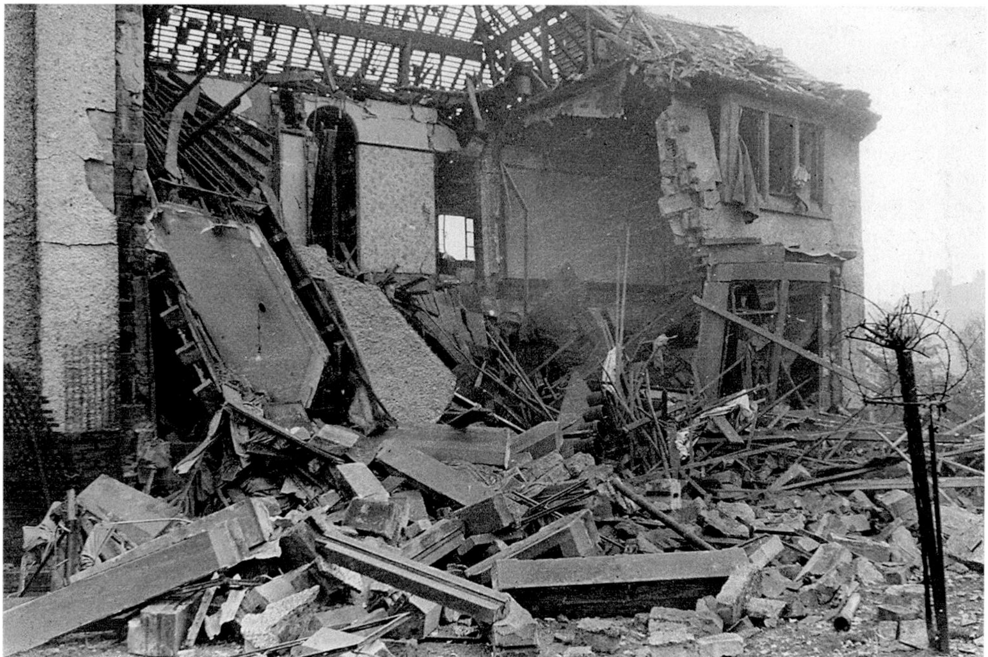

Air Raid Damage at Hale Barns, Altrincham, 23 December 1940

The first and second photographs here show bomb damage caused by an air raid on McEwens Garage at Hale Barns on 23 December 1940; the third image shows the garage today; and the fourth image shows the premises prior to the war. During the war, Mr Martin McEwen Sr was a member of the Auxiliary Fire Service, and the car and trailer were used as fire appliances with a fire service pump. Note the sandbags around the building.[11]

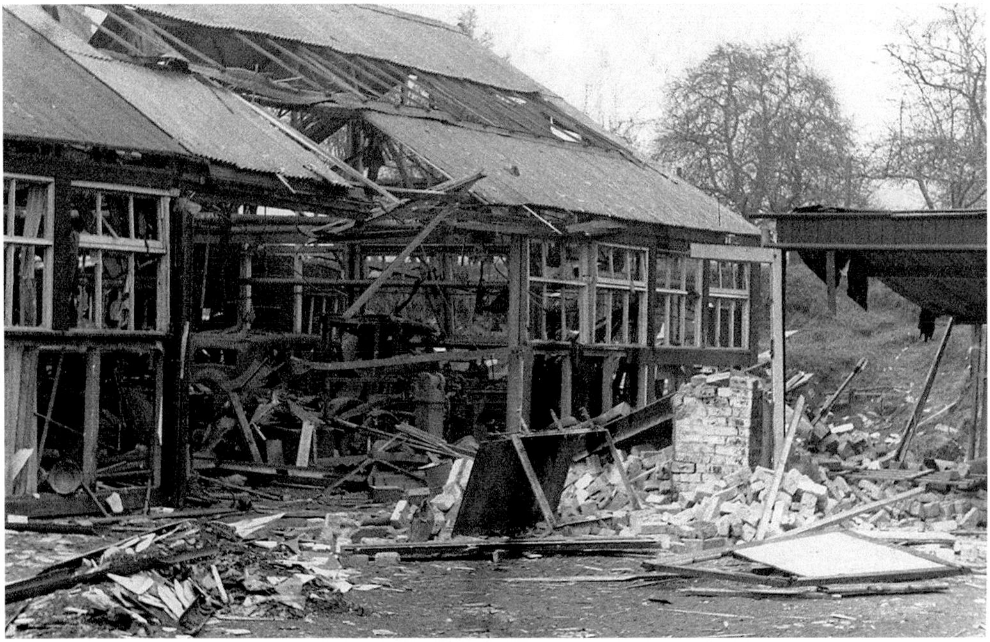

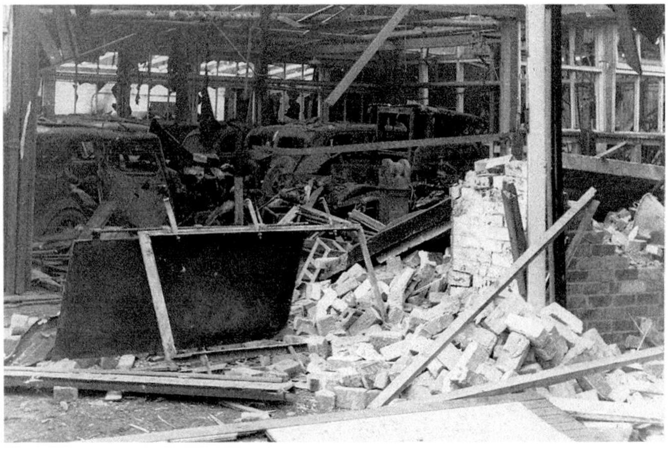

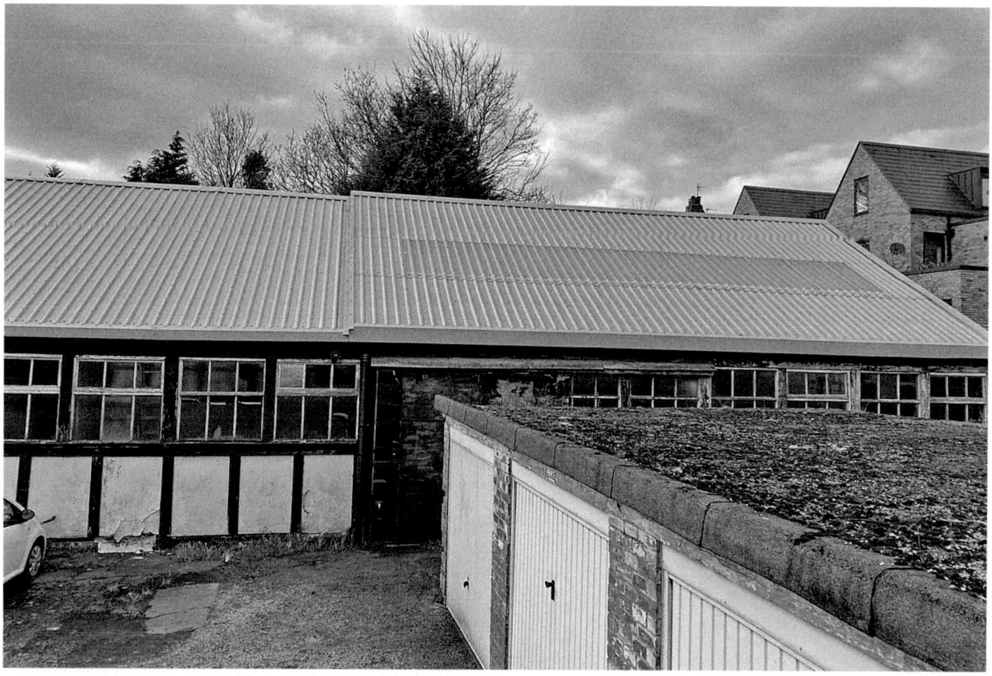

McEwens Garage, Hale Barns, in the present day. (Martin McEwen collection)

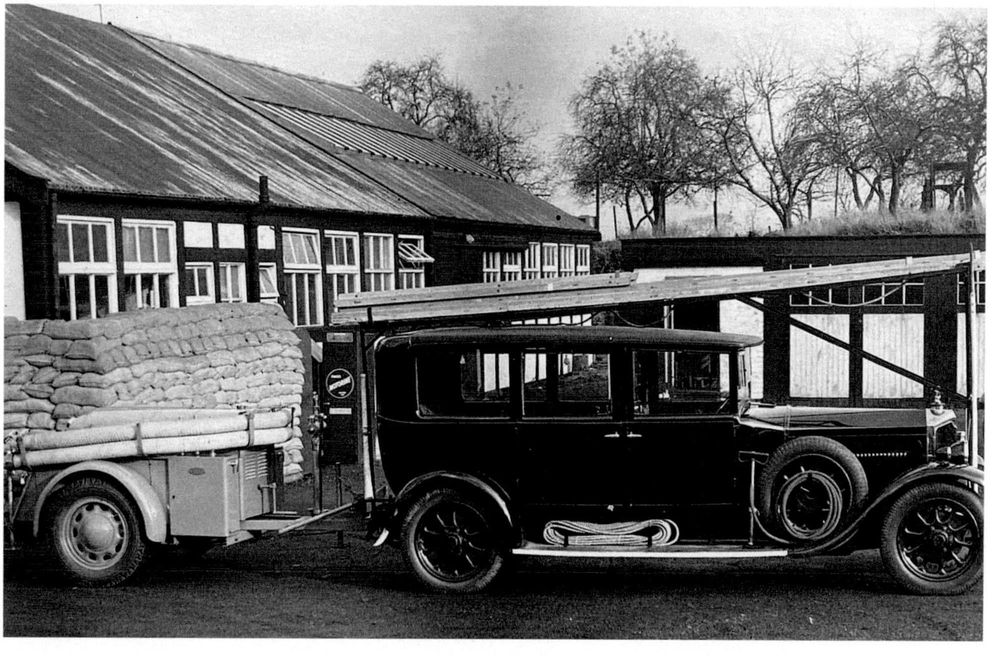

McEwens Garage before the war, with sandbags, car and trailer. (Martin McEwen collection)

Air Raid Damage at Over Alderley on 23 December 1940

Harold Worth, aged 46; his brother Israel, 32; and his wife Mary, 48, all died at Acton Farm, Hocker Lane, Over Alderley, during the Manchester Blitz on 23 December 1940.

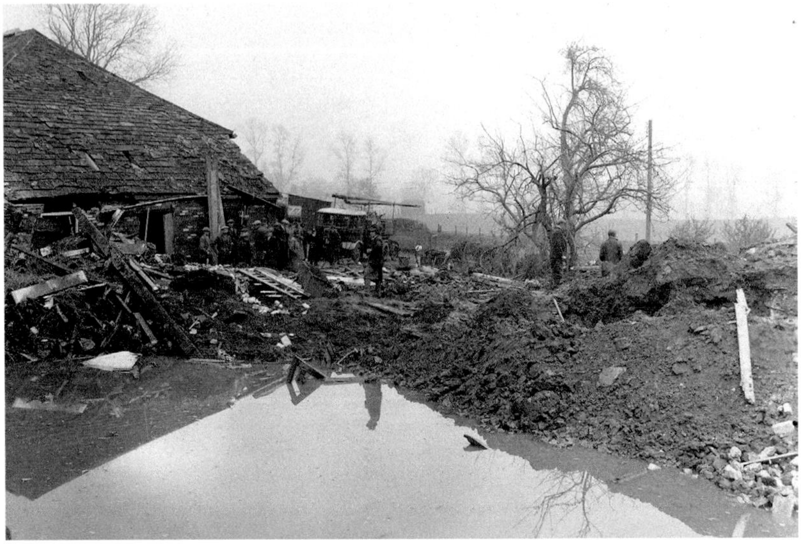

A crater made by a parachute mine at Acton Farm, Over Alderley.

Air Raid Damage at Cheadle, 4 February 1941

These photographs show damage to house property caused by a high-explosive bomb.

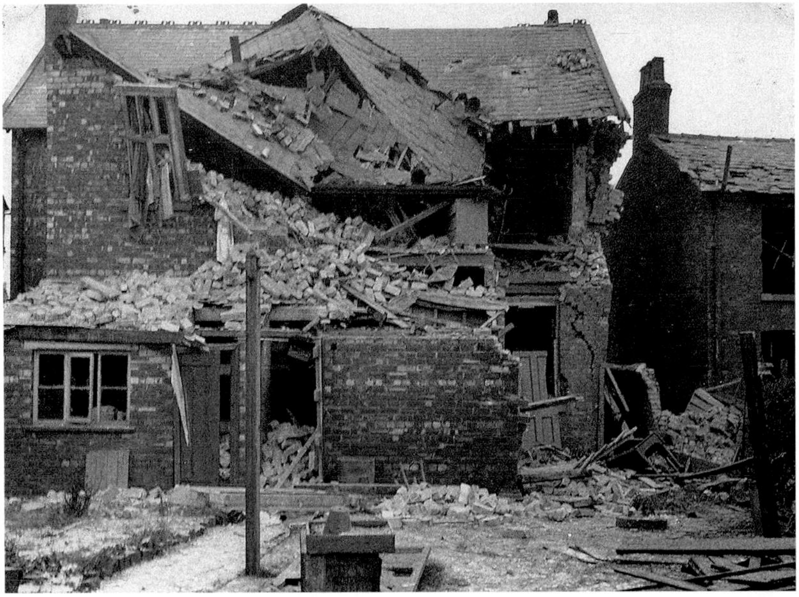

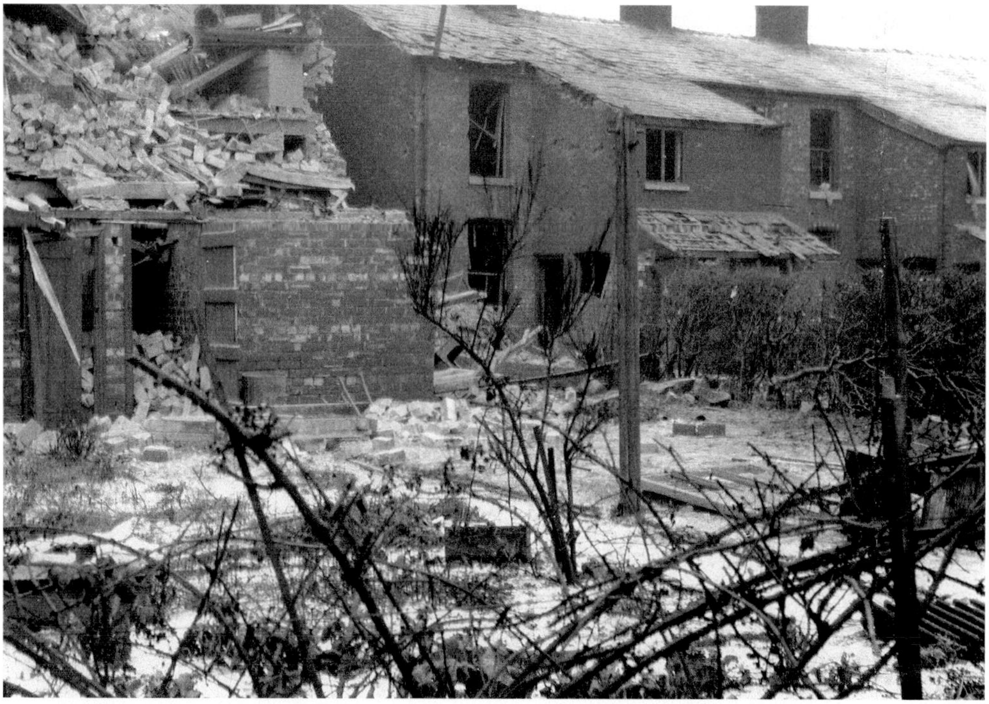

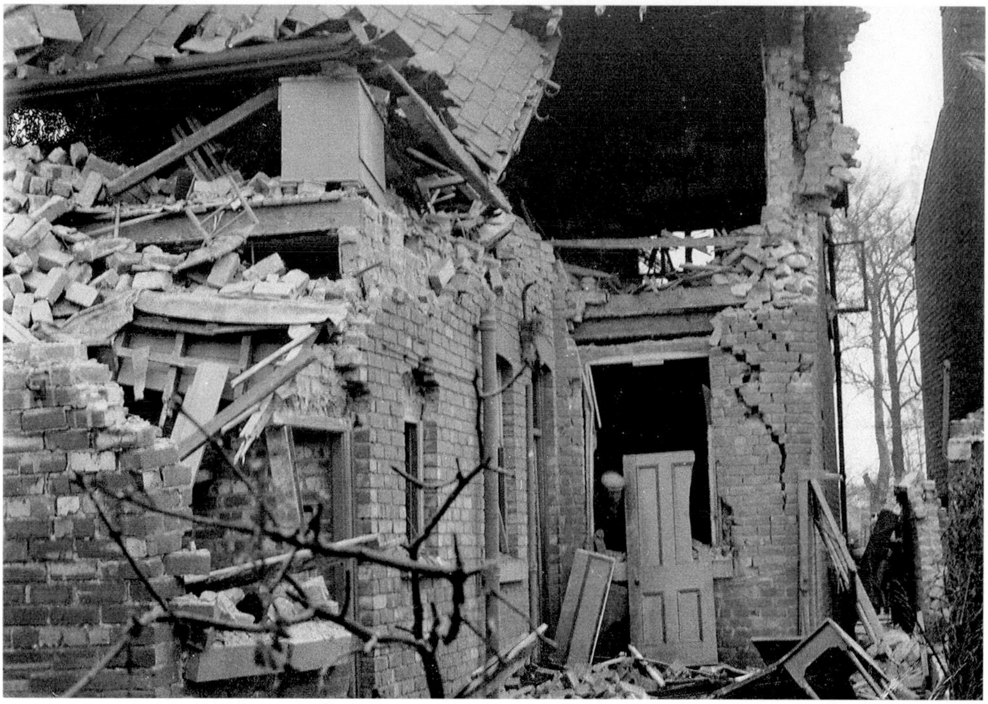

Air Raid Damage at Bowdon, 28 August 1940
'Southwold', in South Downs Road, Bowdon, was damaged in an air raid.

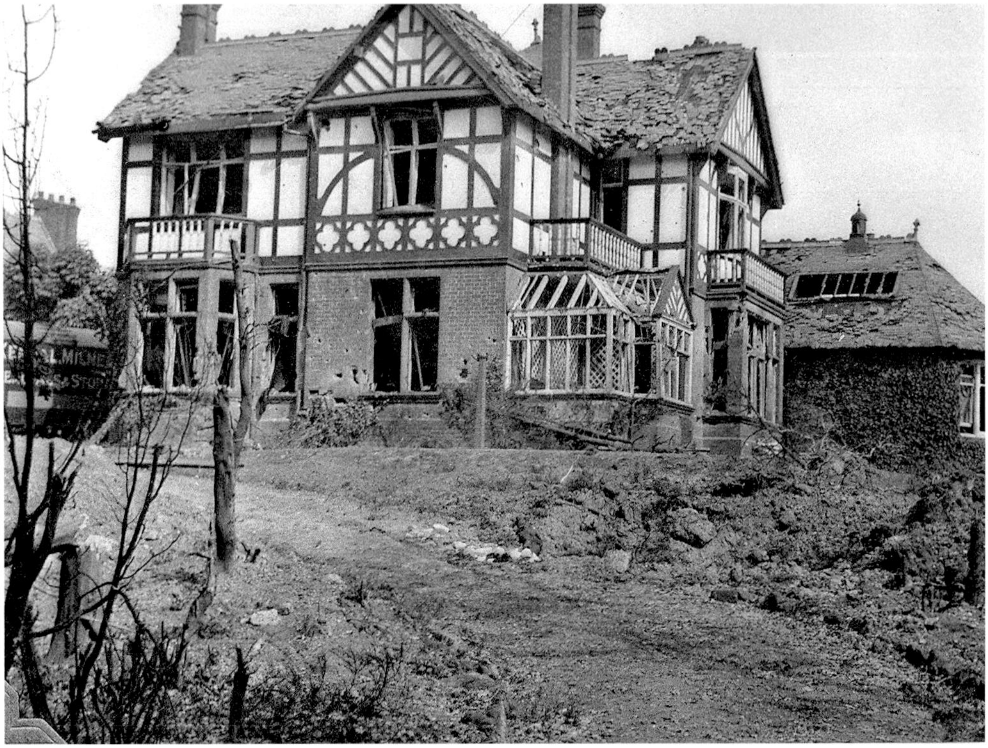

Air Raid Damage at Wilmslow, 30 August 1940
Damage caused by a high-explosive bomb to the detached house 'Brathay' in Macclesfield Road, Wilmslow, on 30 August 1940.

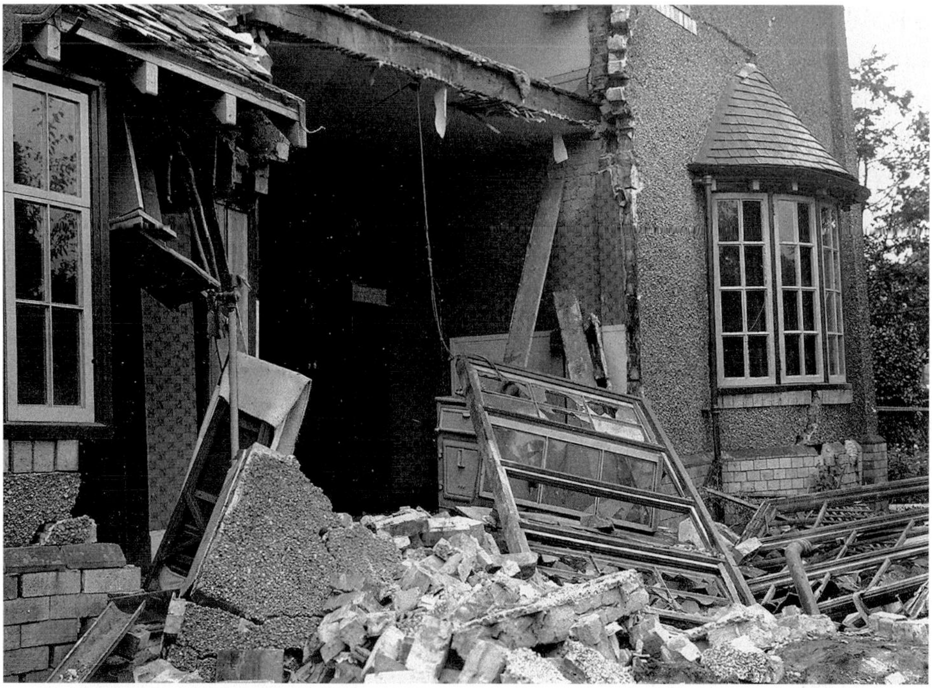

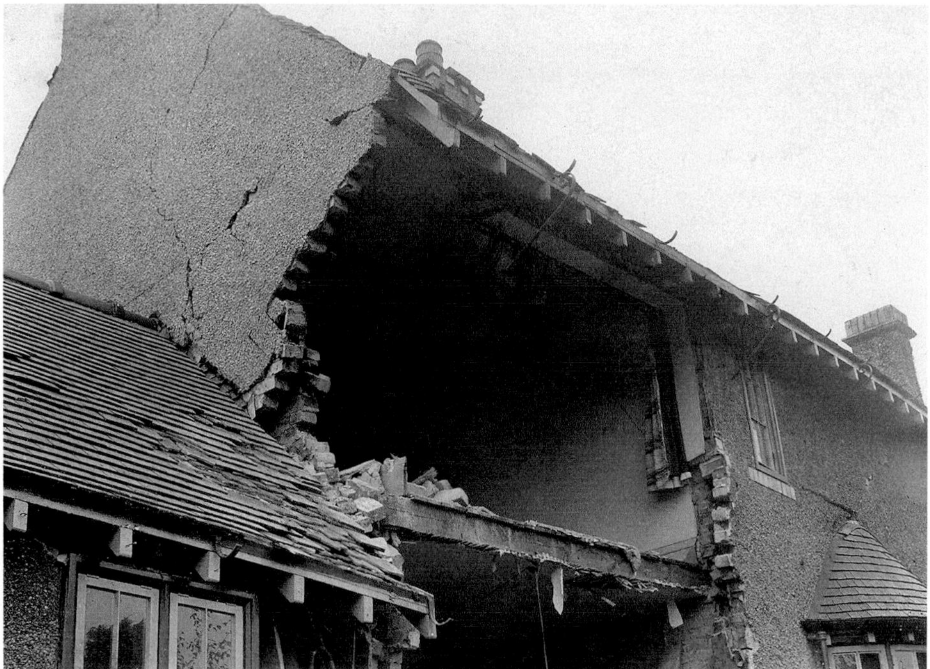

Air Raid Damage at Grappenhall, 11 September 1940

At the foot of a lake in Centre Park, Lakeside Drive, near Warrington, formerly known as Arpley Meadows, sits a memorial to sixteen people who tragically lost their lives when attending a gala in September 1940. The gala was organised by the Thames Board Mills factory, a large paper, paperboard and carton manufacturer located on the banks of the River Mersey and employing hundreds of locals. Over 2,500 people were present at the event and many were killed or injured when a lone German bomber, following the Manchester Ship Canal, passed overhead and released two bombs. Perhaps the crater in Knutsford Road, Grappenhall, that this lorry drove into was caused by the Arpley Meadows bombing.[12]

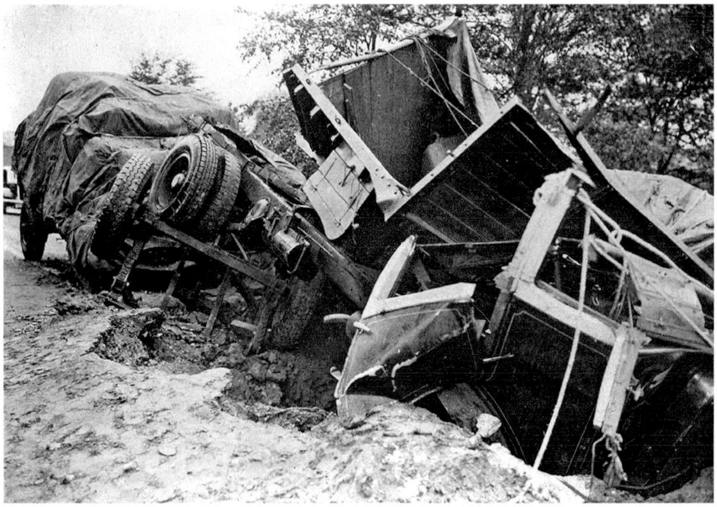

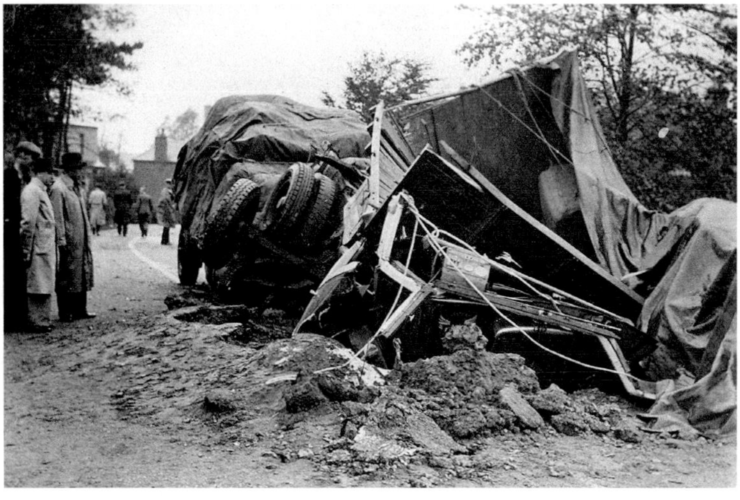

Air Raid Damage at Timperley, 28 August 1940

Damage to a semi-detached house in Kelsall Drive, Timperley. This raid of 28 August 1940 was during the peak of the Battle of Britain (June–September 1940):

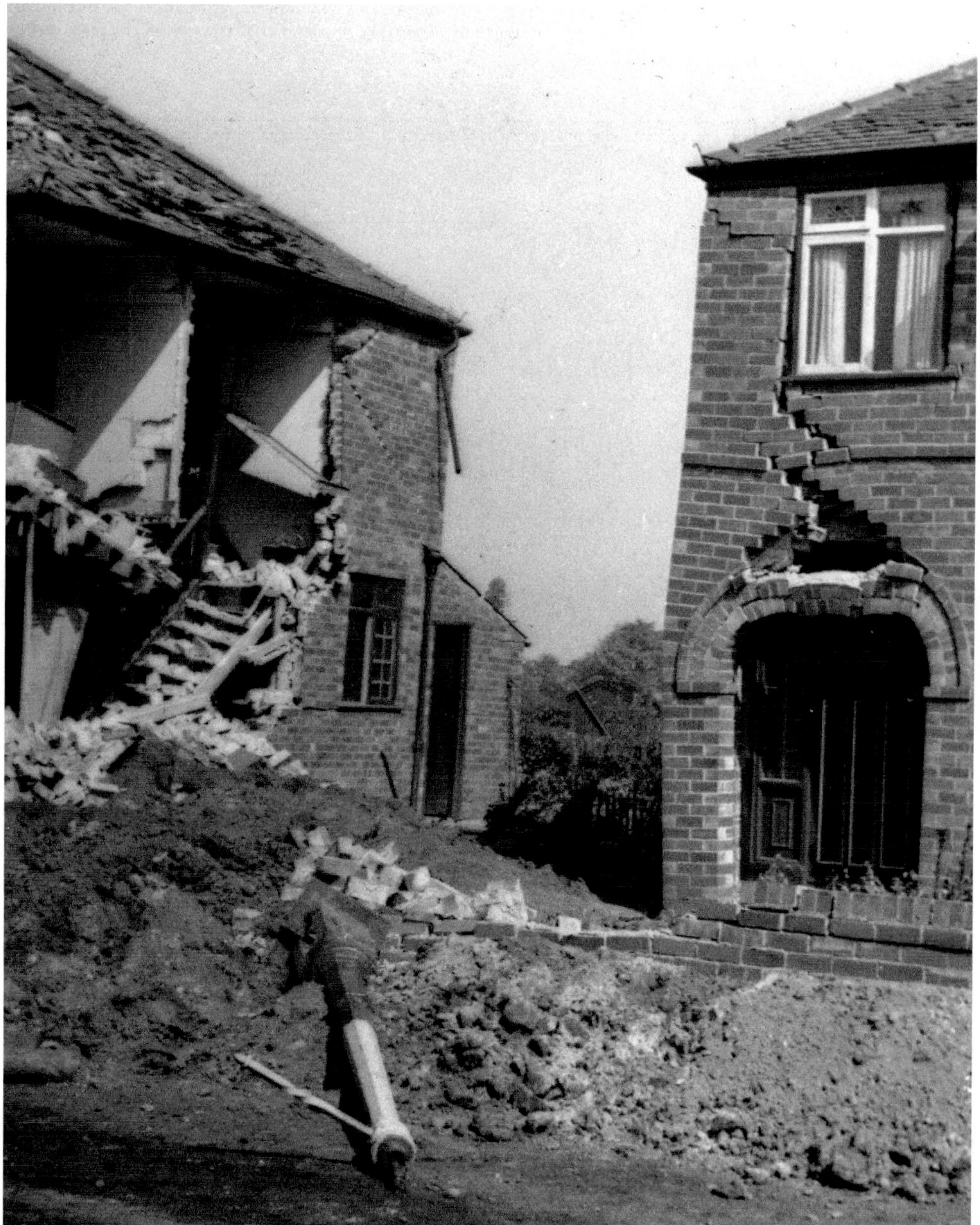

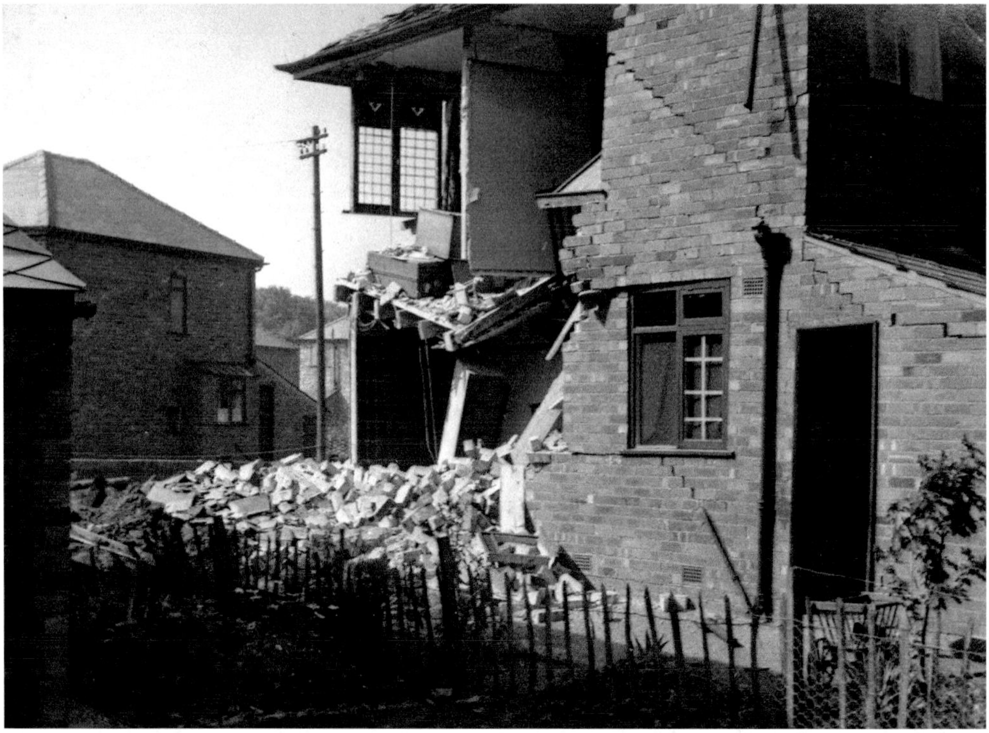

> The Luftwaffe air power consisted of a total of 2,669 aircraft; 1,015 were bombers. Up against this, our own RAF had 704 single-engined fighters, including Spitfires and Hurricanes, alongside 440 bombers. By early August 1940, German raids had become focused on British airfields and the aircraft industry. On 1 August, the Germans issued 'First Directive 17' for the conduct of air and sea warfare against England' (Great Britain) … By this time, the skies around Southern Britain were already accustomed to aerial battles. On 13 August, the German Luftwaffe launched an attack on Britain of approximately 1,500 aircraft, and this was swiftly followed on August 15th by an even larger attack of 1,270 fighters and 520 bombers, which was directed towards British air bases and their support infrastructure, including air defence targets, aircraft factories, repair depots and anti-aircraft sites, all of which would have included many targets in Cheshire, most notably the Rolls-Royce factory in Crewe.[13]

The targets also included Birkenhead docks, Crewe railway works, ICI at Northwich and the heavy industry at Stockport. Cheshire was on a few of the routes to Liverpool and Manchester, which led to indiscriminate bombing and dropping of unused bombs when bombers were returning from the cities.

Air Raid Damage at Timperley, 23 December 1940

Three photographs showing damage caused by a high-explosive bomb at Kingsley Road.

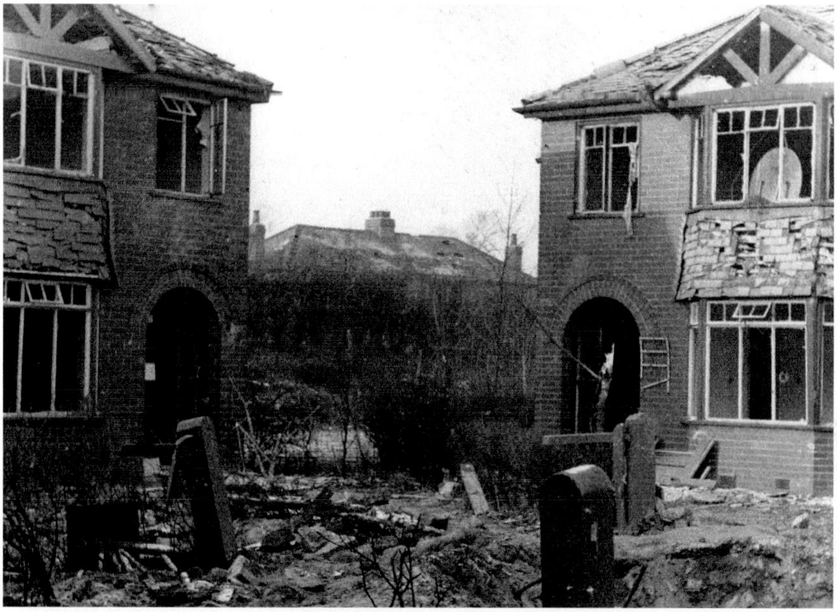

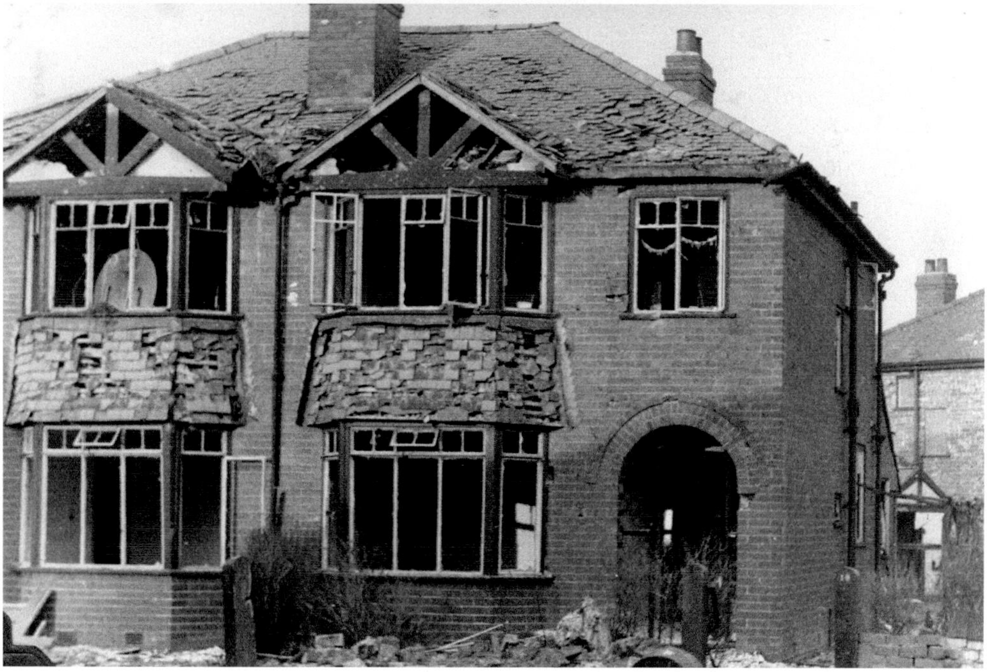

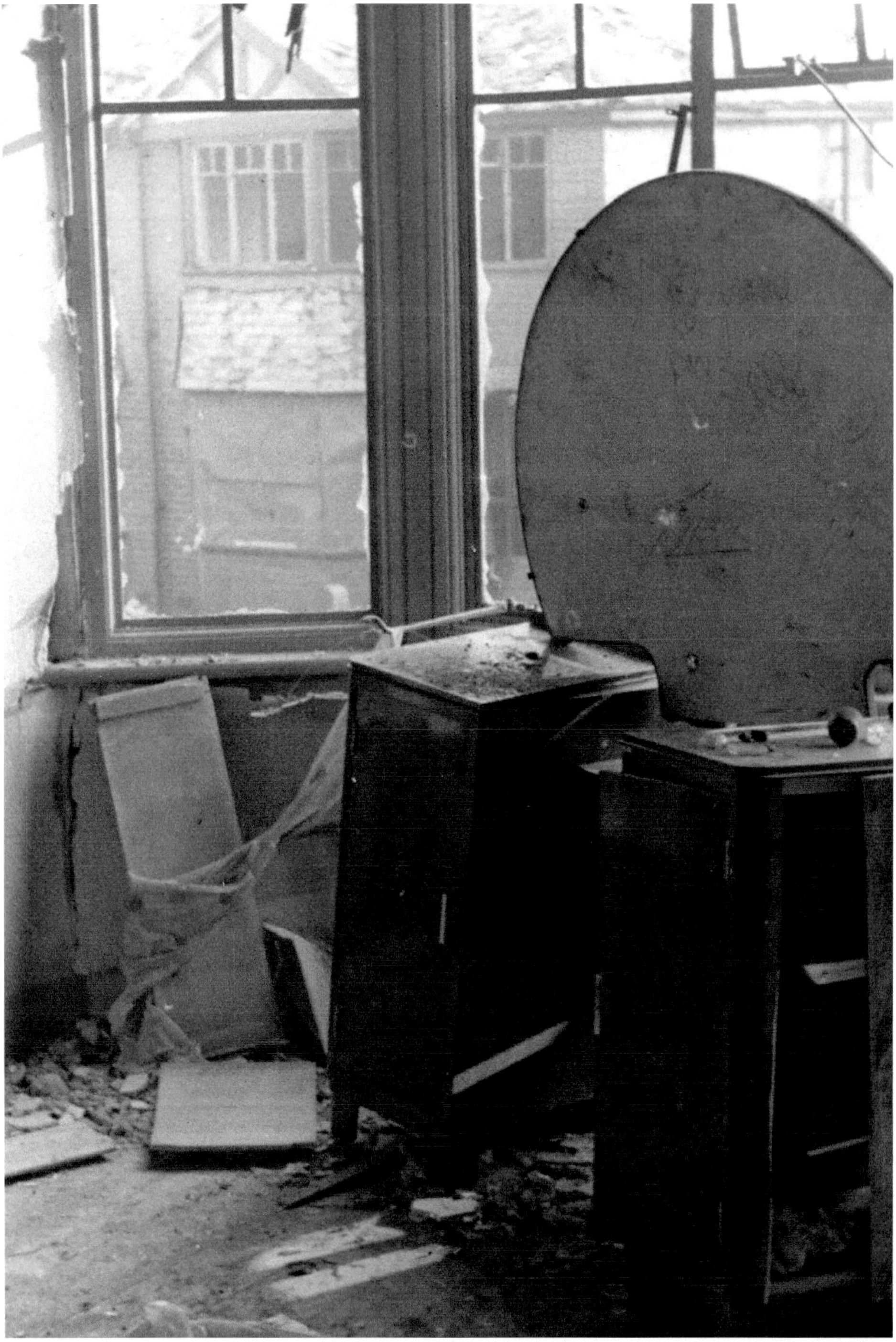

Bomb damage in Kingsley Road, Timperley.

Air Raid Damage at London Road, Appleton, 28 October 1940

Photographs showing the damage caused by a 560lb high-explosive, delayed-action bomb. Two bombs were dropped in the rear of 294 London Road, Appleton, at 12.15 a.m. on 28 October 1940, but only one would explode, at 4.30 p.m. that day. A bomb disposal unit removed the other bomb on 12 November.

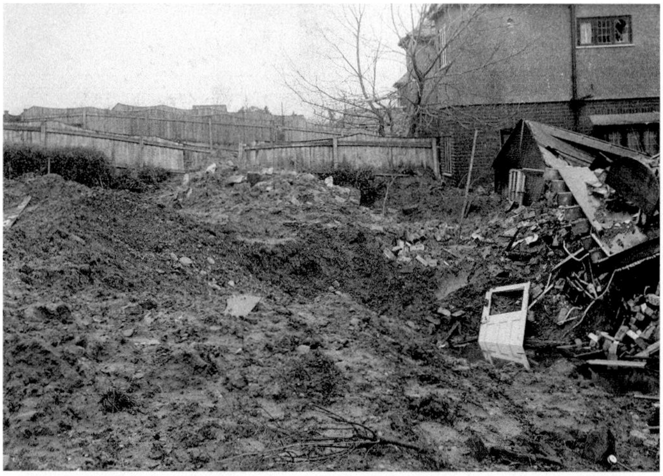

The crater left behind at 294 London Road.

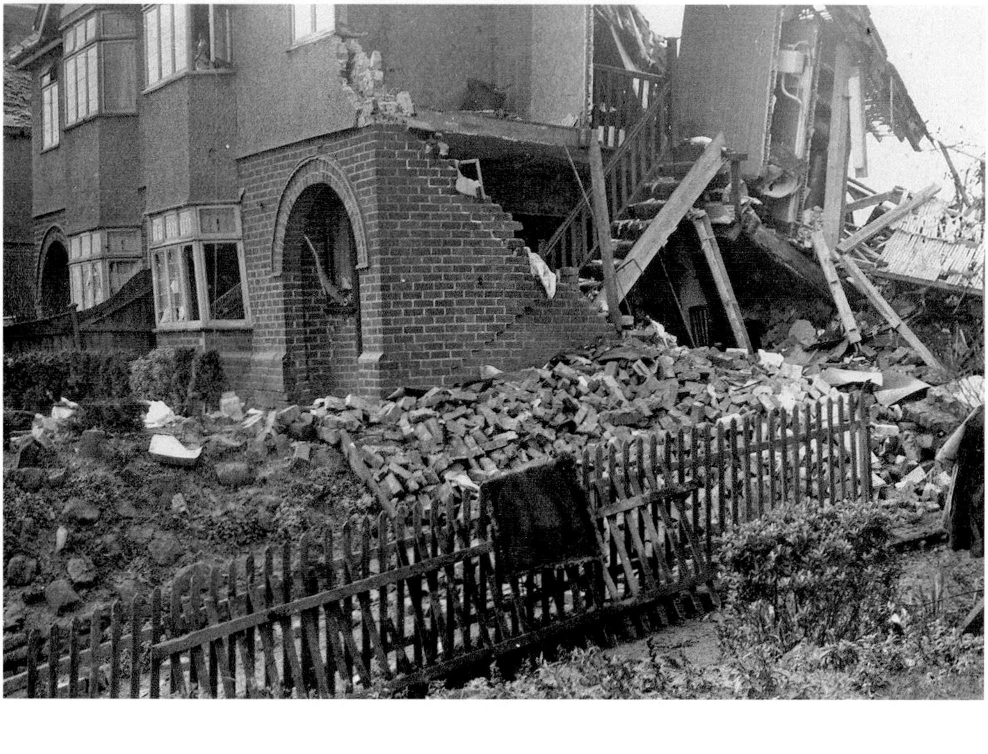

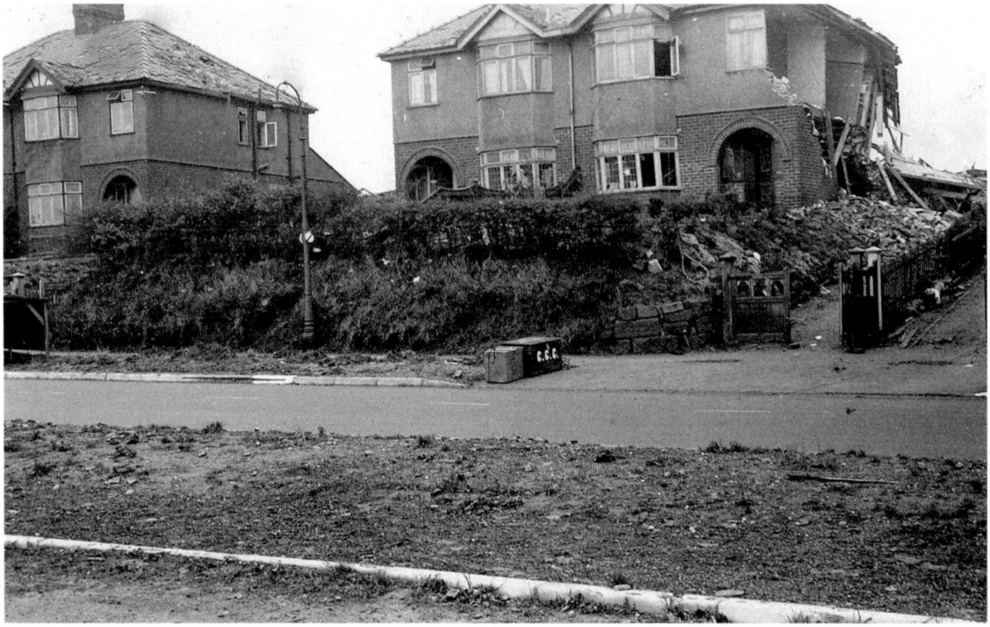

Damage to 294 London Road, Appleton.

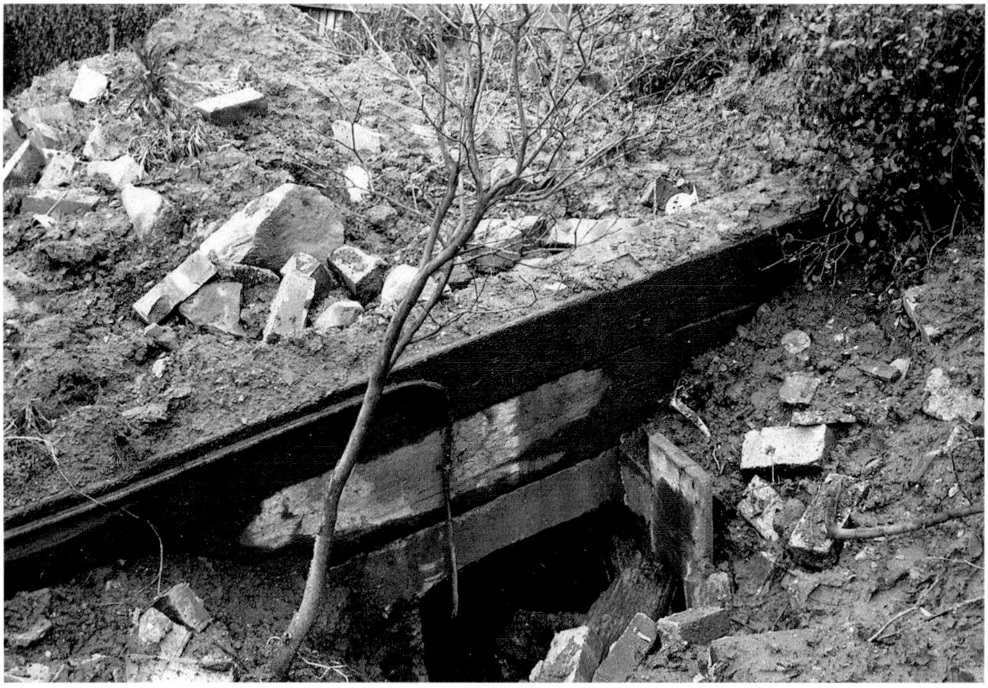

An air raid shelter after the bombing in 294 London Road, Appleton.

5

The Wirral and West Cheshire

Air Raid Damage at Frodsham, 28 November 1940

One of the most horrifying nights of the Blitz for Frodsham was 28 November 1940. The air raids sounded just before 19:30 hours, and in the distance over Liverpool, explosions could be heard, while anti-aircraft batteries fired shells constantly to defend the surrounding villages. Over forty bombs were reported in Frodsham, including in Warrendale, Beechlands, Castle Park, Queensway, Overton Hill and Five Crosses. A whole row of cottages near Mersey View was severely damaged, and three

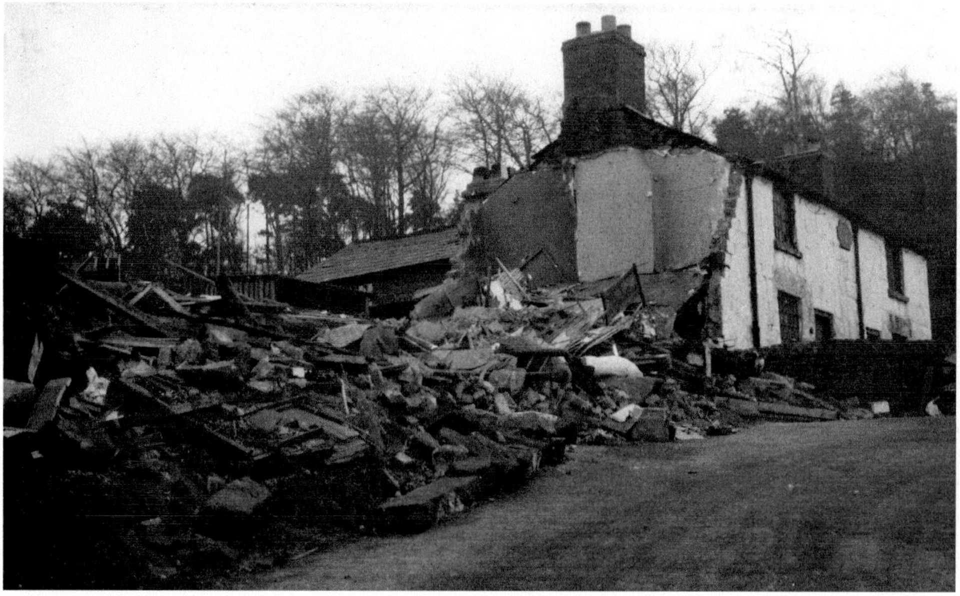

The damage caused to Bate Cottages, Mersey View, by a HE bomb.

occupants – Mrs Annie Bate, her son Francis and her brother Harry Parker – were all sadly killed. The bombing lasted almost eight hours before the all-clear sounded in the early hours of the following day.

Air Raid Damage at Aston, Near Frodsham, 28 November 1940

Three photographs showing damage caused by a high-explosive bomb to Aston church and its surrounds; the photographs overleaf show the damage done to Aston church itself, while the one below shows the damage to houses nearby.

A parachute mine severely damaged the church on 28 November 1940, including the interior. The roof was partially replaced, but the church remained unusable and continued to be derelict. On 30 May 1949, restoration began, and this was completed in June 1950. The church opened again for services on 27 June.

Until the bomb damage, it was the least-restored Georgian church in the Chester Diocese. The damage primarily affected the south side and the east end of the church, with the south porch and organ chamber in the chancel being destroyed, along with the sundial over the south porch and the stone cross at the gable end. The church received a £35,000 repairs grant from the Places of Worship scheme.[14]

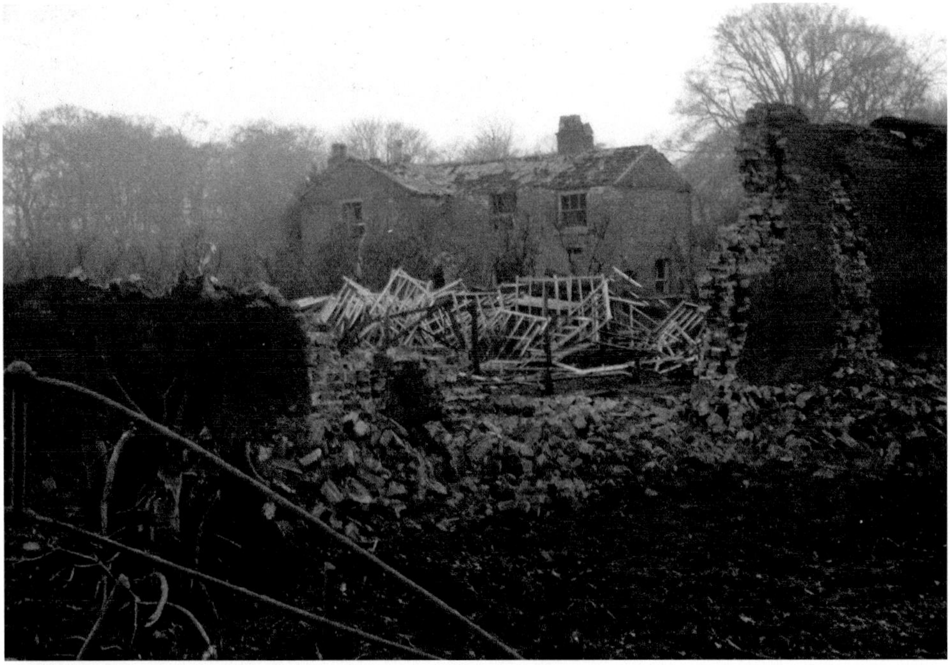

Damage to houses near the church.

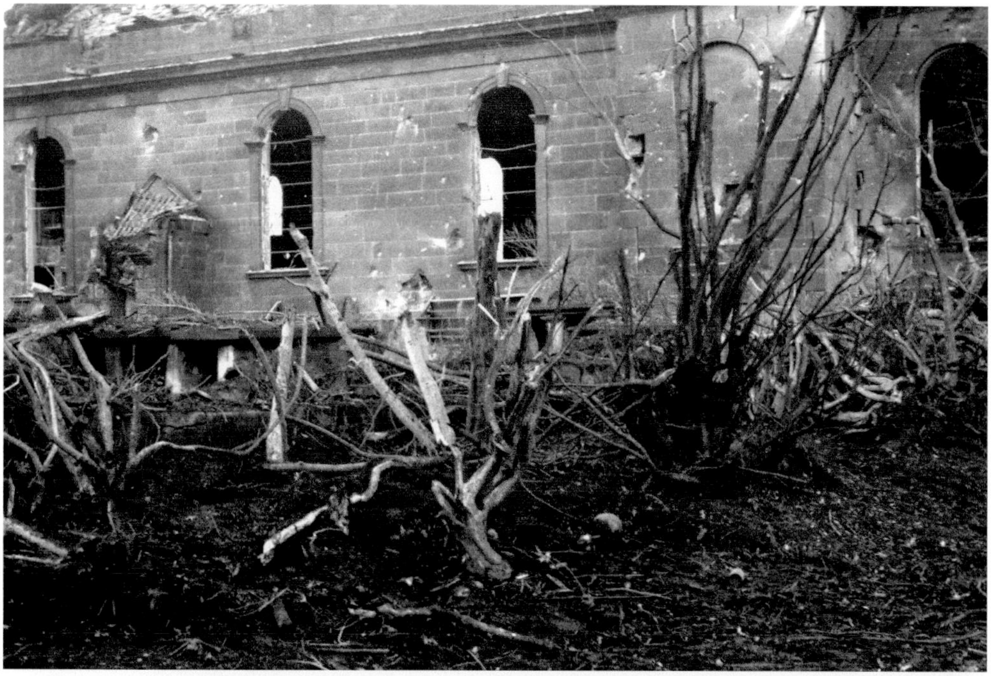

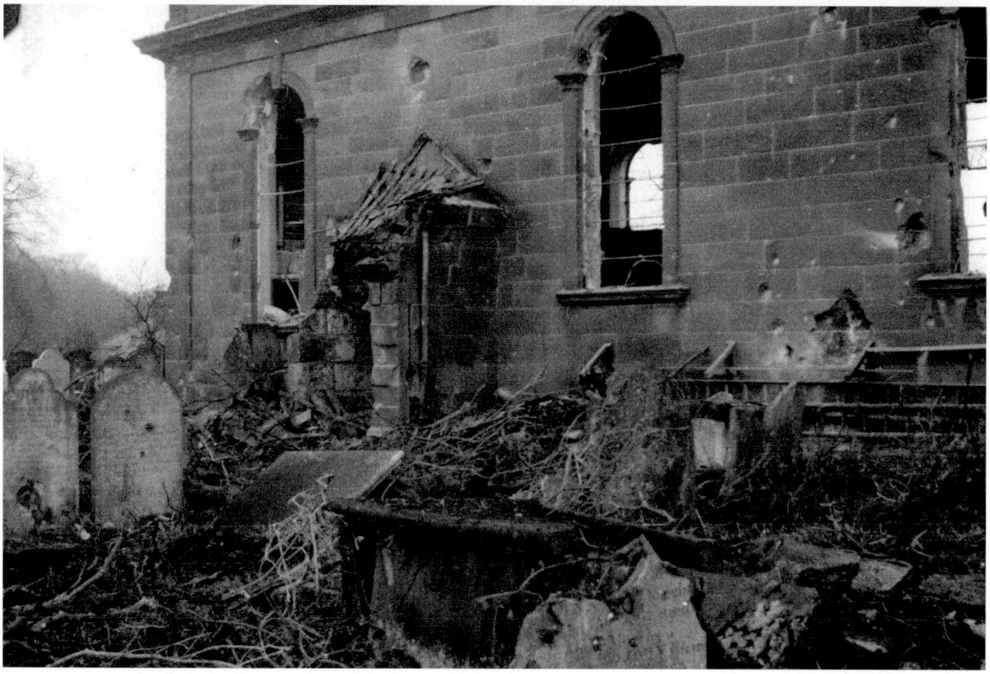

Damage to Aston church.

Air Raid Damage at Barrowmore Hall, Barrow, 29 November 1940
Damage caused by a parachute mine.

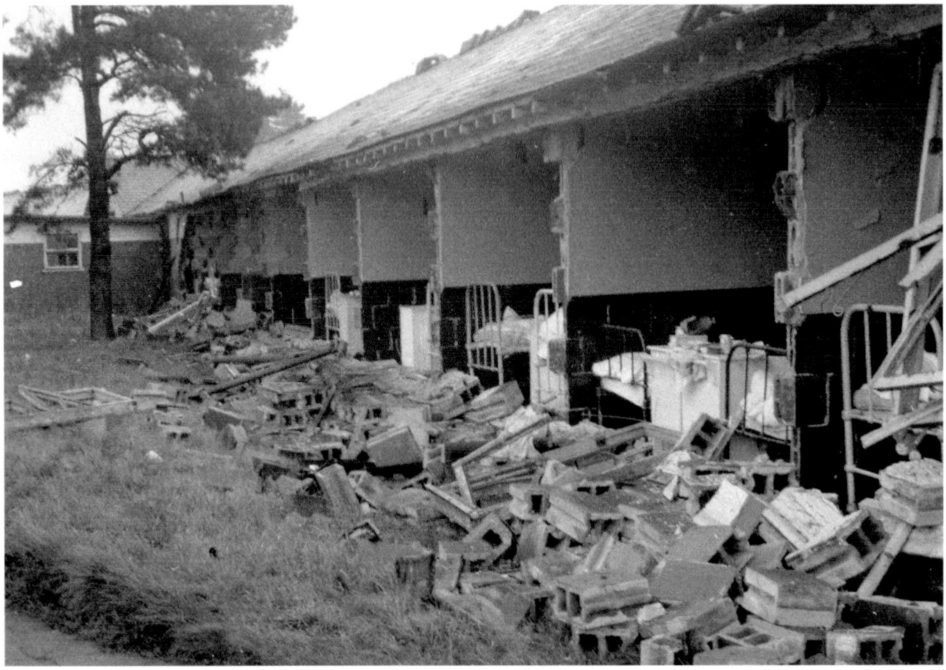

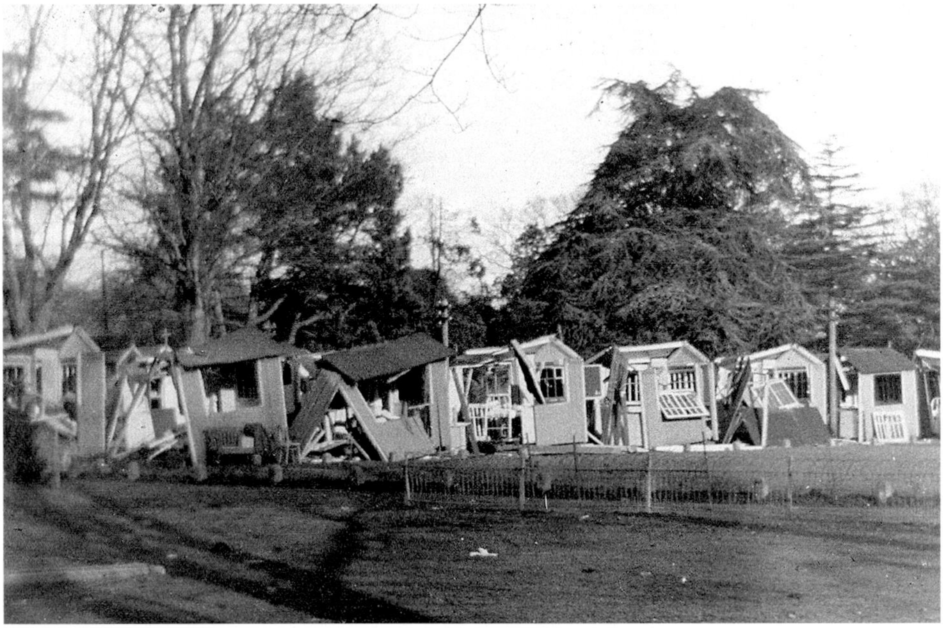

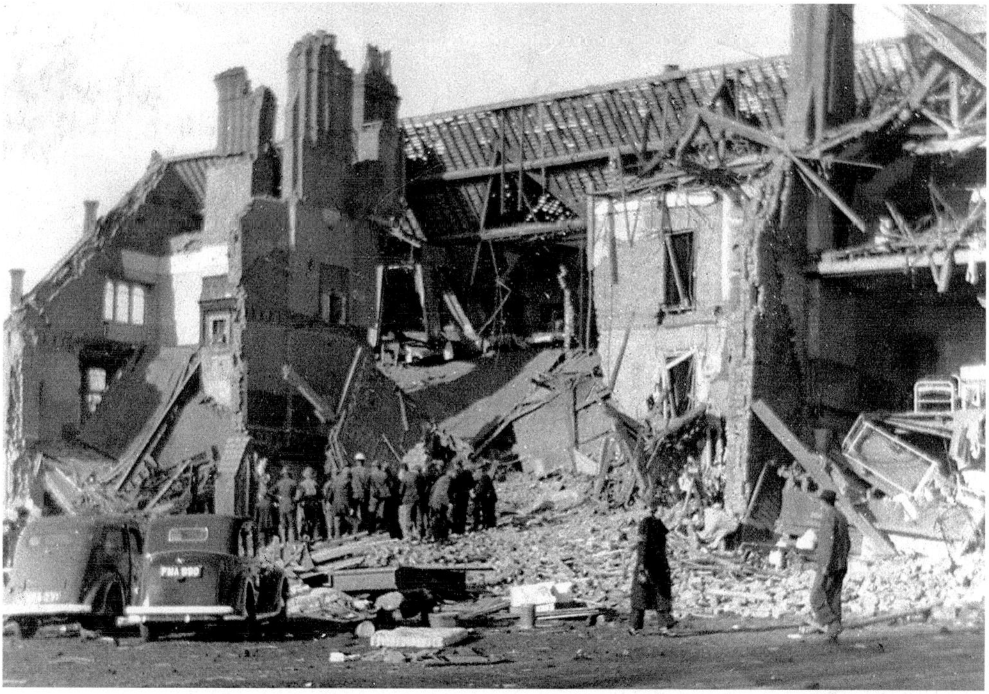

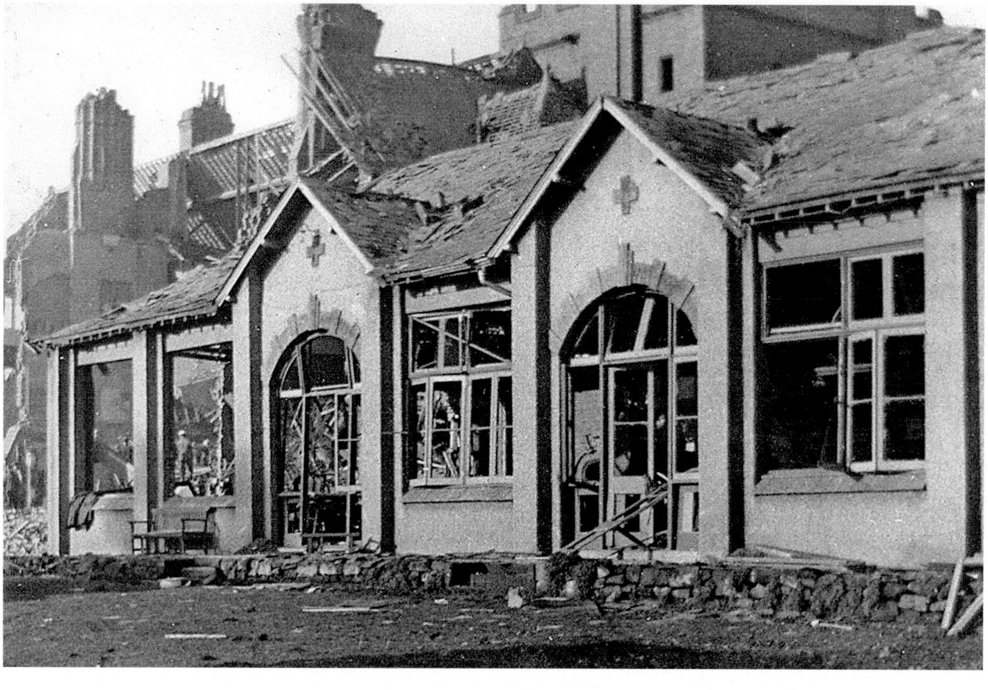

History of Barrowmore Hospital

Liverpool's grandiose late nineteenth-century Barrowmore Hall was converted into a hospital in 1920, and passed to the East Lancashire Committee of the Order of St John of Jerusalem and the British Red Cross Society. It became a haven for ex-servicemen, looking after soldiers injured in the First World War. Known as The Sanatorium, it specialised in treating tuberculosis, and the number of patients treated there had more than doubled by the Second World War. Via a branch known as the Colony, it also provided homes for ex-servicemen with families and dormitory-style arrangements for single men.[15]

In 1931 it was toured by the then Duke and Duchess of York, King George VI and Queen Elizabeth.

It suffered terrible losses and damage after it was hit by a German mine during the night of 29 November 1940. Twenty lives were lost on the premises. The wounded were taken to Chester Royal Infirmary, where they received free treatment.[16]

A new facility was subsequently developed with the support of the Ministry of Health, serving fewer patients overall but carrying out a similar role and function. This was absorbed into the NHS in 1948, after which it took on a broader role carrying out surgical treatment needed across the local region, until it was closed down in 1983.

The Colony side, however, now known as Barrowmore Industries, continues to run today.[17]

Air Raid Damage at Runcorn, 29 August 1940

Runcorn had a significant presence in industry, most notably the ICI works at Weston Point. We know that these works were discussed during Luftwaffe briefings in 1940, but the town itself suffered less frequent air raids than Crewe. Perusing my Luftwaffe maps and books, I see that there is little highlighted for Runcorn. There is, however, a photograph of the Runcorn–Widnes Transporter Bridge – not a primary target, but some bombs did get through.

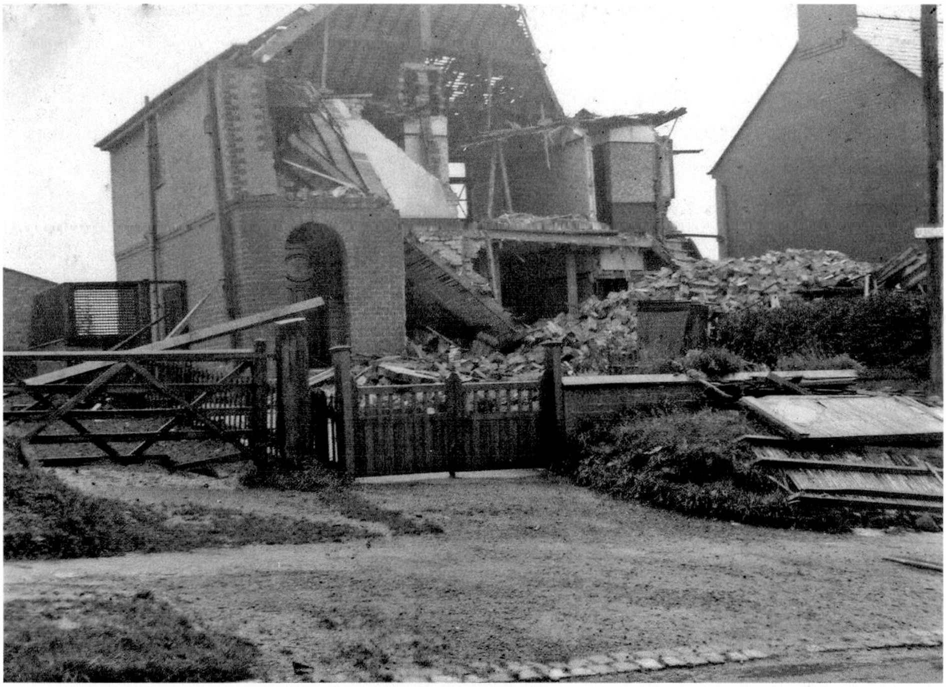

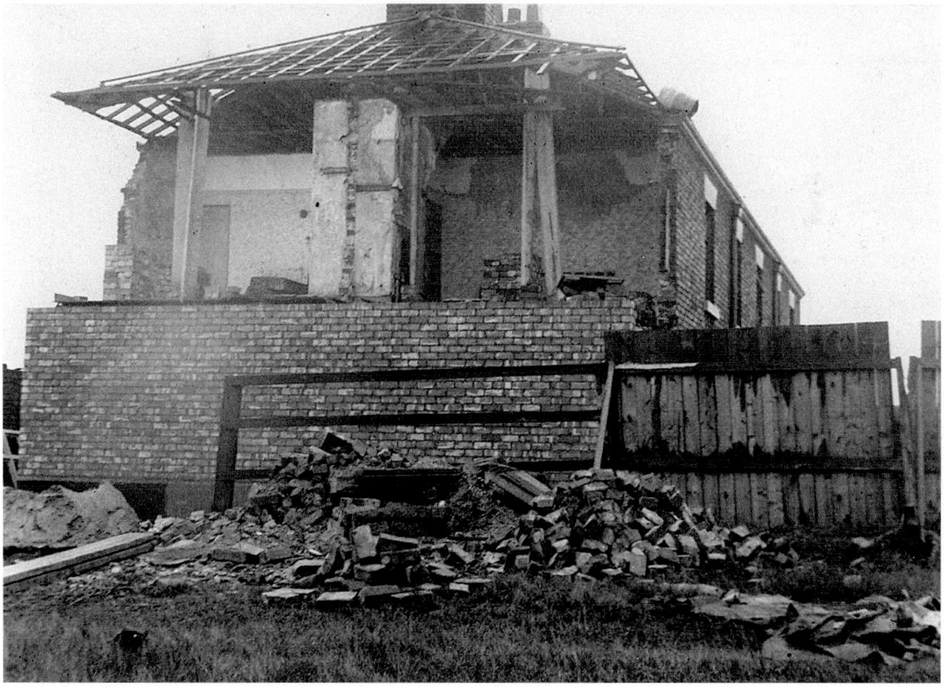

Damage to houses at Halton, Runcorn.

Air Raid Damage at Tattenhall, 28 November 1940

Not many buildings in or around Tattenhall and the surrounding area were destroyed or damaged during the war, but one unfortunate building was: Newton Hall Farm, which the Luftwaffe severely damaged in November 1940, the result of which can be seen in these photographs.

As with many towns and villages in west Cheshire, Tattenhall was close to Liverpool, one of the most heavily bombed cities, which suffered a prolonged bombing campaign in 1940. On the night of 28 November, one parachute mine was dropped on an air raid shelter in Durning Road, Edge Hill, killing 166 people. In a November 2010 issue marking seventy years since the tragedy, the *Liverpool Echo* reported that Churchill described it as the single worst civilian incident in the war.[18]

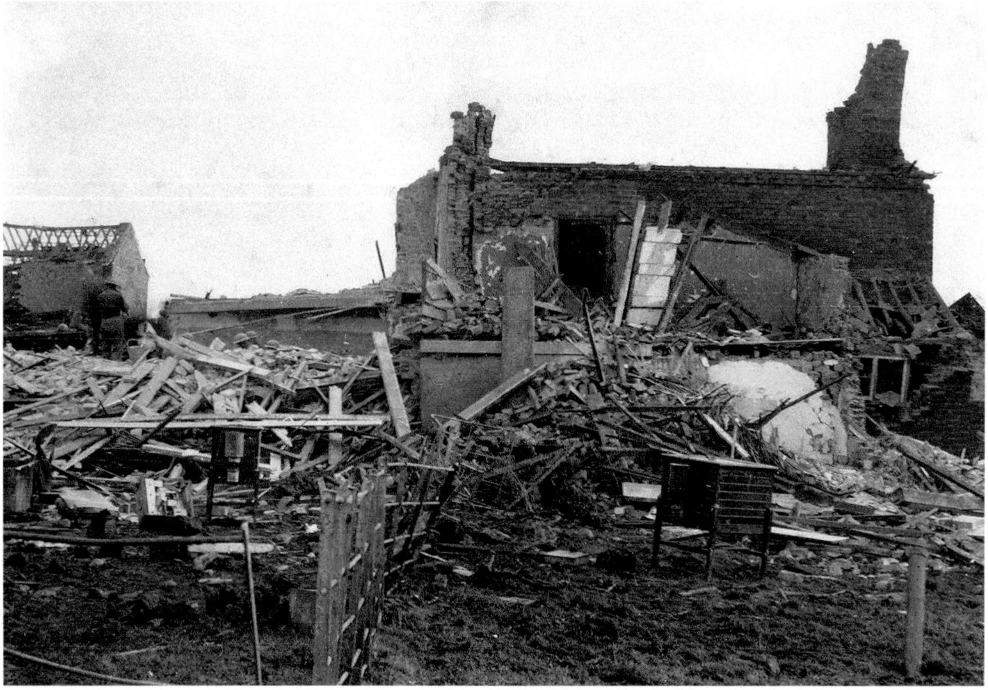

Damage caused by a parachute mine to a farmhouse and buildings at Newton Hall Farm.

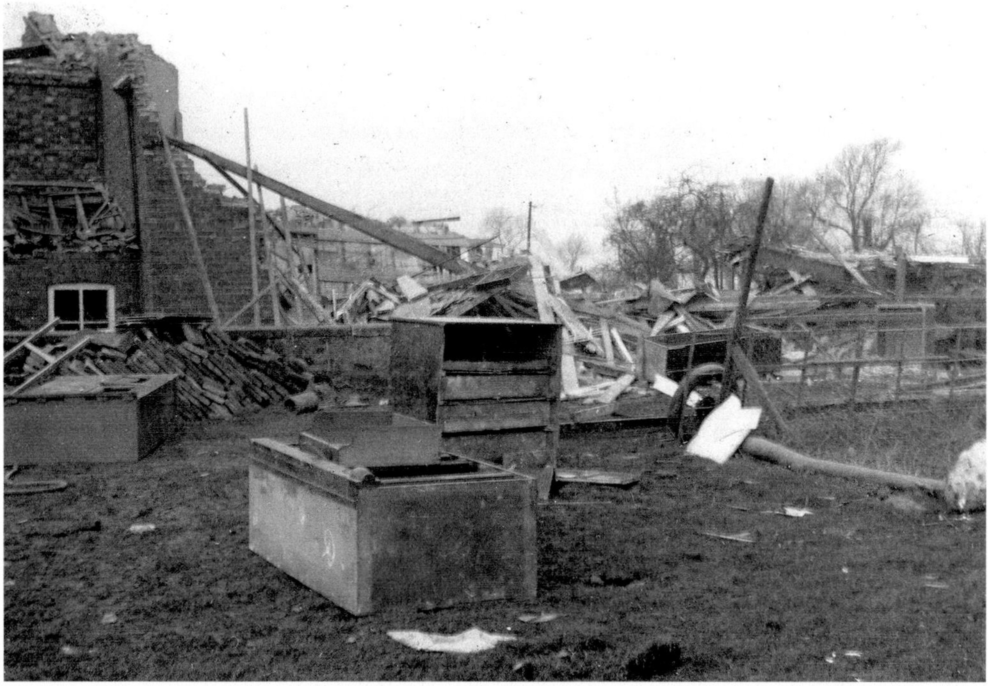

Another shot of the damage at Newton Hall Farm.

Air Raid Damage at Heswall, Wirral, 1 September 1940

An article published in June 2010 in *Heswall Magazine* recounted how the town suffered bomb damage during that fateful Whitsun holiday in May 1941:

> Liverpool and Merseyside were the most bombed areas outside London, and a ferocious onslaught on Liverpool commenced at the beginning of May 1941. Heswall residents grew accustomed to seeing an eerie red glow in the night sky as Liverpool and Birkenhead burned. The air raid siren, located on top of the clock tower in the Children's Hospital, wailed frequently to warn the population to take shelter. As May progressed, they must have felt fortunate not to have suffered any actual bombing, especially since bombing decoys were established on each side of Heswall with the intention of deceiving German bombers into thinking that the River Dee was the River Mersey. Decoy buildings and lights were constructed on Burton Marsh to simulate Garston Dock, on the seaward side of Heswall Golf course to imitate Lime Street railway marshalling yard, and at Thurstaston to imitate Bootle Dock. Perhaps from the perspective of Heswall inhabitants, it was fortunate that these decoys were not very successful in fooling the German bombers.[19]

The first bomb fell near Heswall in July 1940. In September 1940, two absconders from the Heswall Nautical School had set fire to a barn and hay and straw ricks at the neighbouring Oldfield Farm in the hope that the flames would attract planes that would then bomb the school! St Fillan's School ... was taken over by the Soldiers, Sailors & Airmen's Families Association (SSAFA) to provide respite for the families of serving men, especially those who had been bombed out of their homes. As the bombing proceeded in Liverpool and Birkenhead, there was an influx of over 10,000 bombed-out people into the Wirral. A complaint was made ... stating that the shops in Heswall were unable to cope with the increased population and that the resulting demand threatened the local food supply. Heswall's luck in avoiding bombing came to a tragic end on the nights of 30th and 31st May 1941.[20]

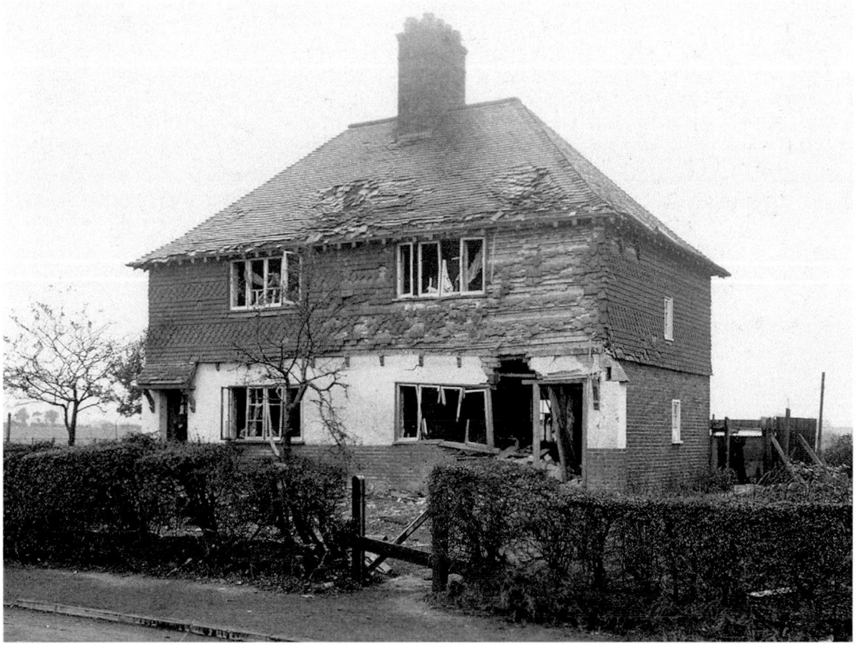

Damage to Ridings Cottage, Brimstage.

Air Raid Damage at Bromborough Police Headquarters, Wirral

Bromborough police divisional headquarters was full of buildings, including offices, married quarters, staff rooms and garages. On 16 September 1940 it was bombed, with one device landing in the main square and causing damage to the garages and the vehicles therein. There was also some damage to the buildings and houses within the grounds.

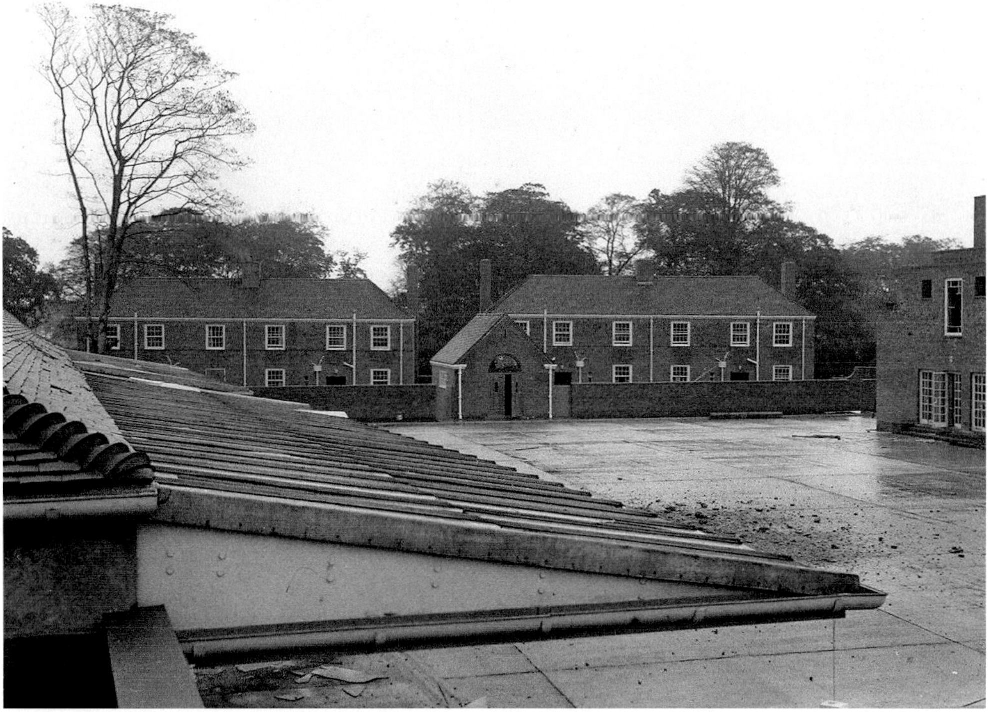

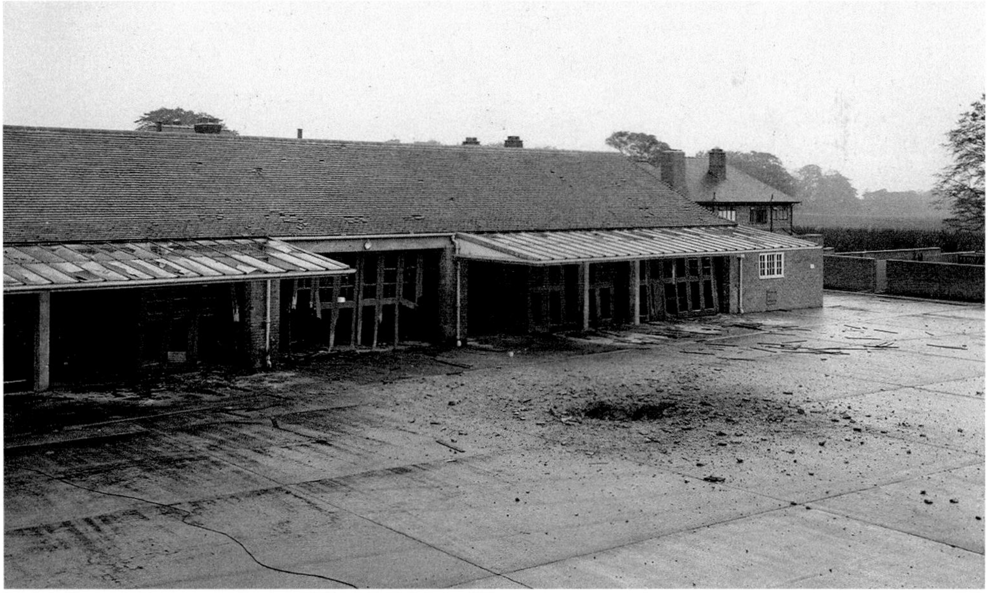

Damage to the police headquarters in Bromborough.

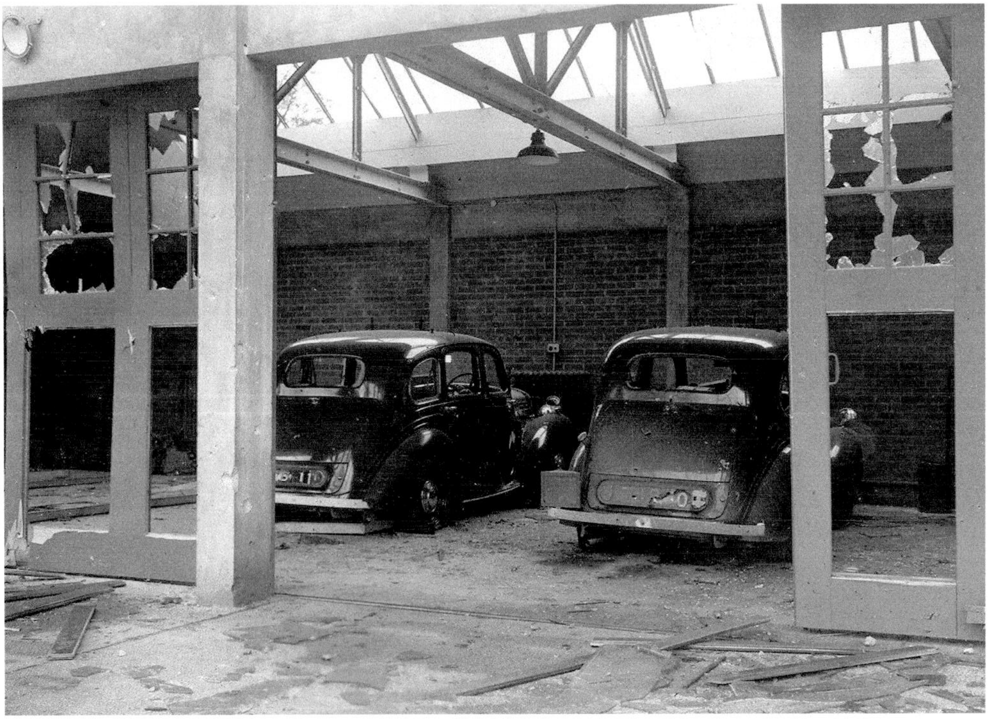

Another view of damage to the headquarters.

Air Raid Damage at Lower Bebington, 23 November 1940
Two photographs showing damage caused by high-explosive bombs to a house in Stanton Estate, Lower Bebington, on 23 November 1940.

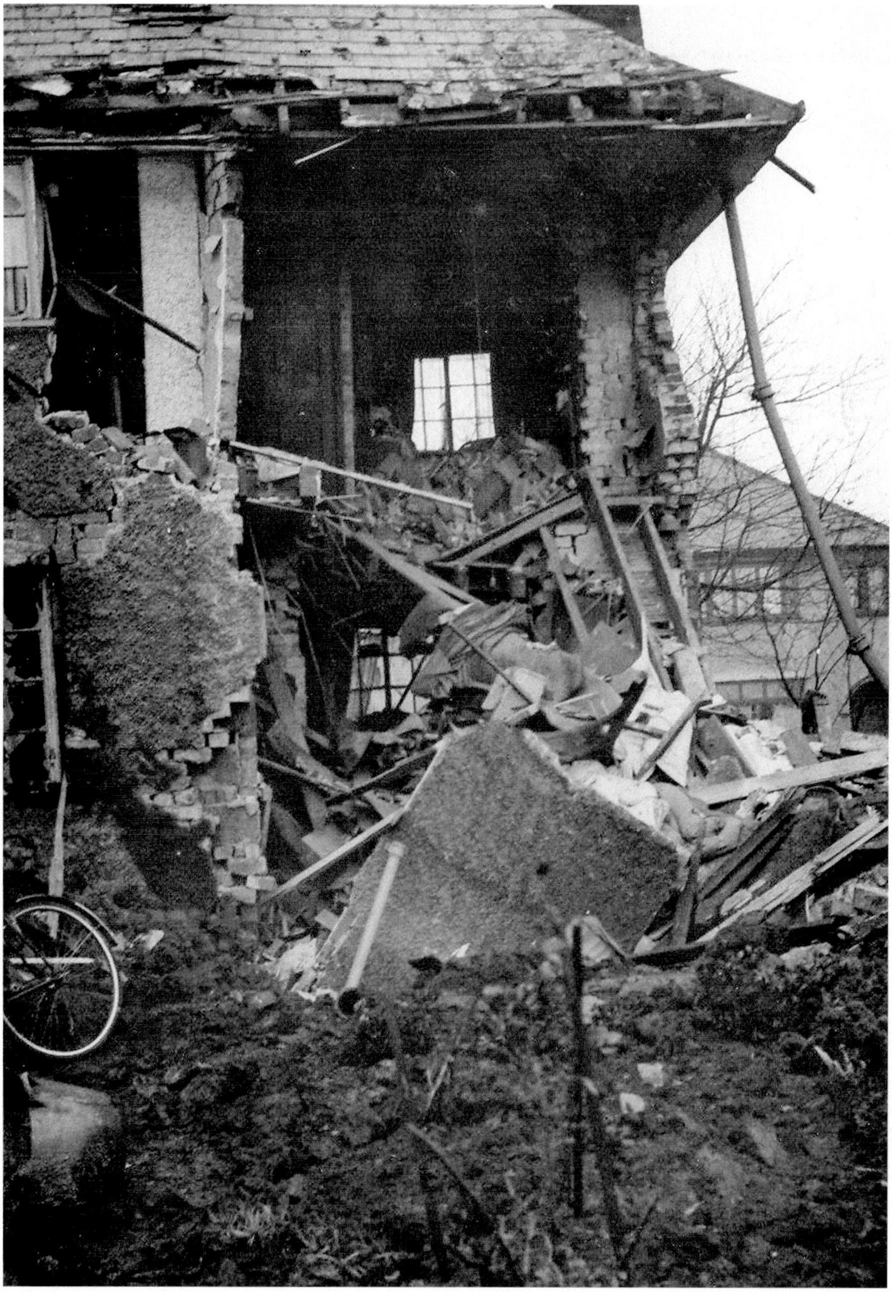

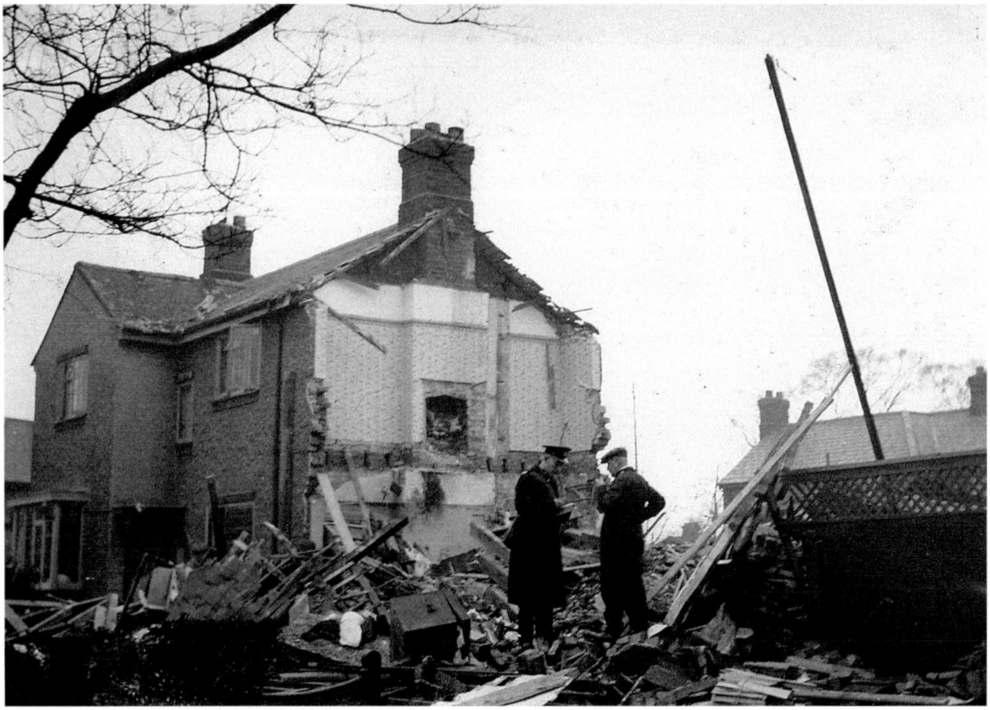

Damage caused by HE bombs in Stanton Estate, Lower Bebington.

Air Raid Damage at Higher Bebington, 28 November 1940

Three photographs showing damage caused by high-explosive bombs to a house at the junction of Heyville Avenue and Holmville Avenue, Higher Bebington, on 28 November 1940, and a modern photograph. Bebington, along with other areas in Wirral, experienced bombing as part of the Blitz. Holmville Avenue and Heyville Avenue in Bebington were directly impacted by these raids, suffering significant damage and casualties.

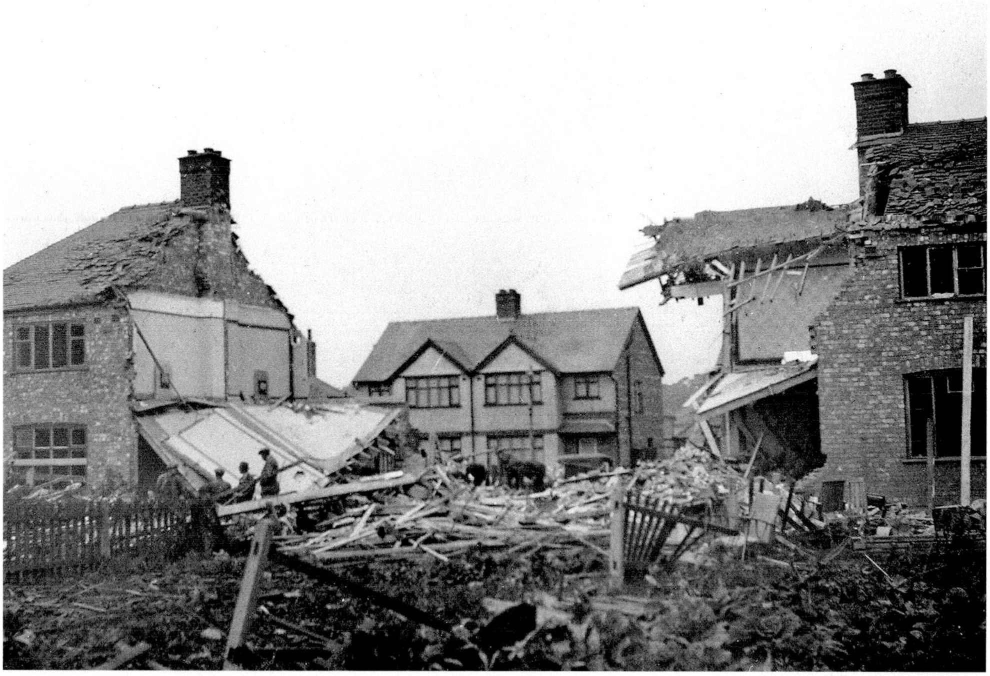

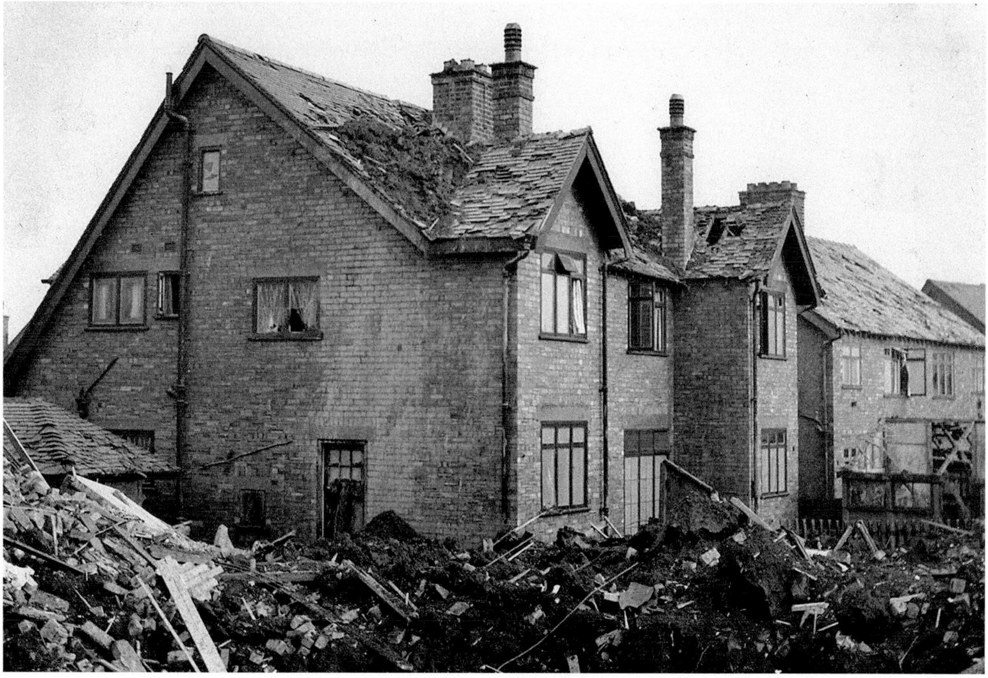

Heyville Avenue and Holmville Avenue, Higher Bebington.

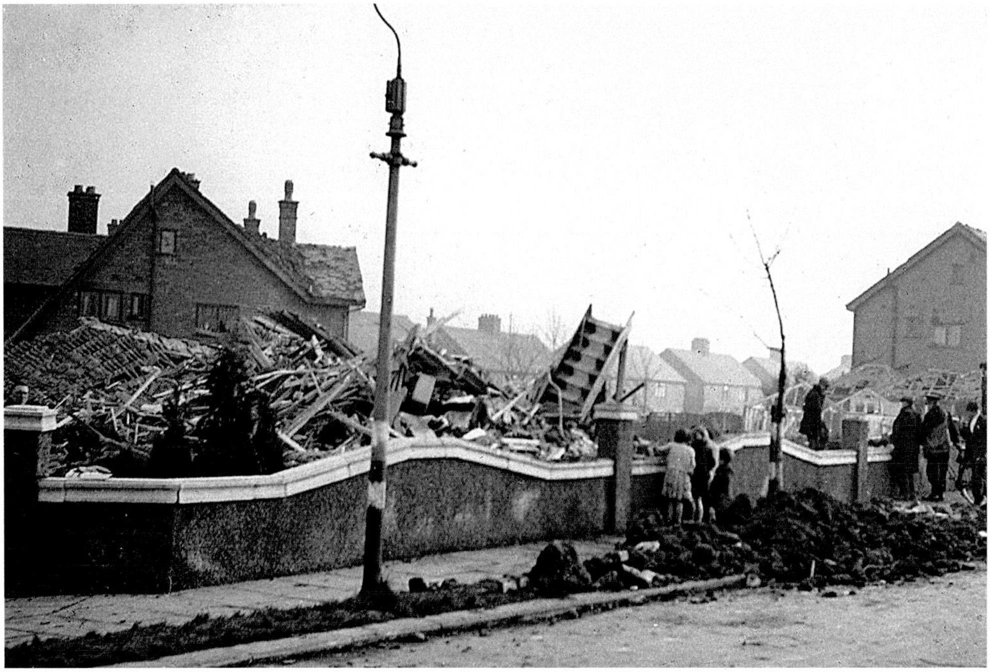

More damage to property in Heyville and Holmville Avenues.

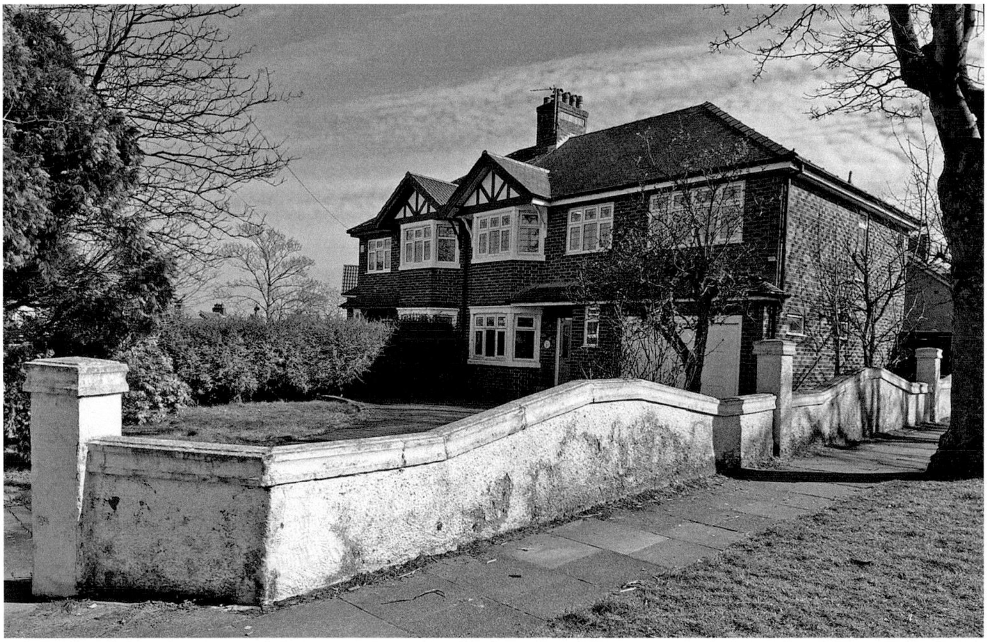

Heyville Avenue and Holmville Avenue, Higher Bebington, in the present day. (Authors' collection)

Air Raid Damage at Bebington, 7 April 1941

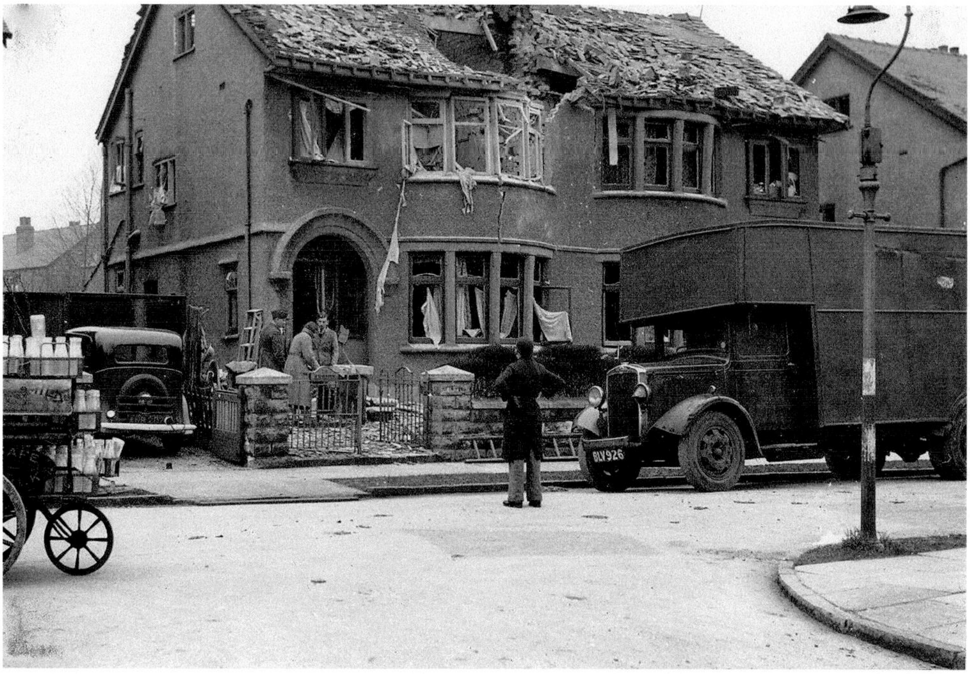

Damage caused by HE bombs in 'Woodbourne' Boulevard, Bebington, Wirral, on 7 April 1941. The correct address is Woodburn Boulevard, but it is spelt incorrectly in the album.

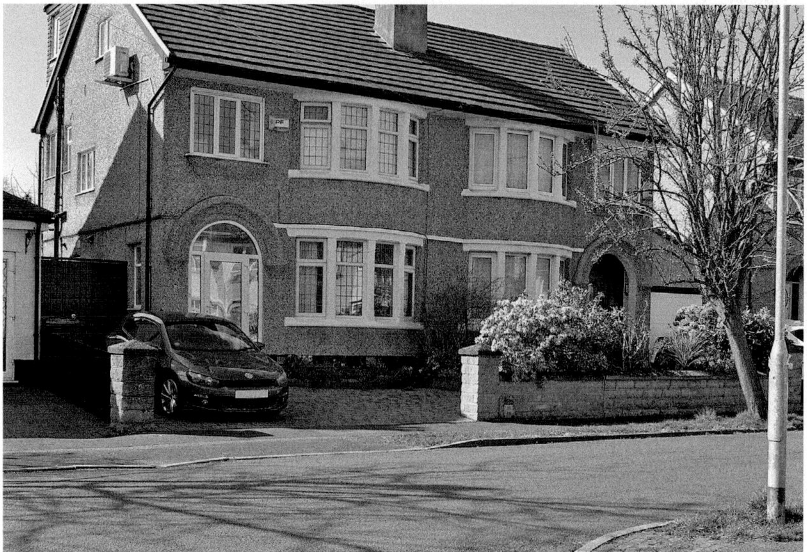

The same view in the present day. (Authors' collection)

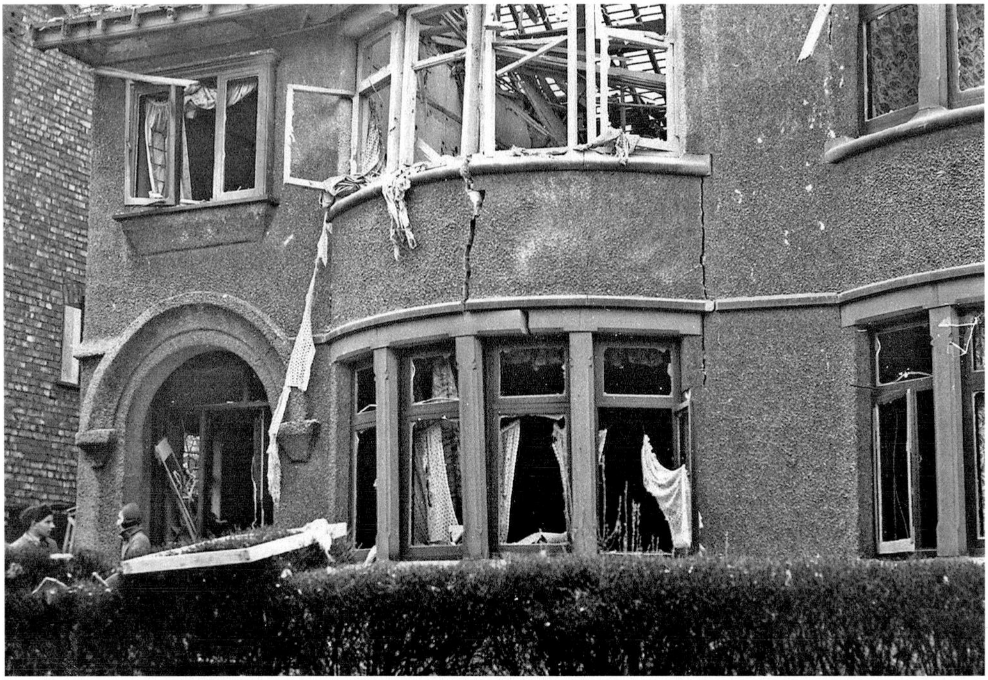

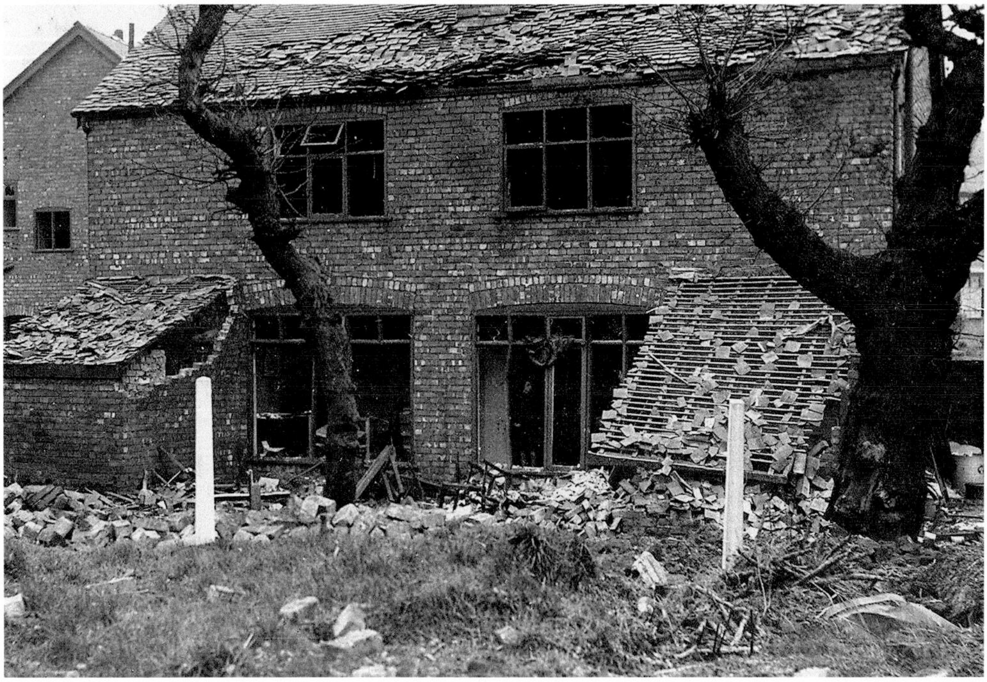

Woodburn Boulevard, Bebington.

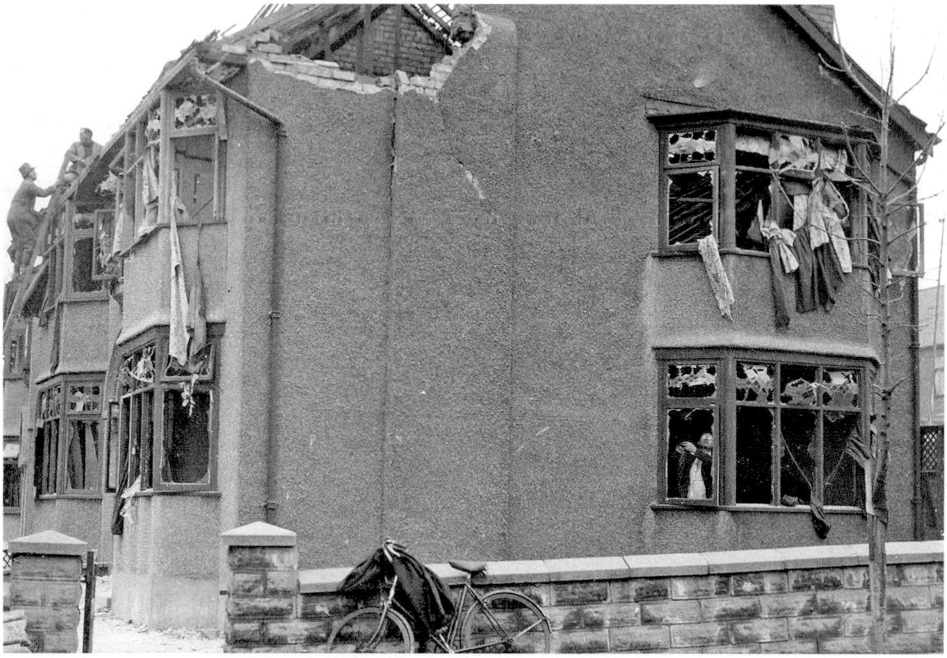

3 and 4 Woodburn Boulevard, Bebington.

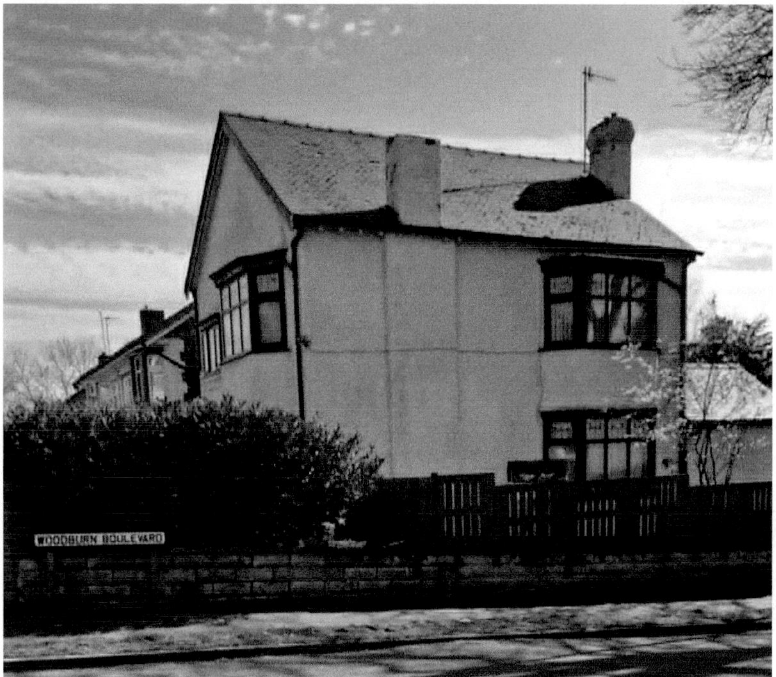

The same view in the present day. (Authors' collection)

Shot-Down Bomber at Bromborough, 8 October 1940

A German Junkers Ju 88 bomber aircraft that was shot down at Bromborough, Wirral Division.[21]

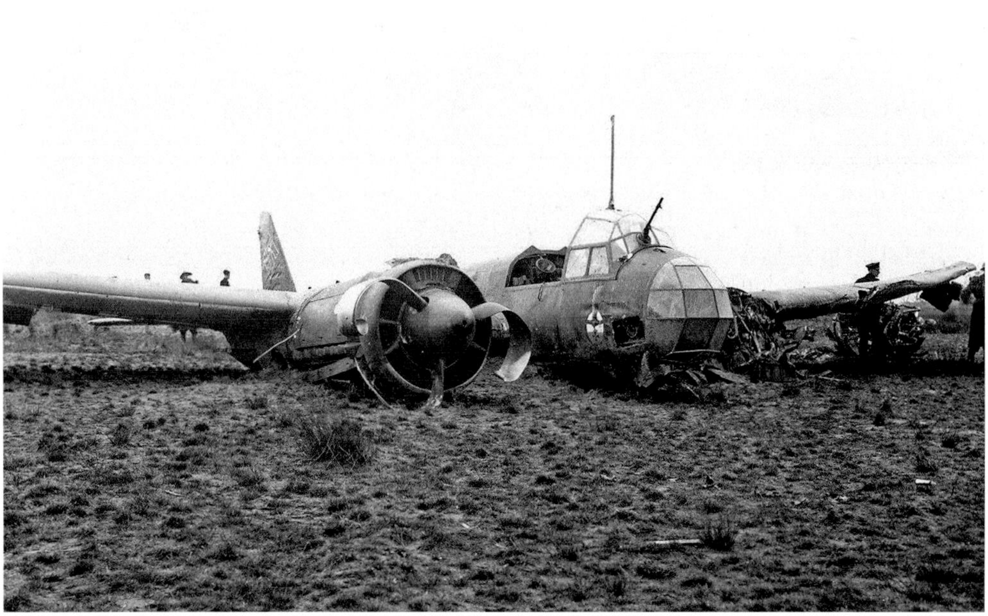

Shot-down bomber at Bromborough.

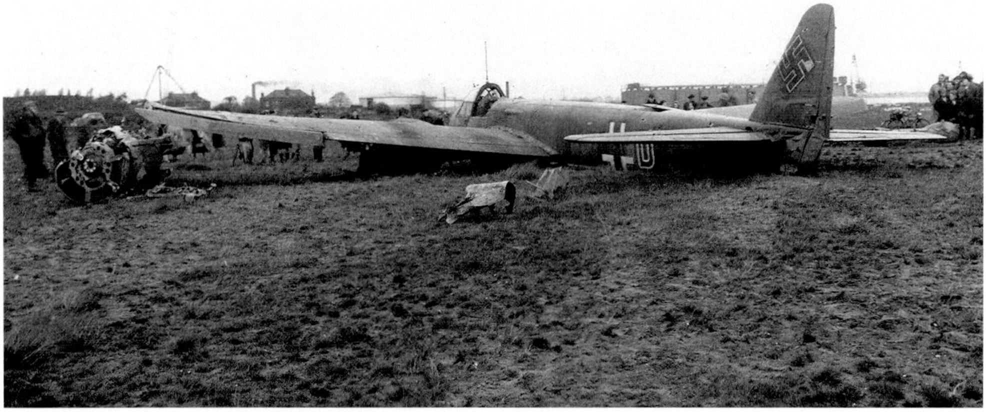

Crashed bomber with the engine lying nearby.

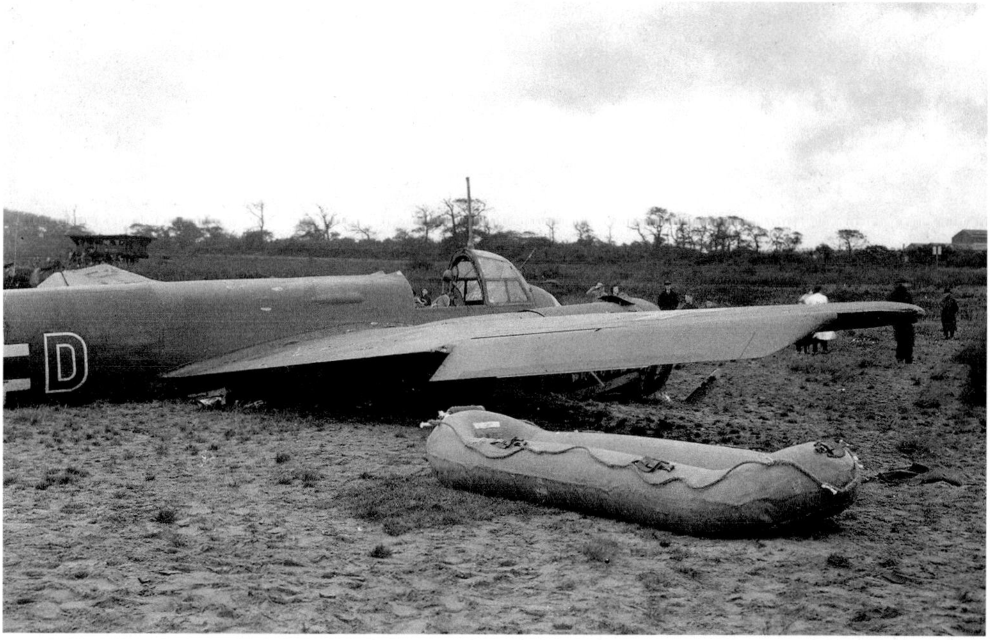

Shot-down bomber at Bromborough with its life raft, which inflated during the crash. The whole story is below.

On 8 October 1940, a Junkers Ju 88 travelled from France to bomb and document damage on military targets across Merseyside, successfully avoiding fighters on its way north. Lookout Les Jones saw the aircraft flying along the River Mersey from his post atop Liverpool's George Henry Lee department store, and alerted Squadron Leader H.W. 'Tubby' Mermagen at Speke, who ordered out three Hurricanes from No. 312 (Czech) Squadron, flown by Flight Lieutenant D.E. Gillam, Pilot Officer A. Vasatko and Sergeant J. Stehlik. Meanwhile, No. 289 AA Battery of the 93rd Regiment of the Royal Artillery prepped its guns, at first hesitating in case of hitting friendly fighters, but soon opening fire until ordered to stop, while the Ju 88 tried to retreat to the cover of clouds.

Pilot Officer Vasatko's Combat Report, held in the Public Record Office, details:

> I was Yellow 2 and started close behind Yellow leader, staying about 20 yards behind. On turning over the river, Yellow leader started to climb sharply, and looking round, I sighted the E/A (Enemy Aircraft). I gave full gas, turned to port, and flew about 60 feet below the E/A from quarter, but could not fire due to the presence of Yellow 3. I turned and climbed, then attacked the E/A from the rear

> and above (at about 2 seconds, at 100 yards). Immediately afterwards, I saw Yellow 1 attack E/A from below; I broke away slightly to the right and saw E/A smoking from the starboard engine and gliding downward. I followed at a distance of 1200–1500 feet and approached but could not fire immediately as Yellow 3 was attacking. I then fired a short burst and experienced return fire from the upper gunner. E/A then flew level at a height of 200 feet, and I attacked from the stern and gave a third short burst and saw the E/A fall flat on the ground and slew round to port. It lies on a meadow at the edge of the waterborne Balloon Barrage.[22]

The second German pilot was killed in the action and the aircraft's engine was hit. The pilot tried dumping some of its bombs into the Mersey while firing back at the Hurricanes, but crash landed near Bromborough Dock.

Gateman Harry Gill, who worked at the dock, reported seeing two men climb out of the aircraft and run behind it, where he found them with a third man prone on the ground. They put up no fight and others soon arrived to help secure the scene, including W.A. Rand and R. Thompson from the electrical, fuel and steam depots, and the Local Defence Volunteer (LDV) units of Unilever and Fawcett Preston.

One of the German crewmembers who climbed out had severe injuries, including bullet wounds, and the team who found them treated him as best they could until help arrived. The dead man, Sonderführer H. Lehmann, was buried in Hooton village church, but his body was reinterred in the German military cemetery at Cannock Chase, Staffordshire, in 1962.

Gill found some detailed maps inside the crashed plane, marked to show targets in the Port Sunlight factory and Bromborough Dock. There were great celebrations for the Hurricane pilots who shot down the plane, for whom this was a very successful first action. So many locals wanted to come and congratulate them that the airport had to be closed.[23]

Sometime after the crash, Flight Lieutenant Gillam returned to the site:

> Flight Lieutenant Gillam got into his car and drove to the scene of the crash. There, he cut a badge off the side of the aircraft, together with the Swastika on the starboard side of the fin, for a souvenir. Returning to Speke, it was hung in the hut at the squadron dispersal. After the War, Flight Lieutenant Gillam presented the panel with the Swastika to RAF Finningley. Sadly, following Finningley's closure, the panel is now missing. It has been reported that a paddle from the dinghy, which had a plaque mounted on it, and a painting entitled 'The Fastest Victory' painted by Robert Taylor and signed by Flight Lieutenant Gillam, has been seen for sale on an internet site.[24]

Air Raid Damage at Eastham, Wirral, 20 December 1940

Eastham Hall Farm took a direct hit from a high-explosive bomb, and all the cattle in the farm's shippons were killed. The farm was opposite the Stanley Arms pub, which was named for the local landowners; the pub itself did not suffer from the blast but, as can be seen below and overleaf, the farm was severely affected. The pub, now known as The Montgomery, has a stone stag's head embedded in the wall above the door, which comes from the original Hooton Hall. Eastham had a large contingent of American troops based there in a tented camp.

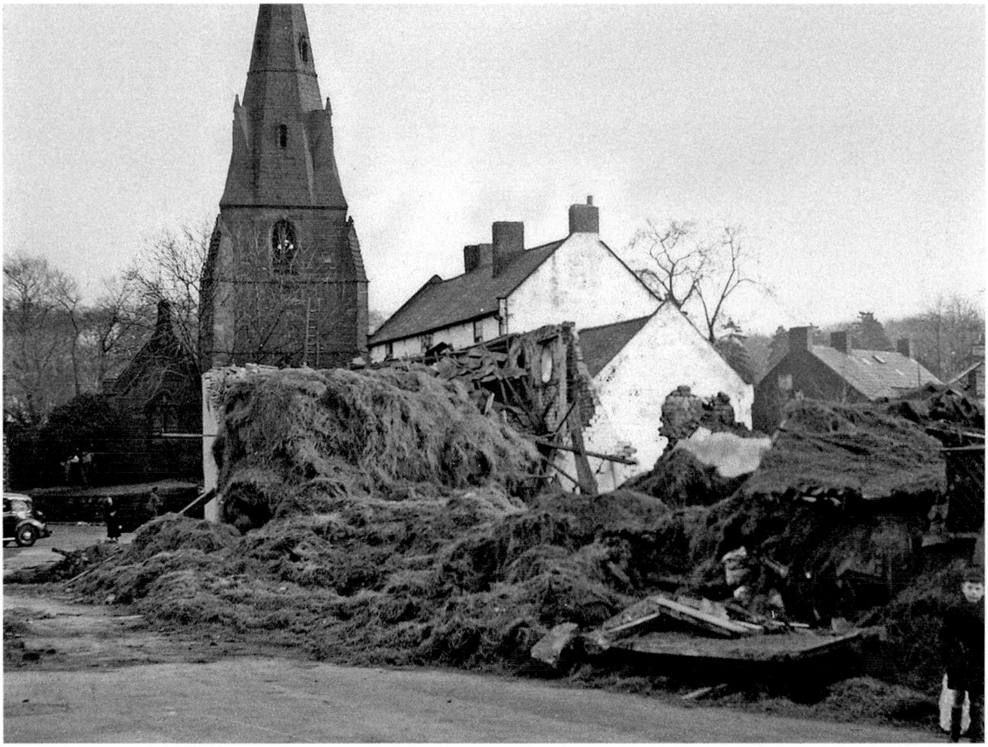

Damage caused by a HE bomb to Eastham Hall Farm.

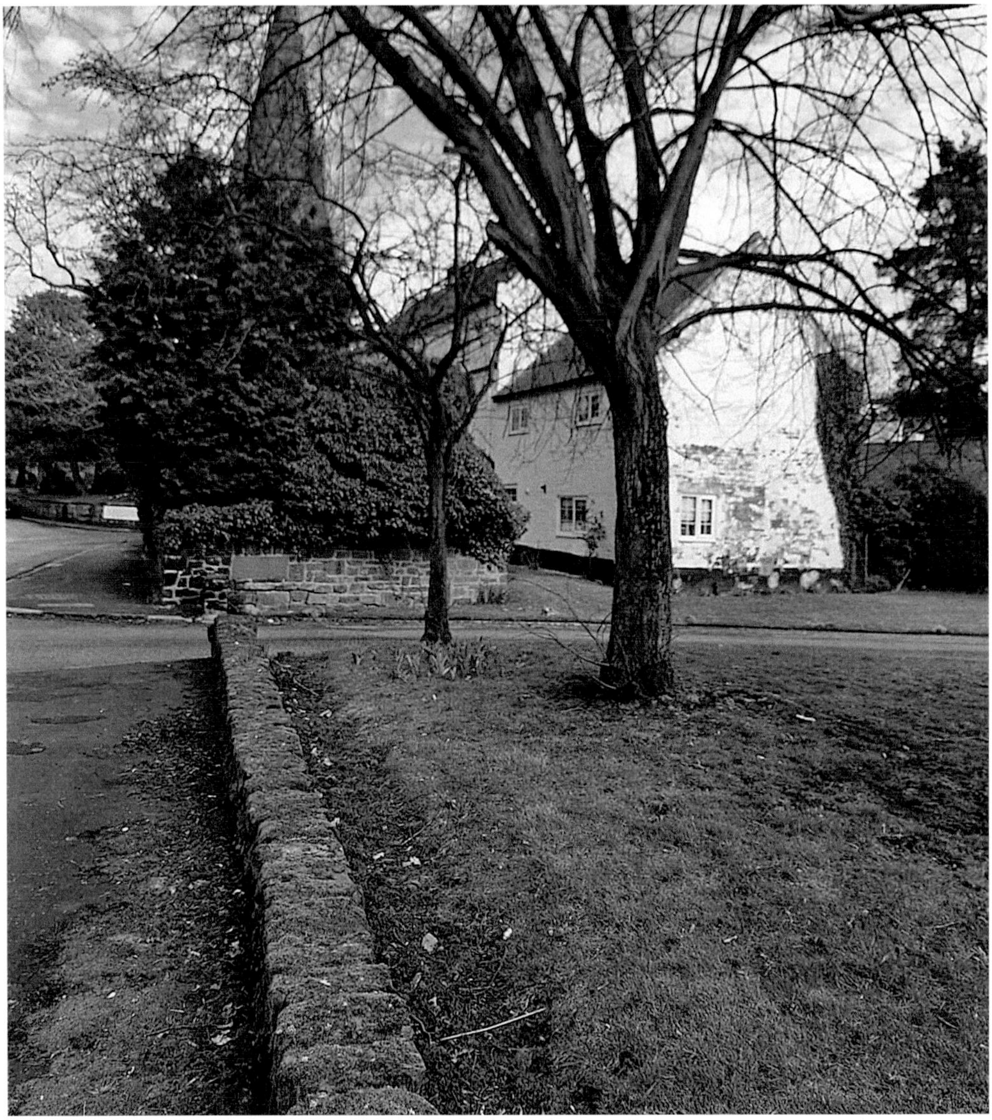

Eastham Hall Farm in the present day. (Authors' collection)

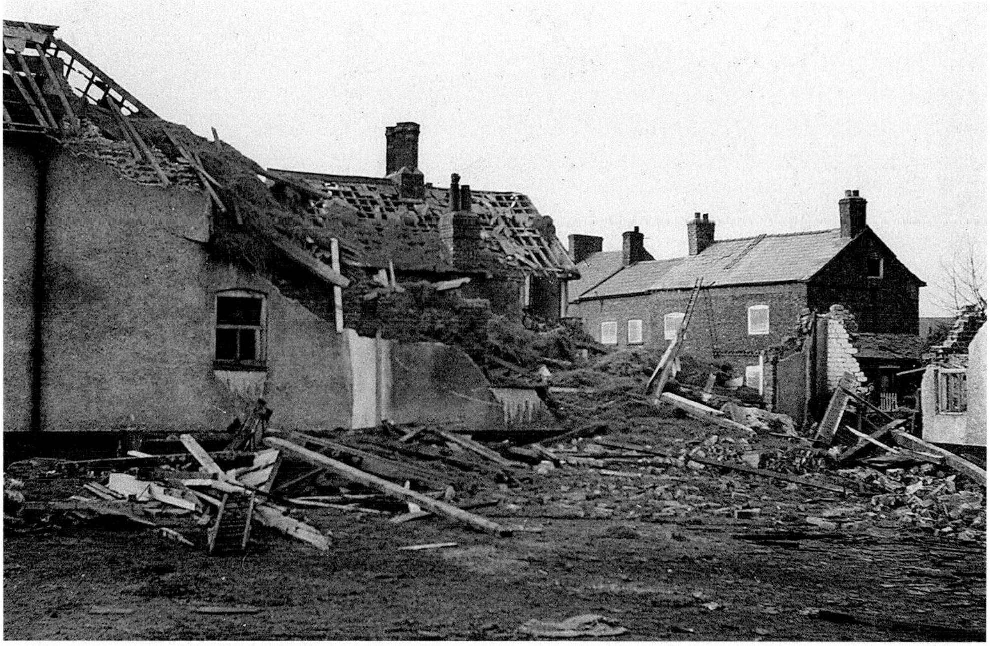

Damage to Eastham Hall Farm.

Air Raid Damage at New Ferry, Wirral Division, 12 March 1941

The damage to the roof of New Ferry police station was caused by the blast from a parachute mine. During the Second World War, the shoreline of New Ferry was significant as the shore fields near the river had an anti-aircraft gun emplacement to defend Liverpool and Birkenhead from German bomber attacks:

> Despite this protection, however, during the 1941 Blitz, a bomb fell on some of the terraced houses on Egerton Road (those on the north side). The houses, only completed a few years earlier, were destroyed.[25]

Following the war, local barracks were used as temporary living accommodation for people made homeless during the Blitz:

> The New Ferry shoreline was also used to construct some of the landing pontoons used for the D-Day landings. These had to be towed around the coast and taken across the Channel as part of the invasion.[26]

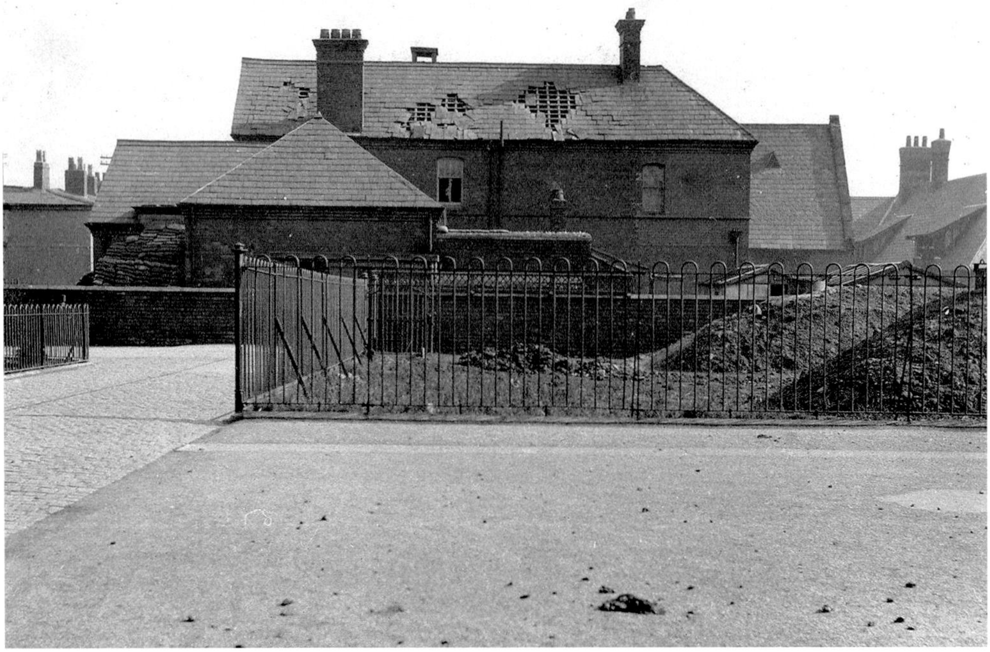

Damage to the roof of New Ferry police station, caused by a parachute mine.

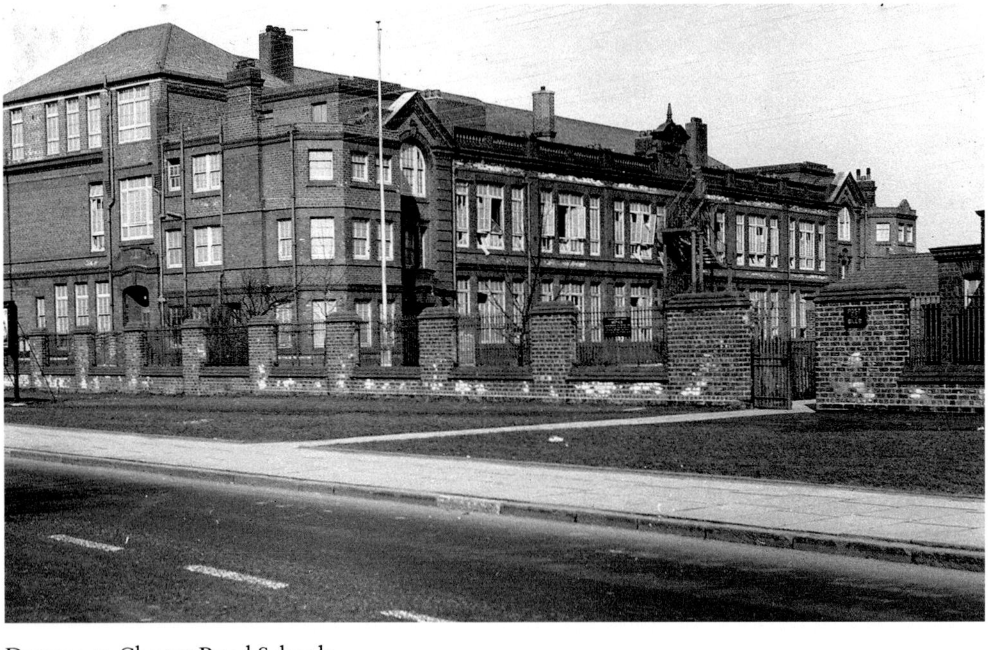

Damage to Chester Road Schools.

Air Raid Damage at Port Sunlight, 17 October 1940

Port Sunlight on the Wirral has been described as 'arguably the finest surviving example of urban planning in Britain'[27] and has remained virtually intact since it was planned by William Hesketh Lever in 1888 – apart from, of course, the damage shown in the photographs overleaf. Lever, who later became Baron and then Viscount Leverhulme, learned his trade in his father's grocery store before opening a soap factory at Port Sunlight with his brother. He then decided to provide a model village for his employees. This was not a new idea as New Lanark had been built in 1800 and Sir Titus Salt had built Saltaire in 1851, but Lever decided to go a stage further and provide first-class houses with plenty of green spaces, public buildings and parkland. These houses would be rented to his employees at a modest price. A considerable amount of work was carried out by twenty-odd different architects, and around 900 exclusive dwellings were built, which are now listed as Grade II. Most still exist in the 130 acres of gardens.[28]

The Lever Brothers became successful and went on to become the multinational company Unilever. But what about their contribution to the war effort? Obviously, soap and all of its derivatives was welcome, but, like many big manufacturing companies, they went even further. When asked if they could put together the vehicles sent as parts from America in the early war years, their immediate answer was yes. They cleared a large section of the works and erected runways, gantries, inspection pits and offices. In just ten days, they were ready to start.

Consignments of Jeeps, Dodge trucks and Ford vans then began to arrive in crates, which took up less shipping space. It was the job of Lever Brothers to assemble them. Over the coming years, they assembled over 1,400 vehicles, later discovering that they had been put to good use in the North African campaign. The works and village suffered greatly at the hands of the Nazis, and on one day 1,000 workers did not turn up for work as their houses had been bombed – however, they were all back at work in less than twenty-four hours. This is the story of one of many companies whose wartime work proved invaluable.

The beautiful Port Sunlight village was somewhat close, as the crow flies, to Liverpool and its docks, and some examples follow of the destructive work the Luftwaffe carried out, showing damage to property in Pool Bank and Boundary Road.

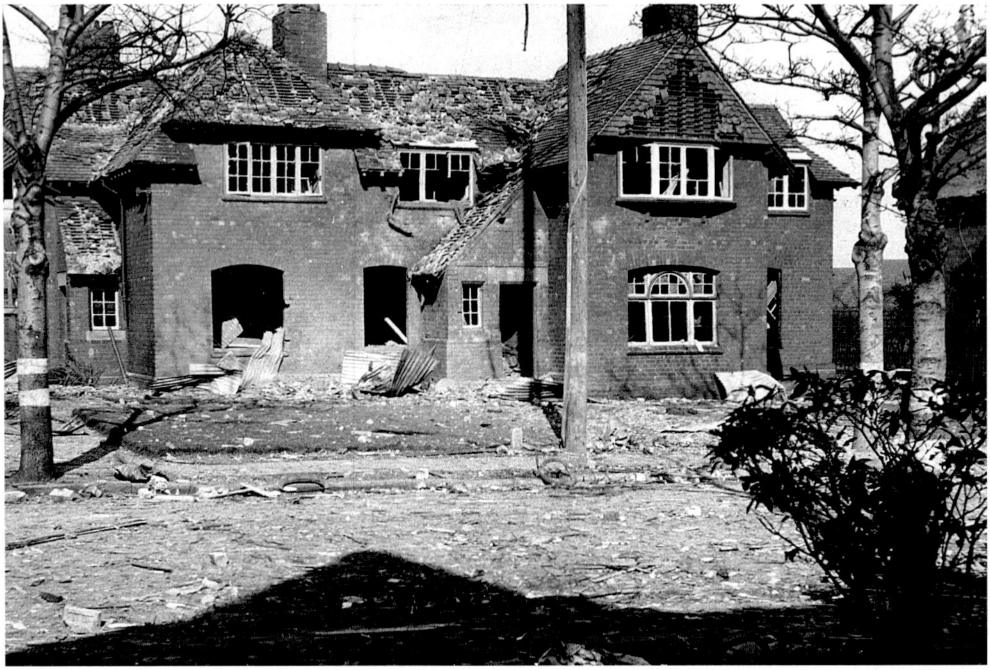

9–13 Bolton Road, Port Sunlight.

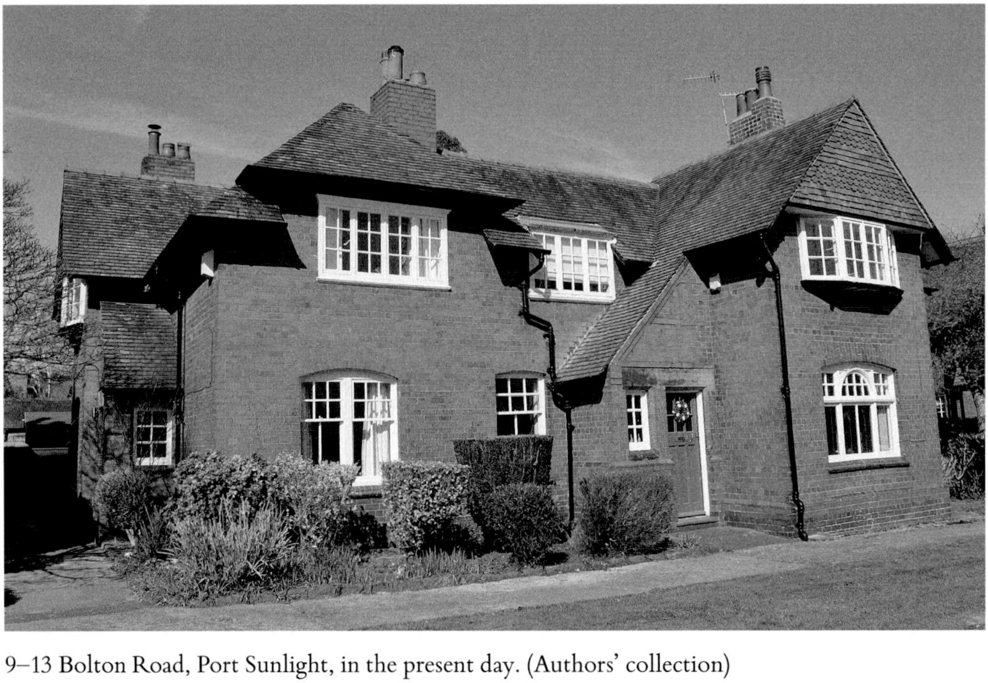

9–13 Bolton Road, Port Sunlight, in the present day. (Authors' collection)

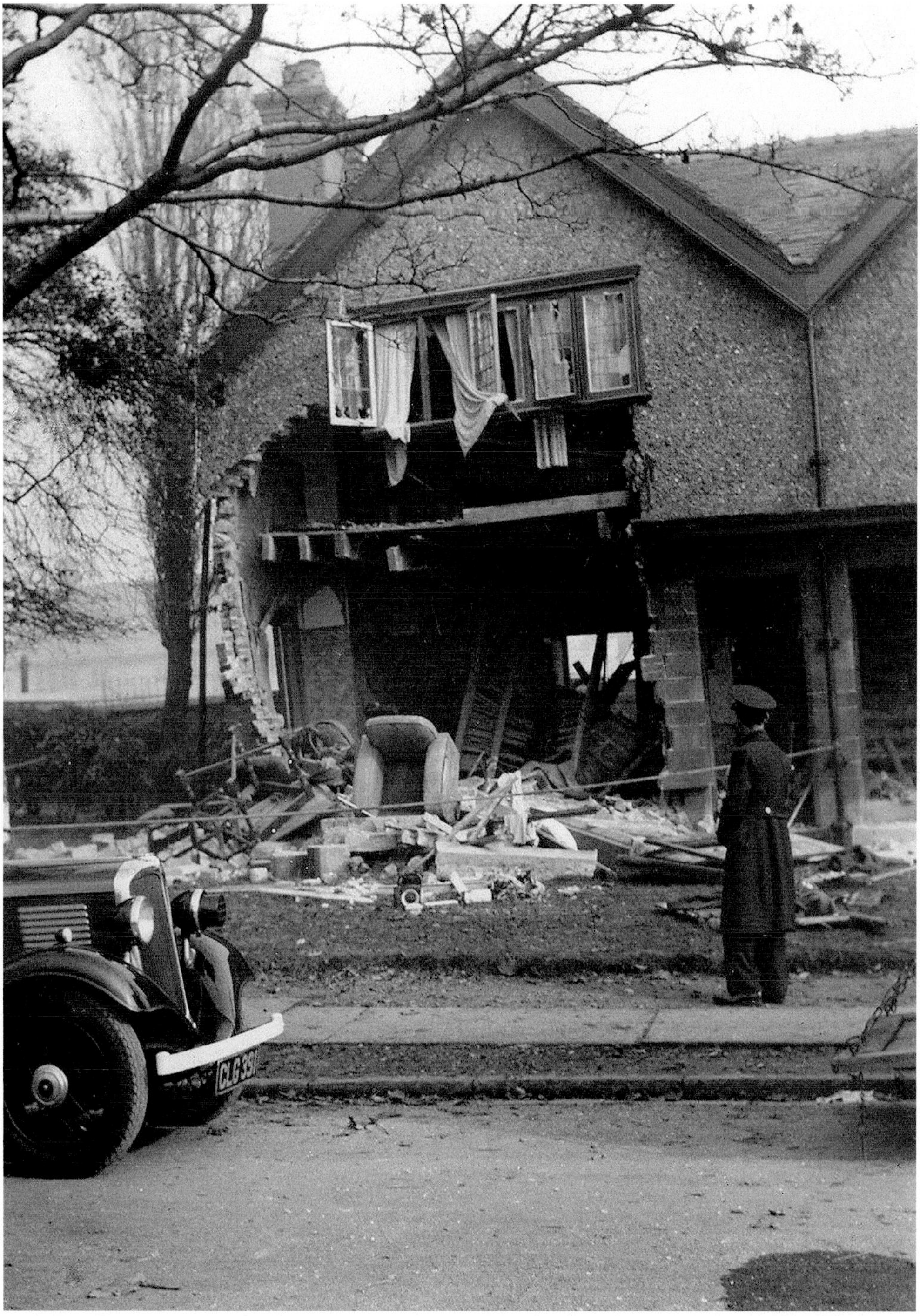

Damage to property in Pool Bank and Boundary Road.

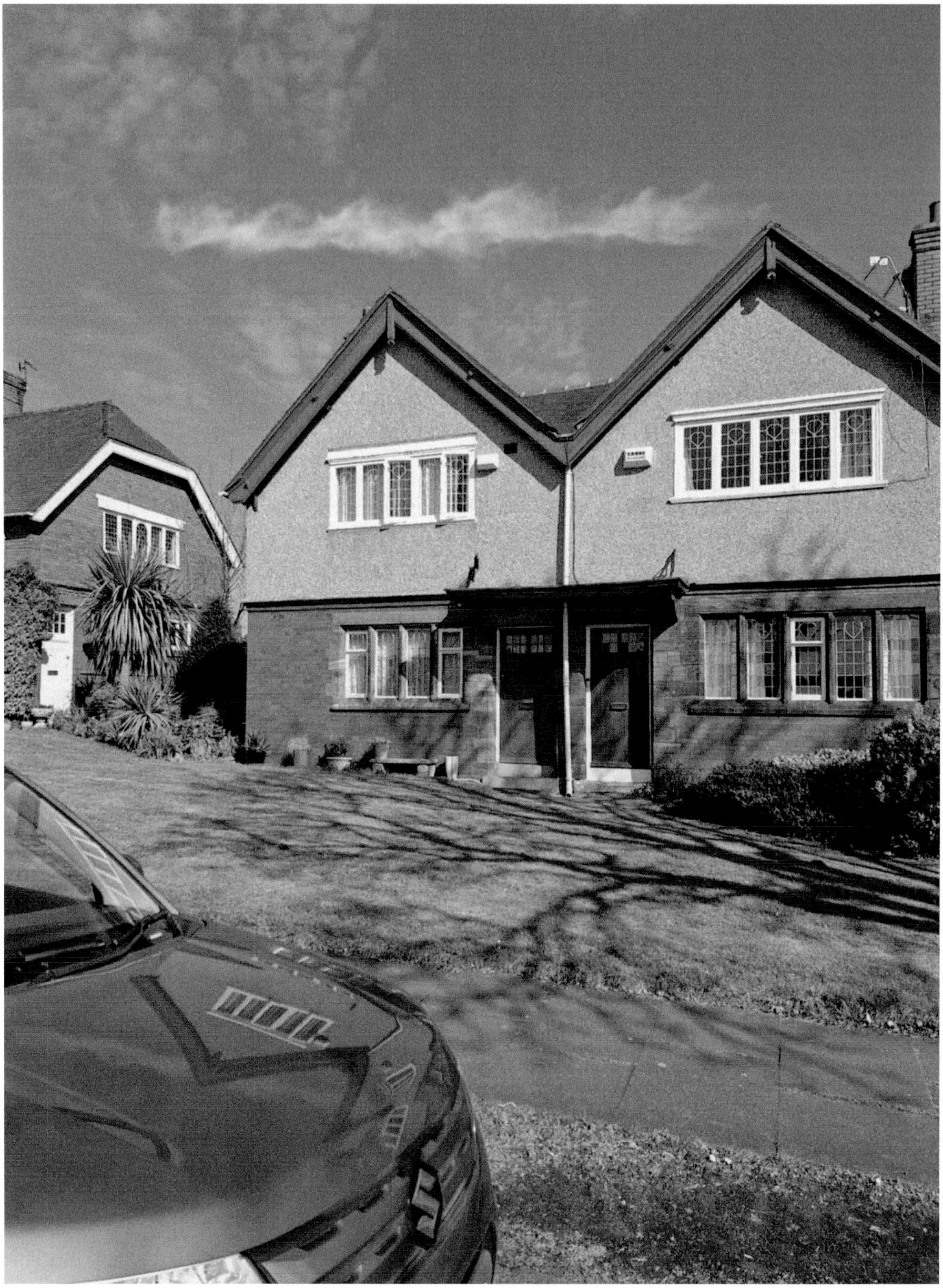

Pool Bank and Boundary Road in the present day. (Authors' collection)

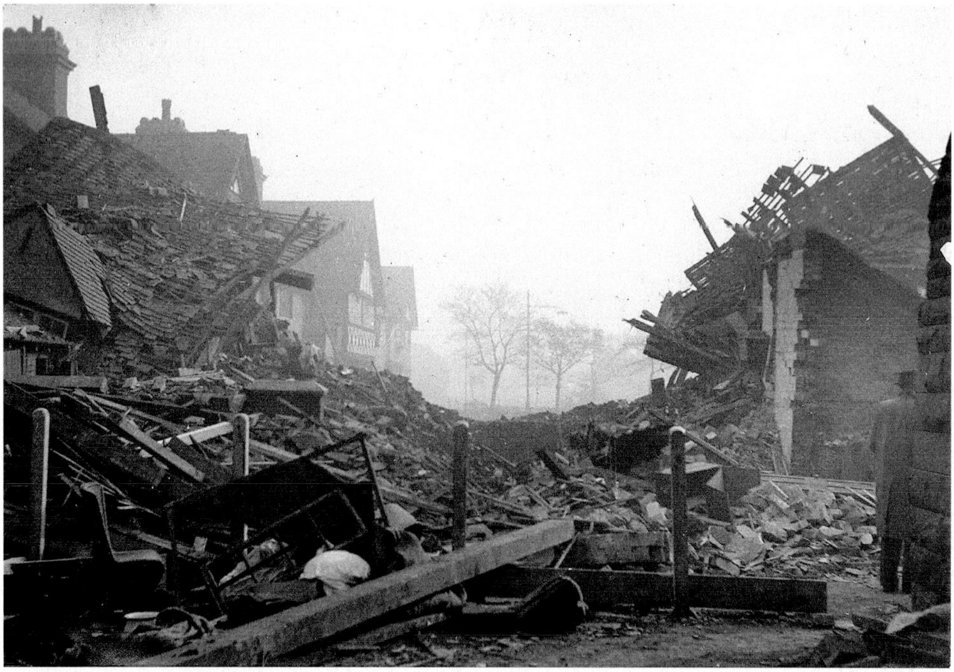

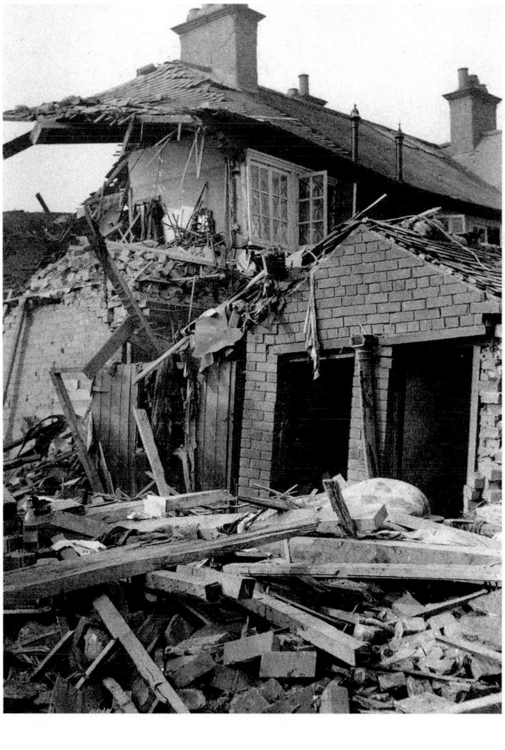

Damage to property in Pool Bank and Boundary Road.

Air Raid Damage at Bridge Street, Port Sunlight, 12 March 1941

Photographs showing damage caused by a parachute mine to a house and a bakehouse.

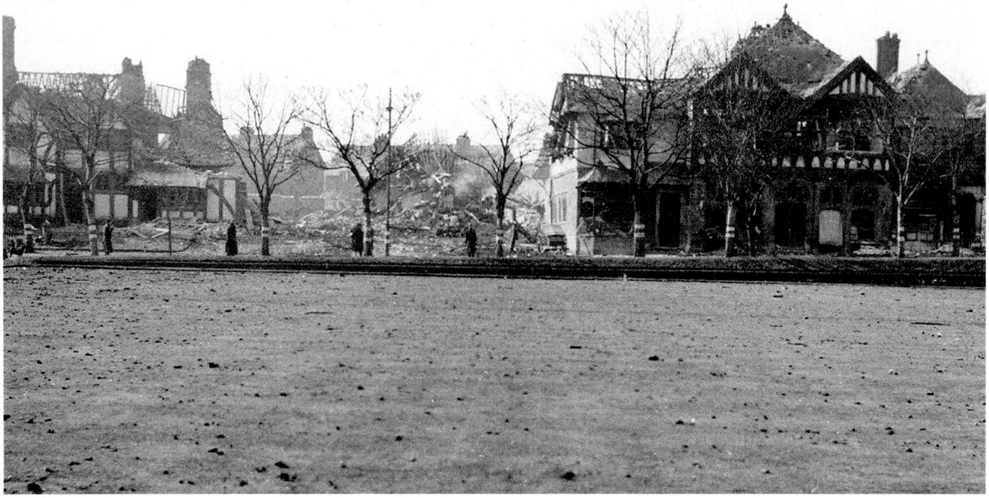

Damage to Port Sunlight by a parachute mine.

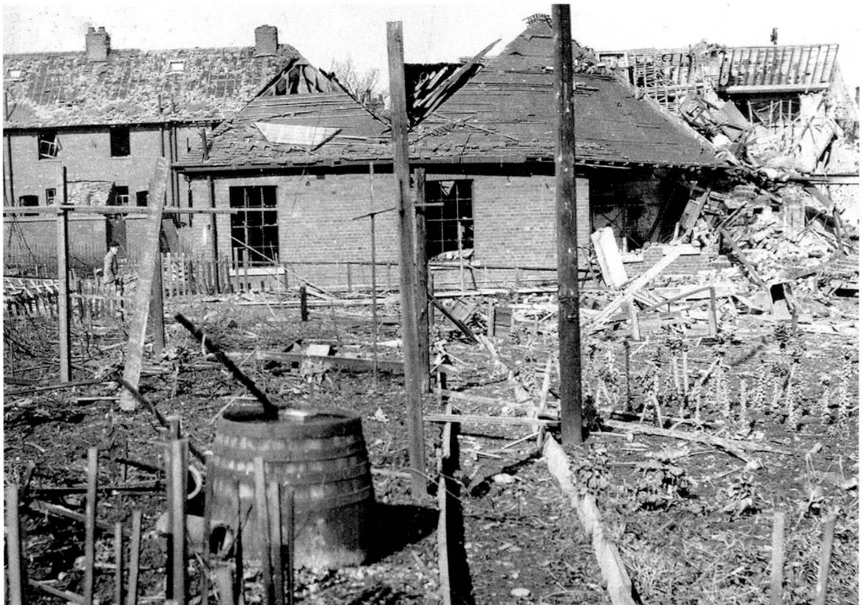

A bakehouse in Port Sunlight.

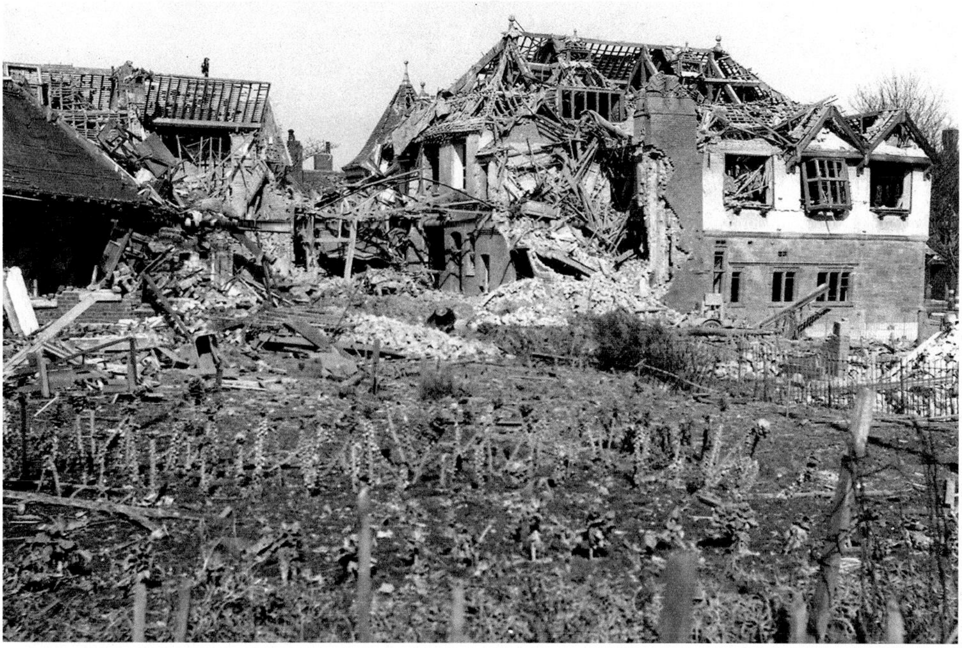

View of Bridge Street, Port Sunlight.

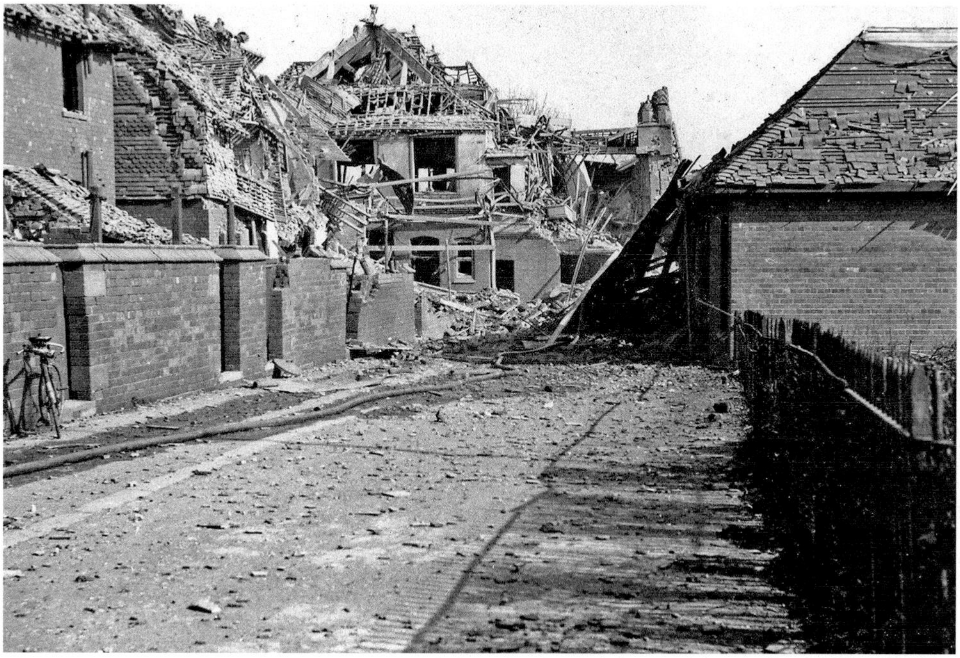

The result of a parachute mine attack.

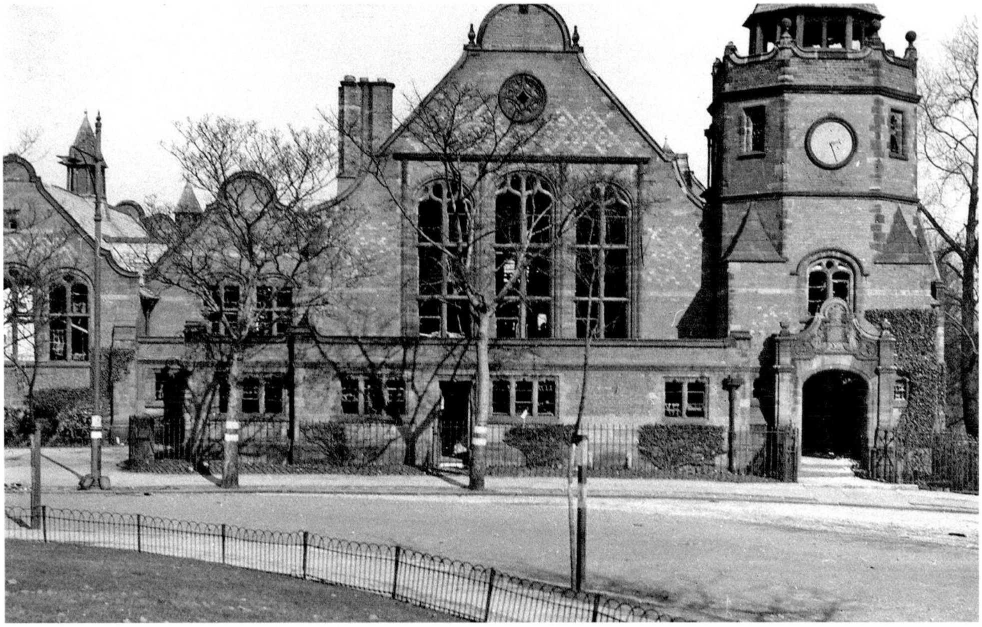

Port Sunlight town centre damage.

Air Raid Damage at Bebington, 12 March 1941

These photographs show the damage caused by a bombing raid; the first three images are of a shops and a house after a parachute mine, while the next two pages are after a HE bomb.

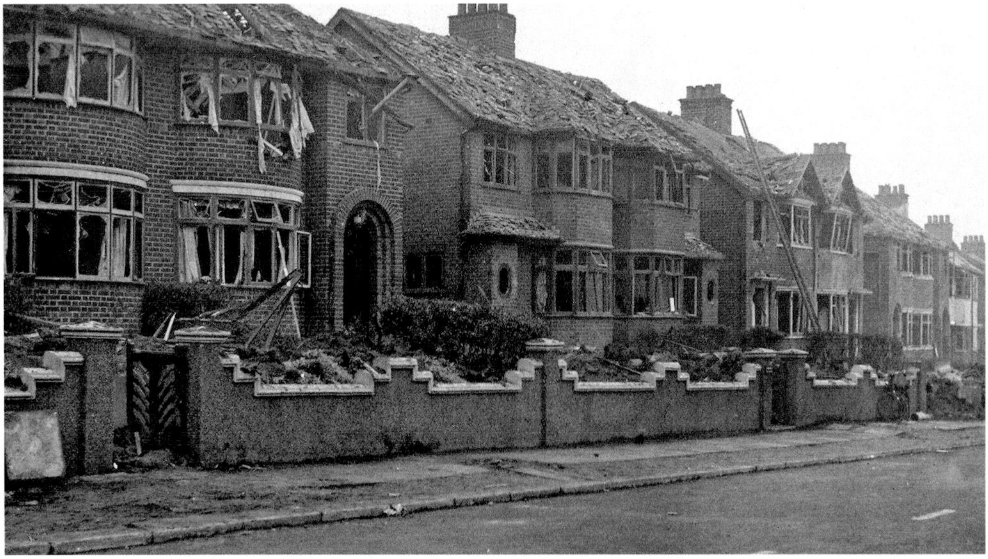

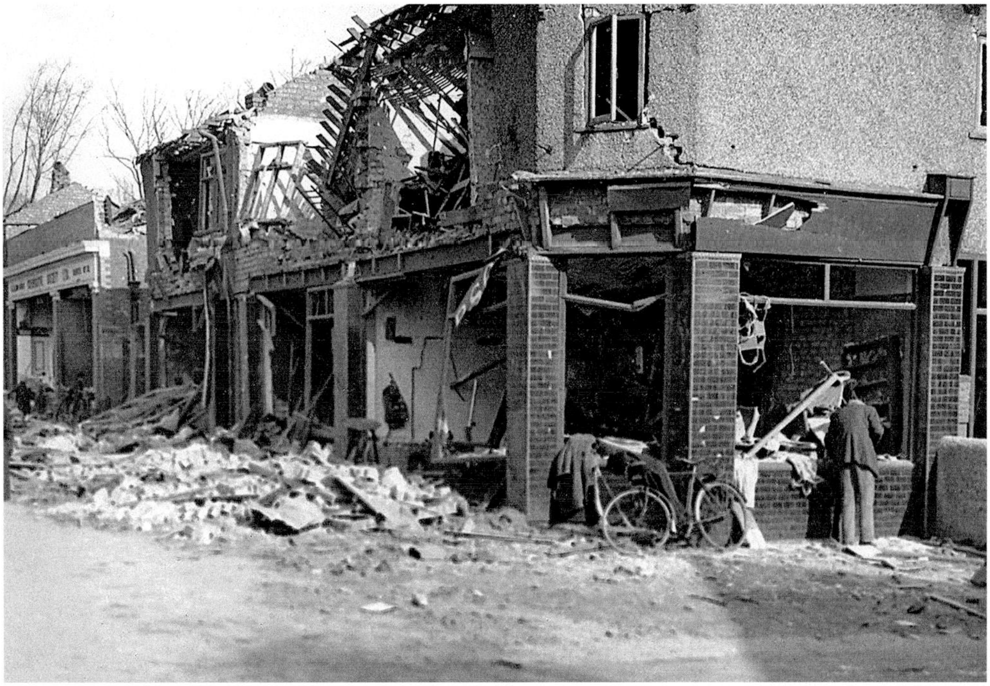

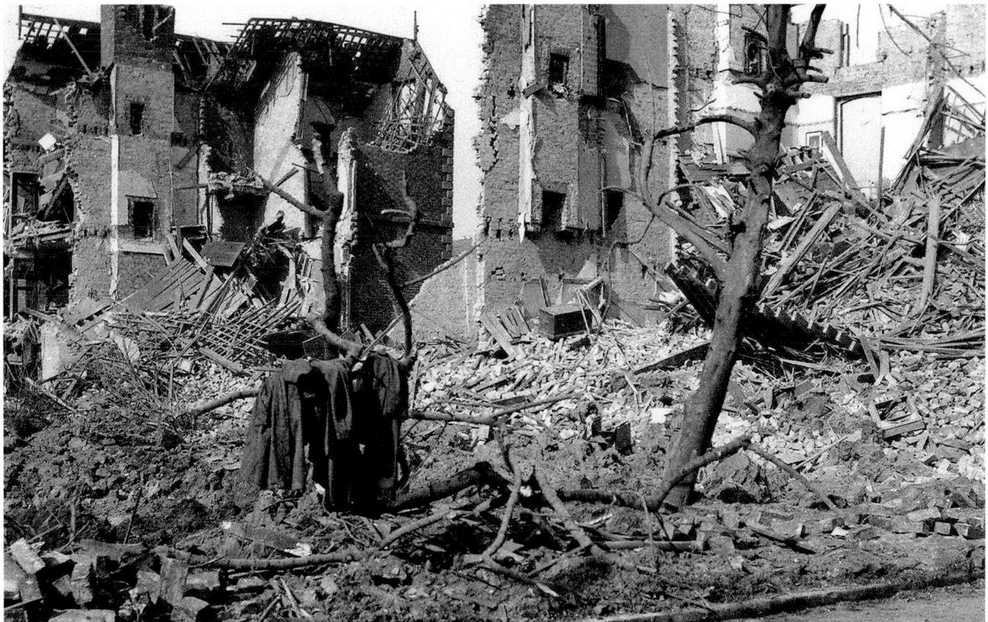

Damage to Town Lane, Bebington.

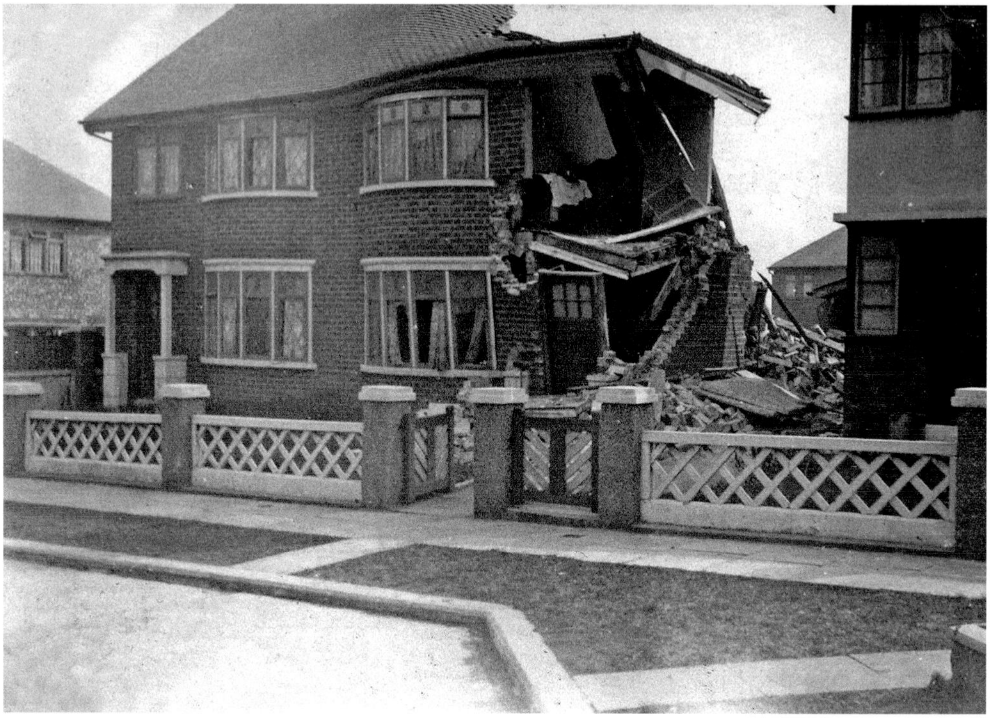

1 Rosefield Avenue, Bebington, after the HE bombs struck.

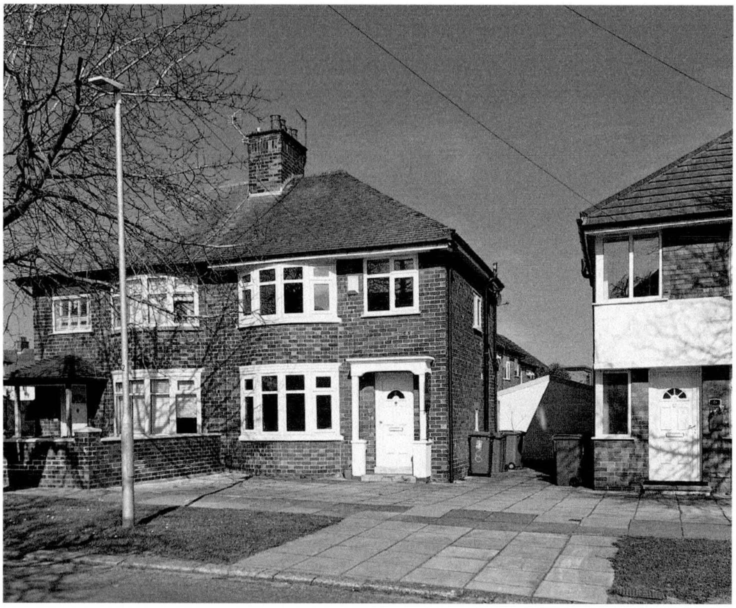

1 Rosefield Avenue in the present day. (Authors' collection)

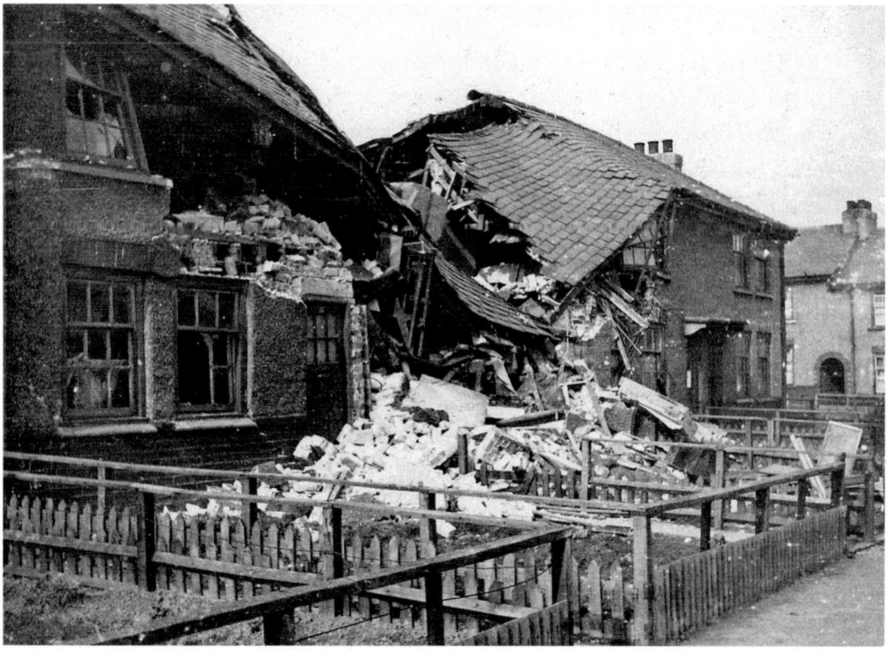

3 Miranda Avenue, Bebington.

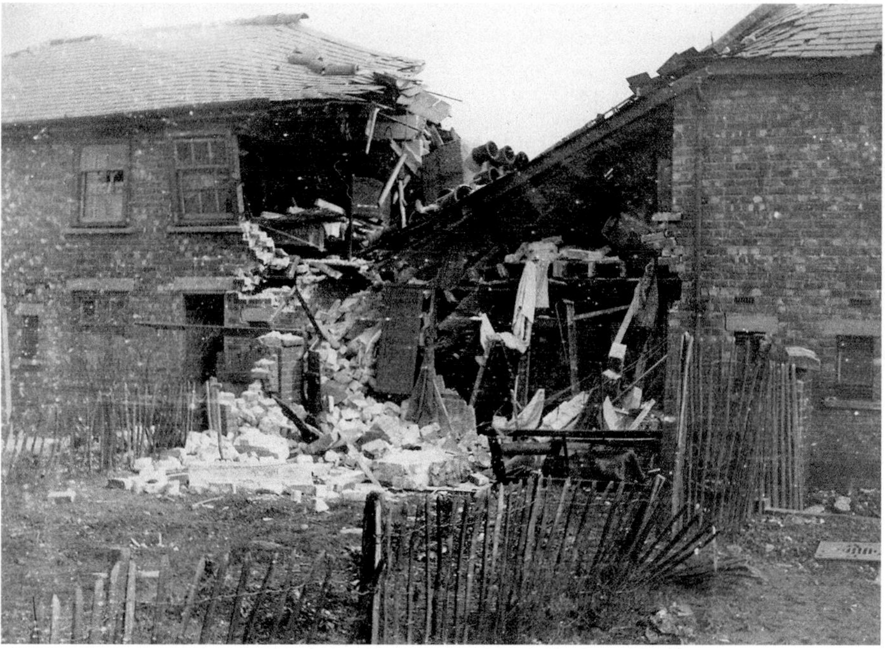

4 Miranda Avenue.

Air Raid Damage at Higher Bebington, Wirral Division, 12 March 1941

A parachute mine fell at the triangular junction of Gayton Avenue, Storeton Road and Thornton Avenue, creating a crater that was 36ft in diameter and 8ft deep. The photographs show the roof of a surface shelter after it had been lifted. Four people were sheltering in there and were uninjured, but a man who was about to enter the shelter was killed. The shelter was 56ft 5in from the centre of the mine crater.

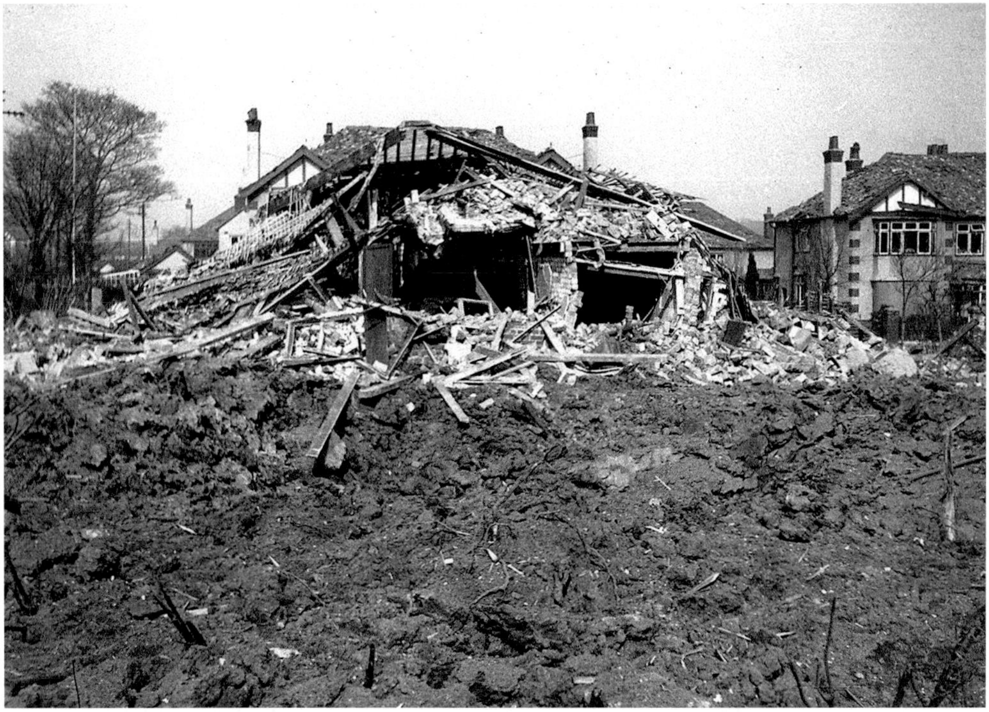

Higher Bebington area houses were wholly destroyed.

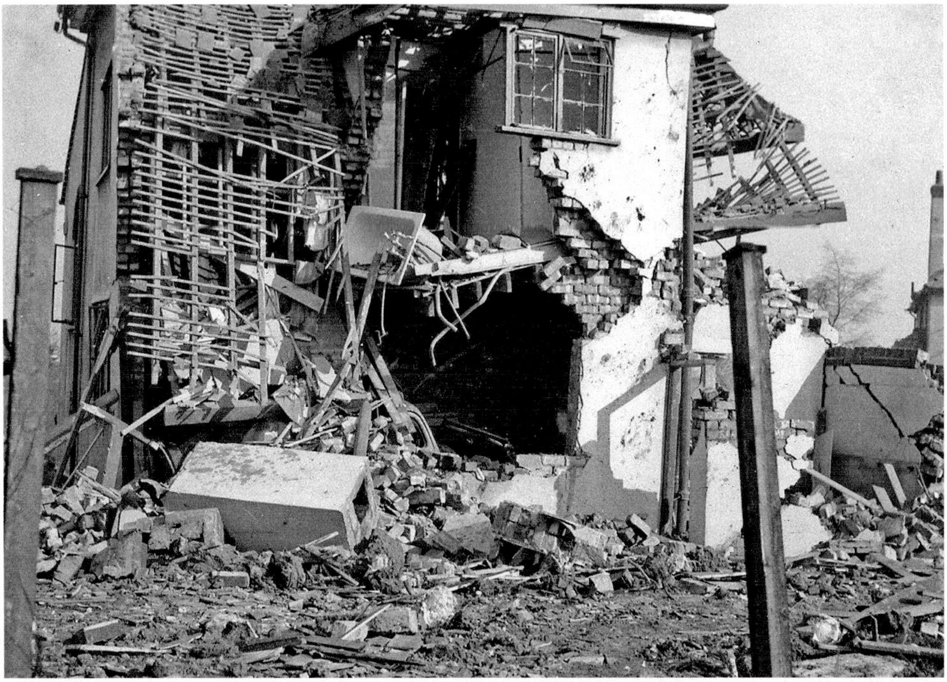

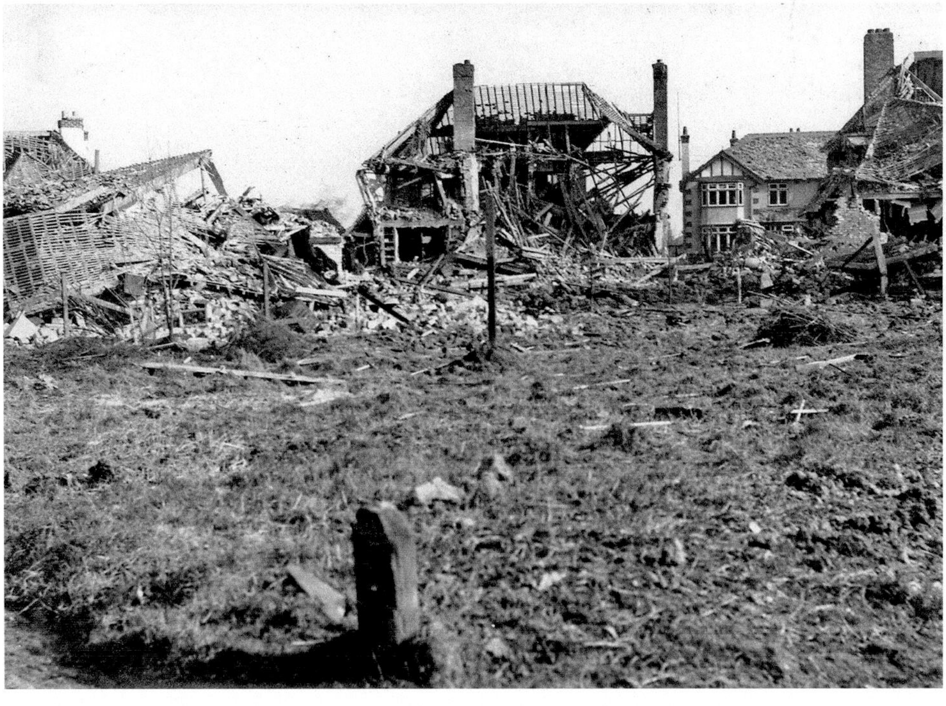

Houses at the junction of Storeton Road, Gayton Street and Thornton Avenue.

Three photographs that show the damage caused by a parachute mine that landed on the roadway of Thornton Avenue, very close to the houses on the previous page. There was a shelter: a three-sided corrugated iron shed with a corrugated iron roof and sandbags reinforcing the side. Six people were in this shelter and were uninjured.

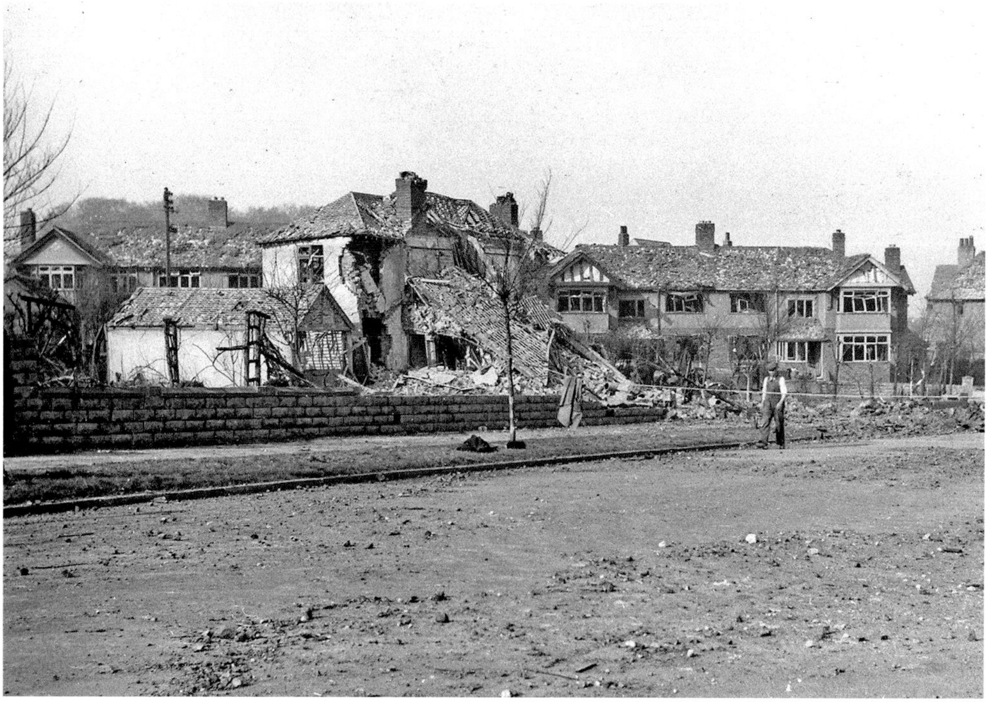

Scene of a parachute mine dropped in the centre of Thornton Avenue.

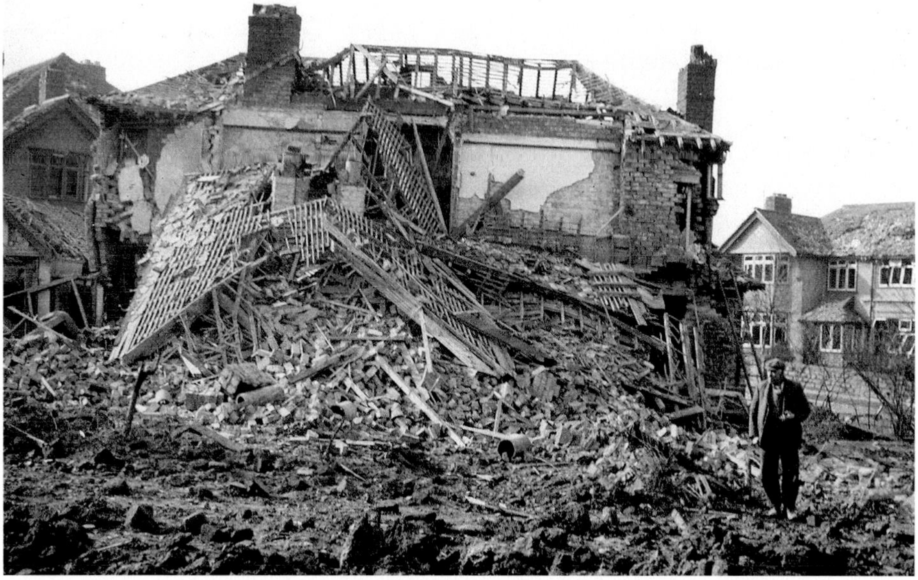

Thornton Avenue area, Higher Bebington.

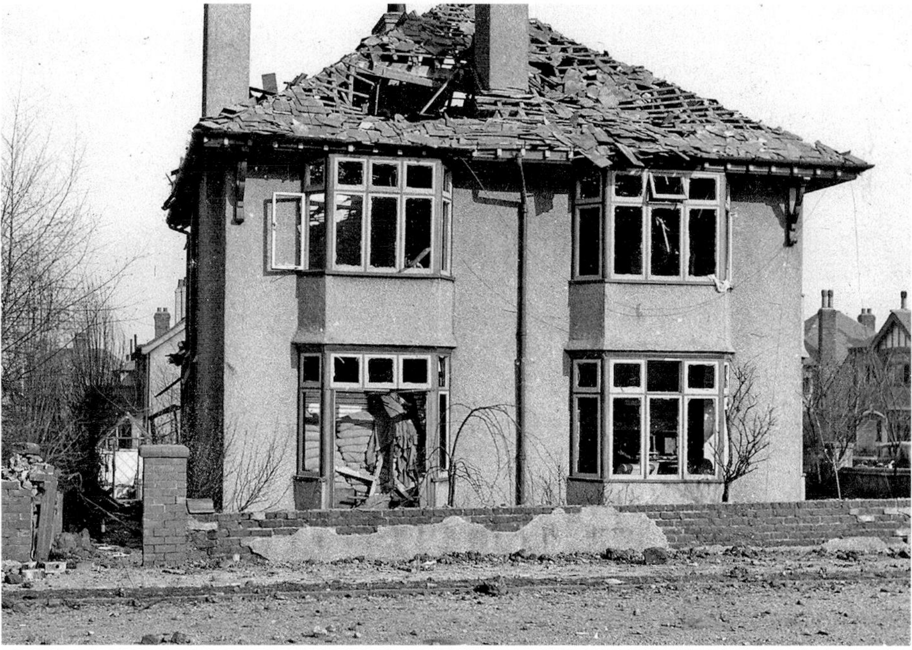

This house was approximately 60ft from the mine crater.

Raid Damage at Links Avenue, Little Sutton, 22 October 1941

Little Sutton, near Ellesmere Port, experienced several bombing raids during the war, including an attack on the bus garage on 17 October 1940, and residents witnessed many aerial dogfights. A raid also took place on the night of 22–23 October 1941, damaging several houses in Little Sutton and Ellesmere Port.

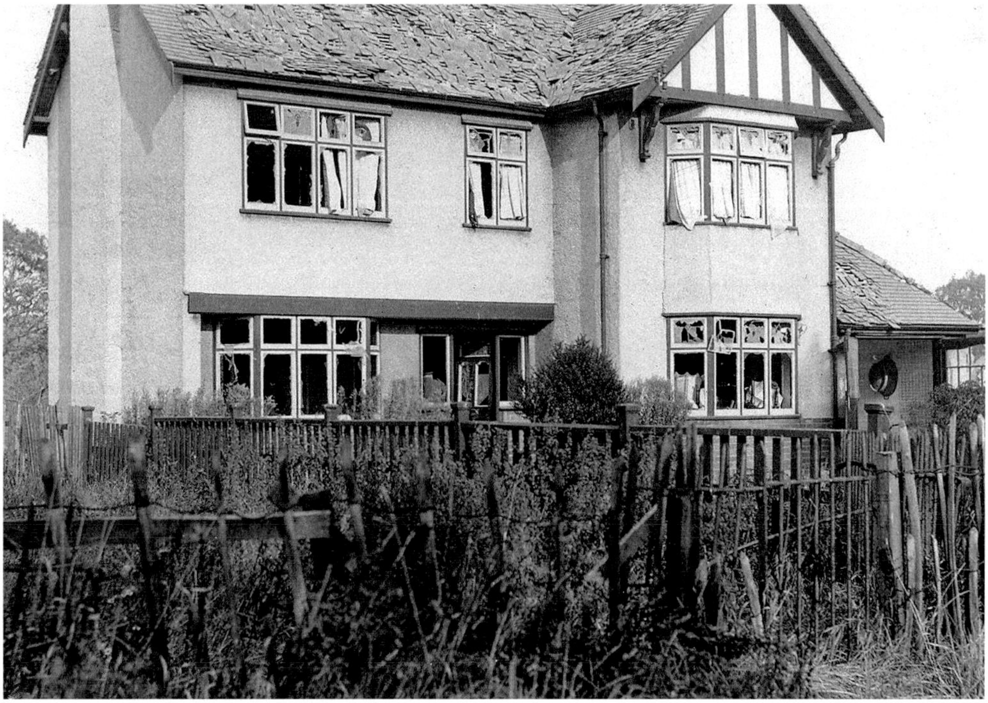

Damage to the front of a detached house.

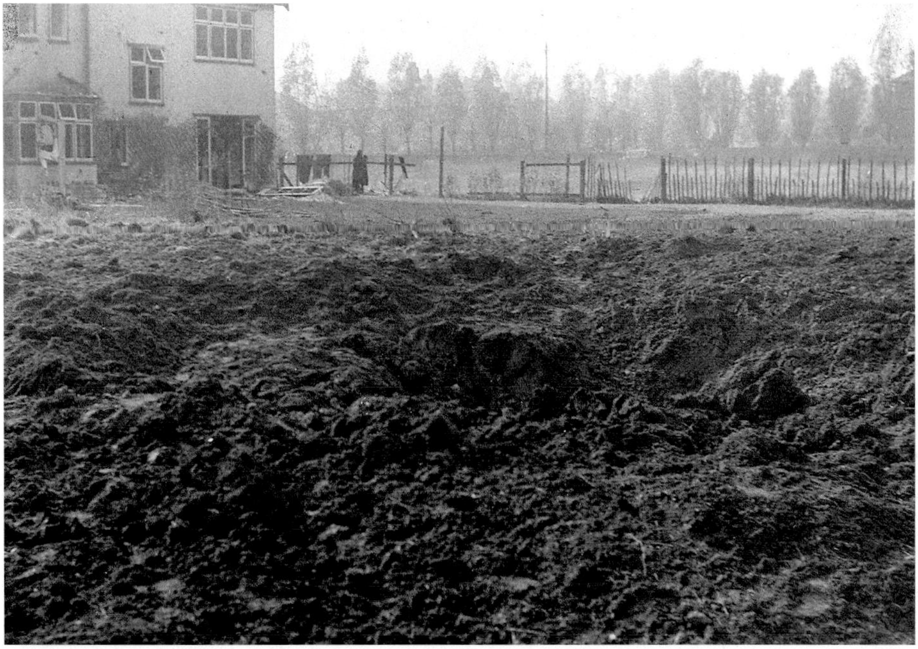

A bomb crater at the rear of the house.

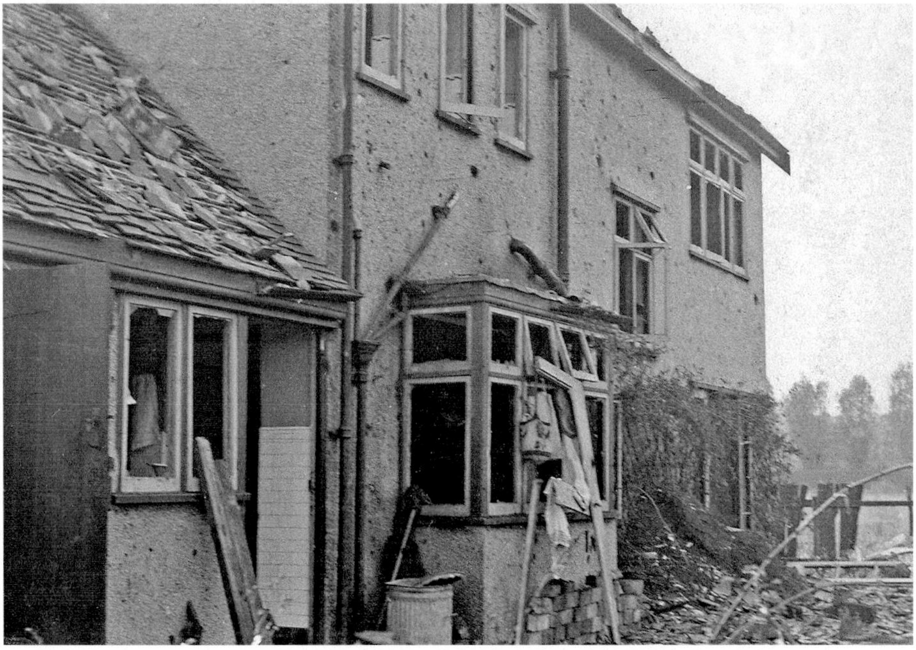

The rear of the house.

Air Raid Damage at Queenswood Avenue, Higher Bebington, 12 March 1941

Four photographs showing damage caused by a parachute mine. This mine dropped at the rear of two semi-detached houses and demolished them. Six people were sheltering in the inside shelter, as shown in photograph three. This shelter was constructed from three ship's boiler plates. None of the people in this shelter were injured.

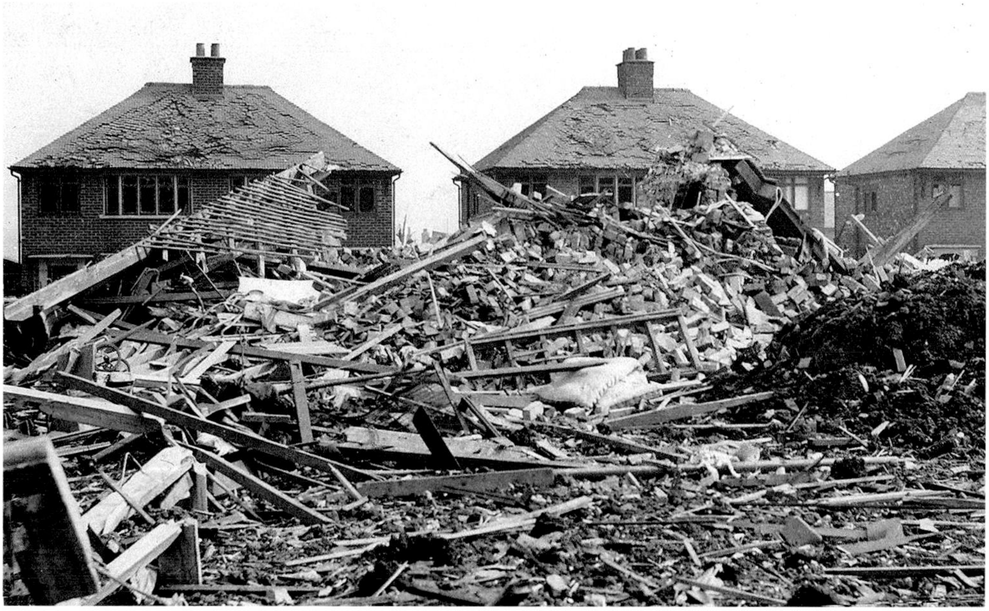

Bomb crater in Queenswood Avenue.

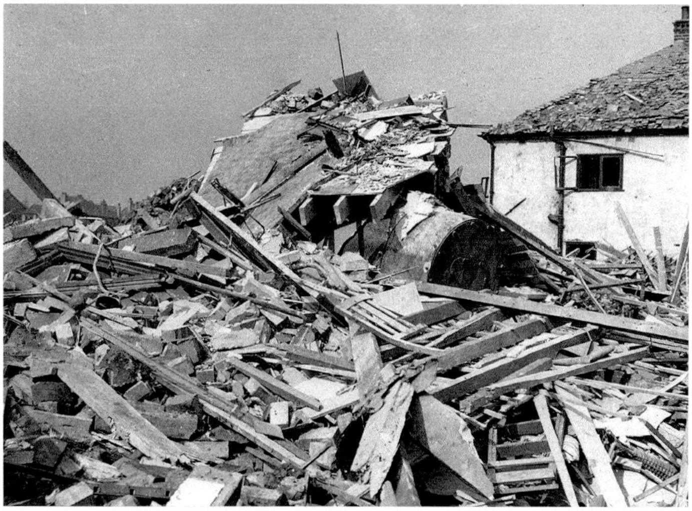

Bomb shelter.

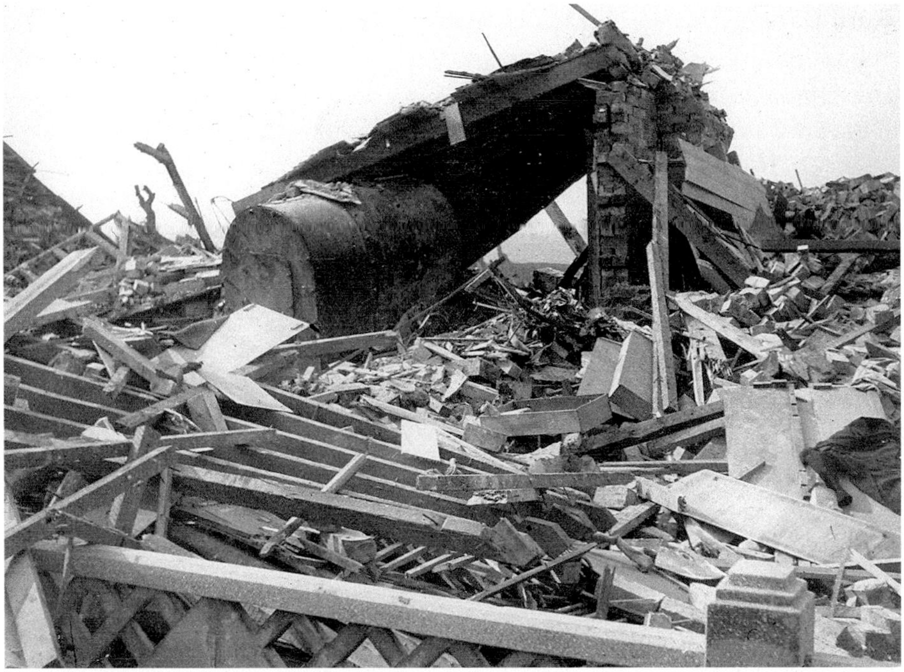

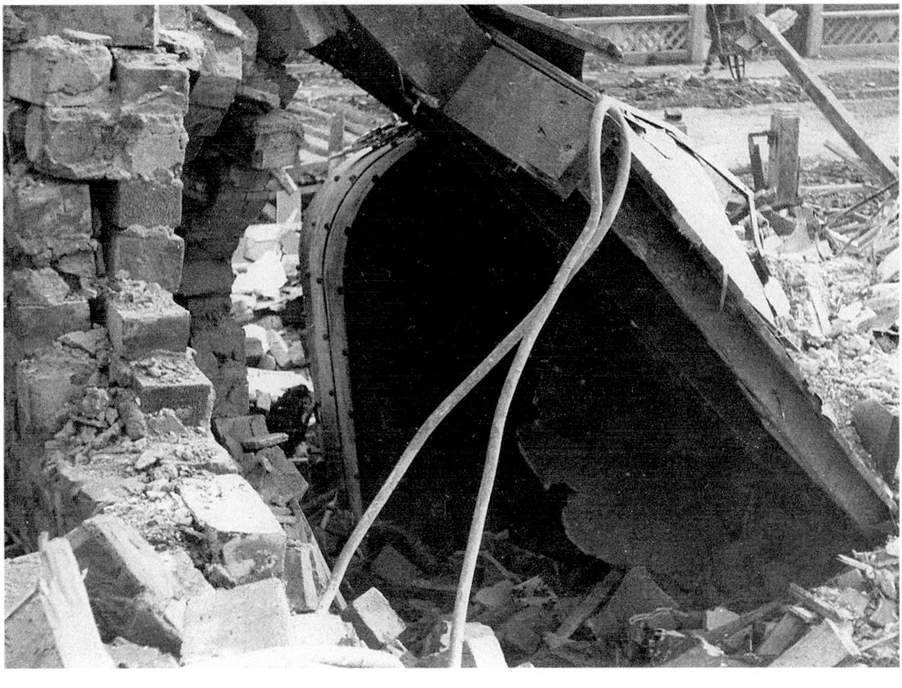

Bomb shelter.

Air Raid Damage at Bebington, 12 March 1941

These photographs show Wirral Grammar School for Girls, Bebington, after it had been hit with a powerful parachute mine.

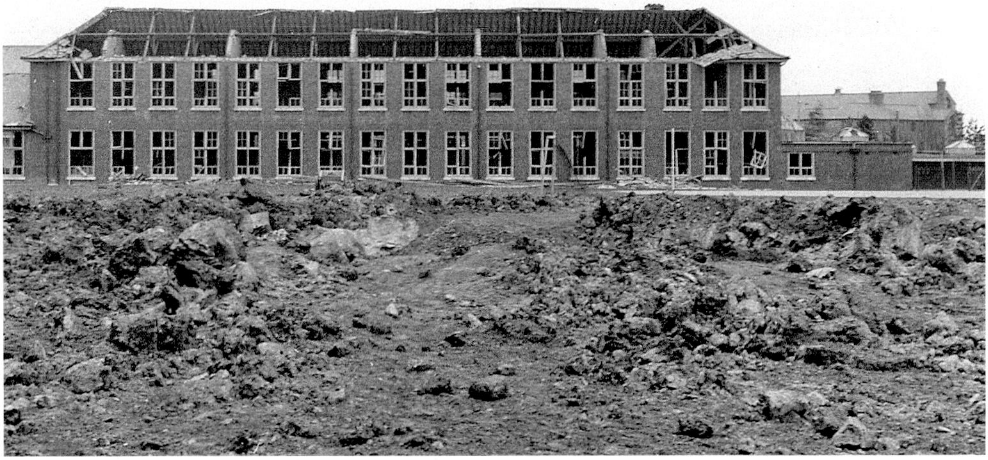

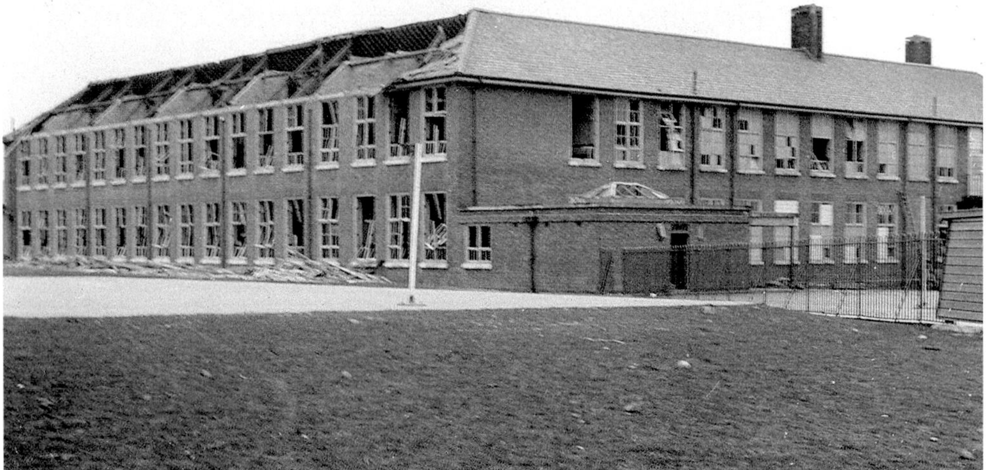

Wirral Grammar School for Girls after the attack.

Air Raid Damage at Greasby, Wirral Division, 7 April 1941

A high-explosive bomb hit a house in Eastway, Greasby, while a woman and her two children slept in the front lower room of this house. Fortunately, they were uninjured.

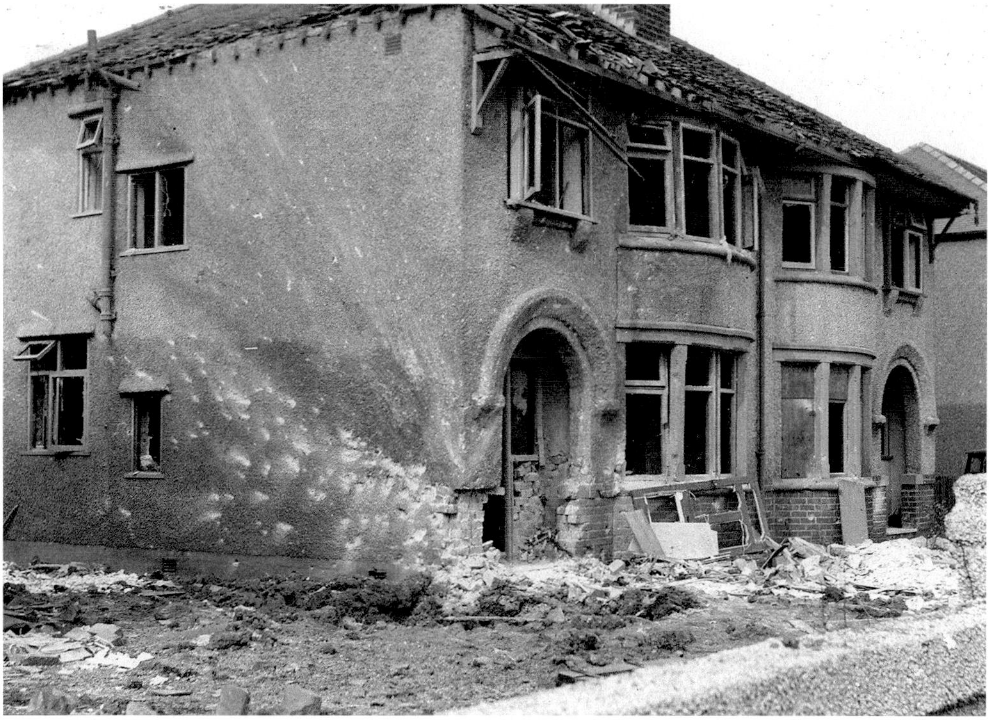

Air Raid Damage in Birkenhead Road, Meols, 2 May 1941

Damage caused by a bomb that dropped in the front garden of the house shown. Note in the second photograph how the bay window is falling away from the house.

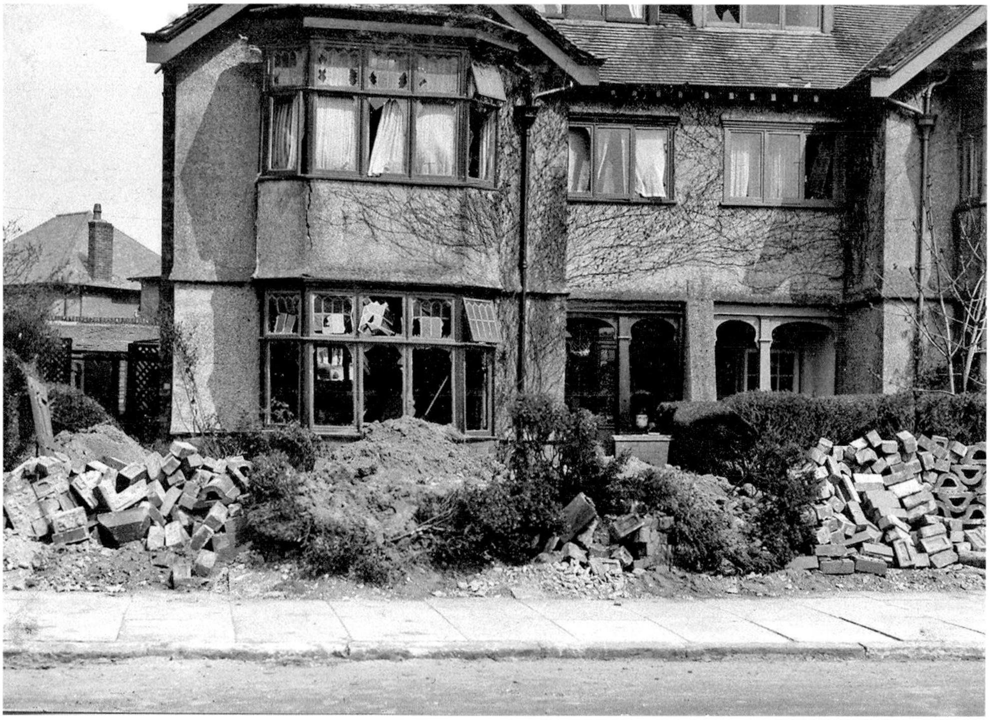

A single bomb was dropped in the garden of this house on Birkenhead Road.

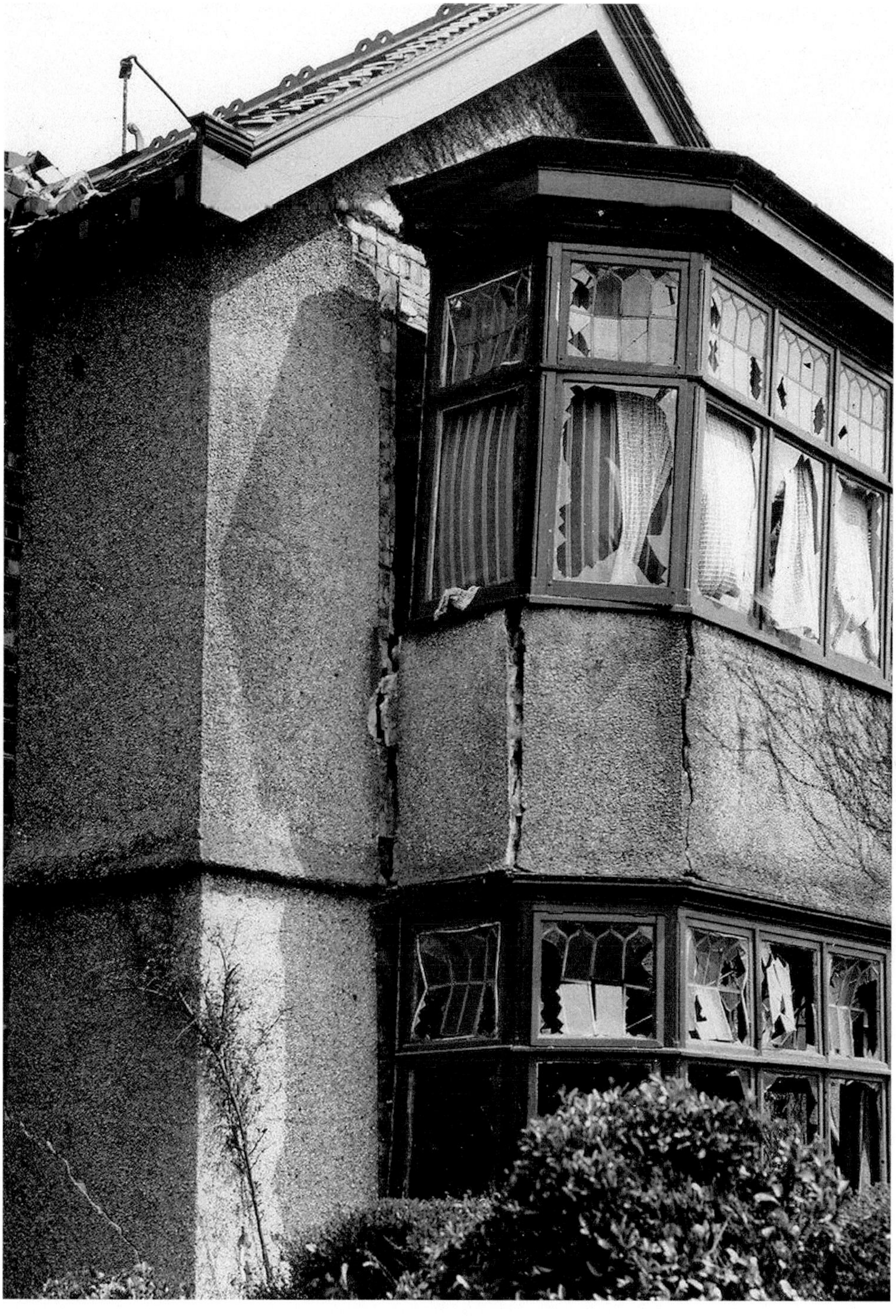

The bay window was forced from the wall by the blast.

Air Raid Damage at Meols, 2 May 1941

Two photographs showing damage caused by bombs to a house in Meols on 2 May 1941. Some of the bombs damaged a church near the railway, as well as a signal box and other nearby buildings. Additional bombs fell on Meols Promenade, which was also severely damaged, and many nearby houses suffered minor damage to roofs and windows. Several houses on Ashley Road were damaged, as can be seen here.

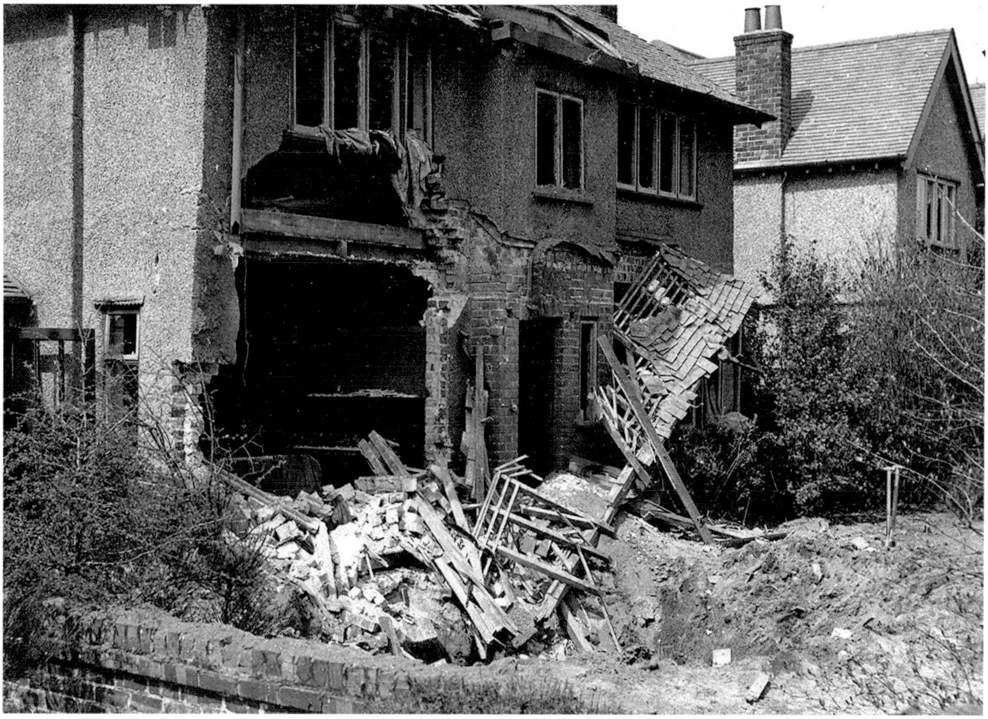

Bomb damage at Meols on the Wirral.

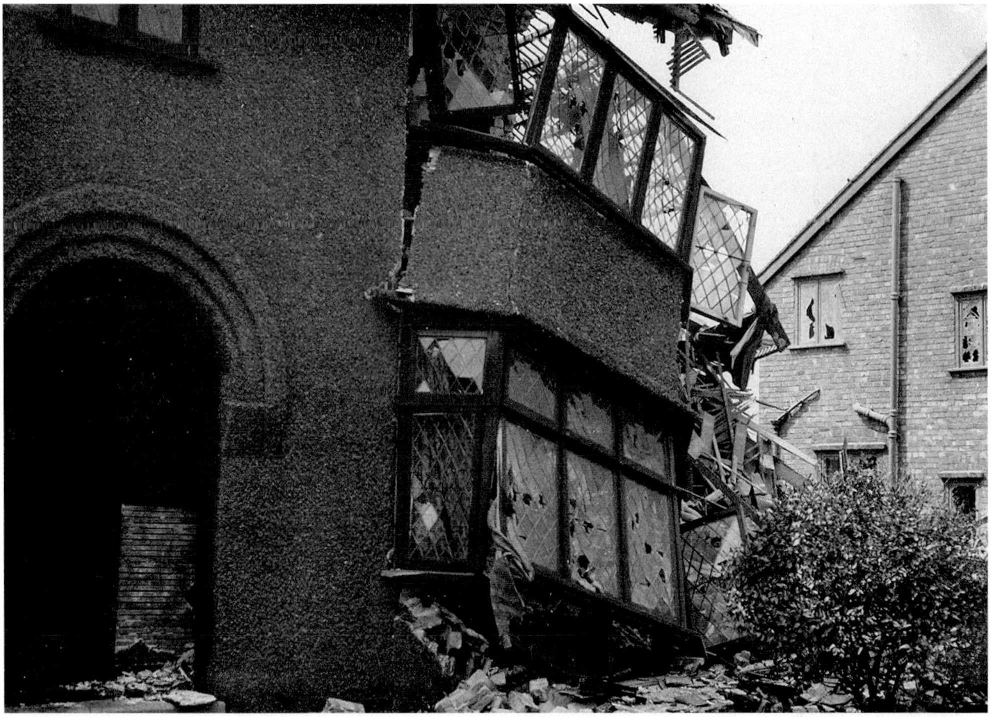

Bomb damage at Meols on the Wirral. Note how few of the leaded panes in the window are broken.

Air Raid Damage at Great Saughall, Wirral Division, 15 February 1941

Three 1,100lb bombs were dropped in fields near The Hermitage, Great Saughall. The first was a delayed-action type and exploded six hours after it was dropped, while the second bomb was removed by the bomb disposal unit on 3 March. It was recovered from a depth of 25ft, having penetrated 23ft of clay and 2ft of sand. The third bomb exploded upon impact.

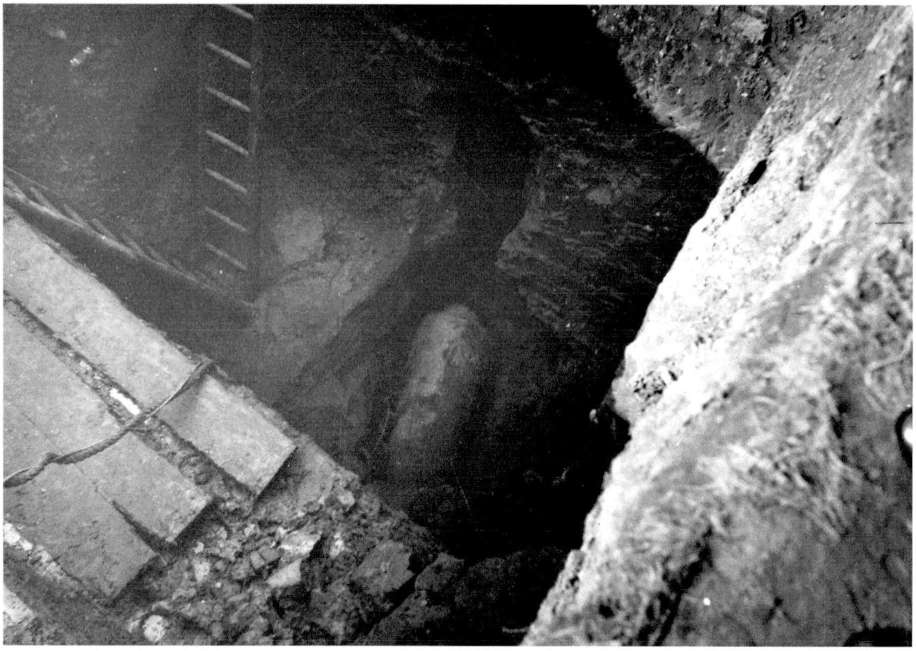

The bomb crater.

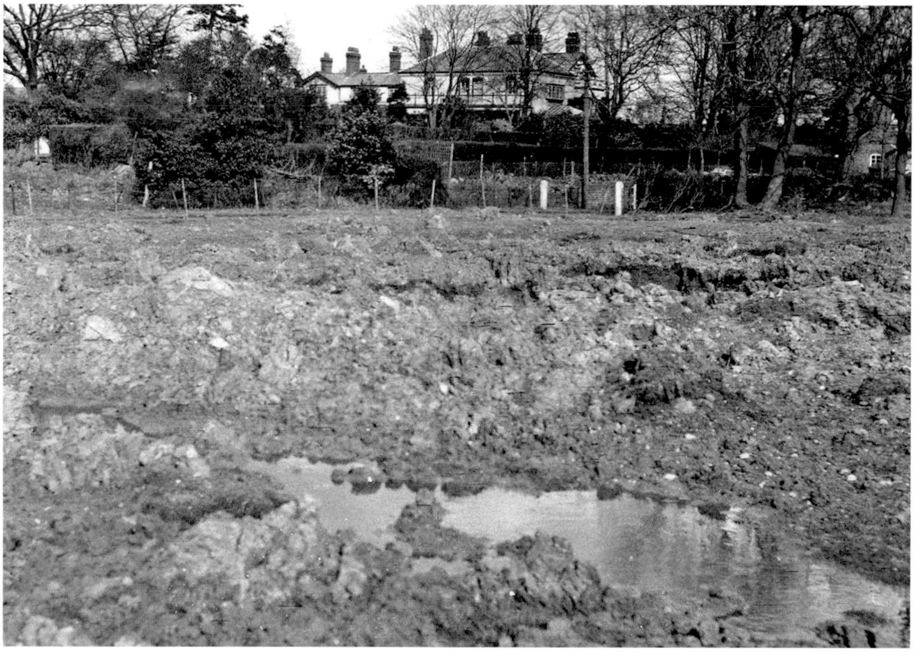

The Hermitage is shown in the background of this photograph.

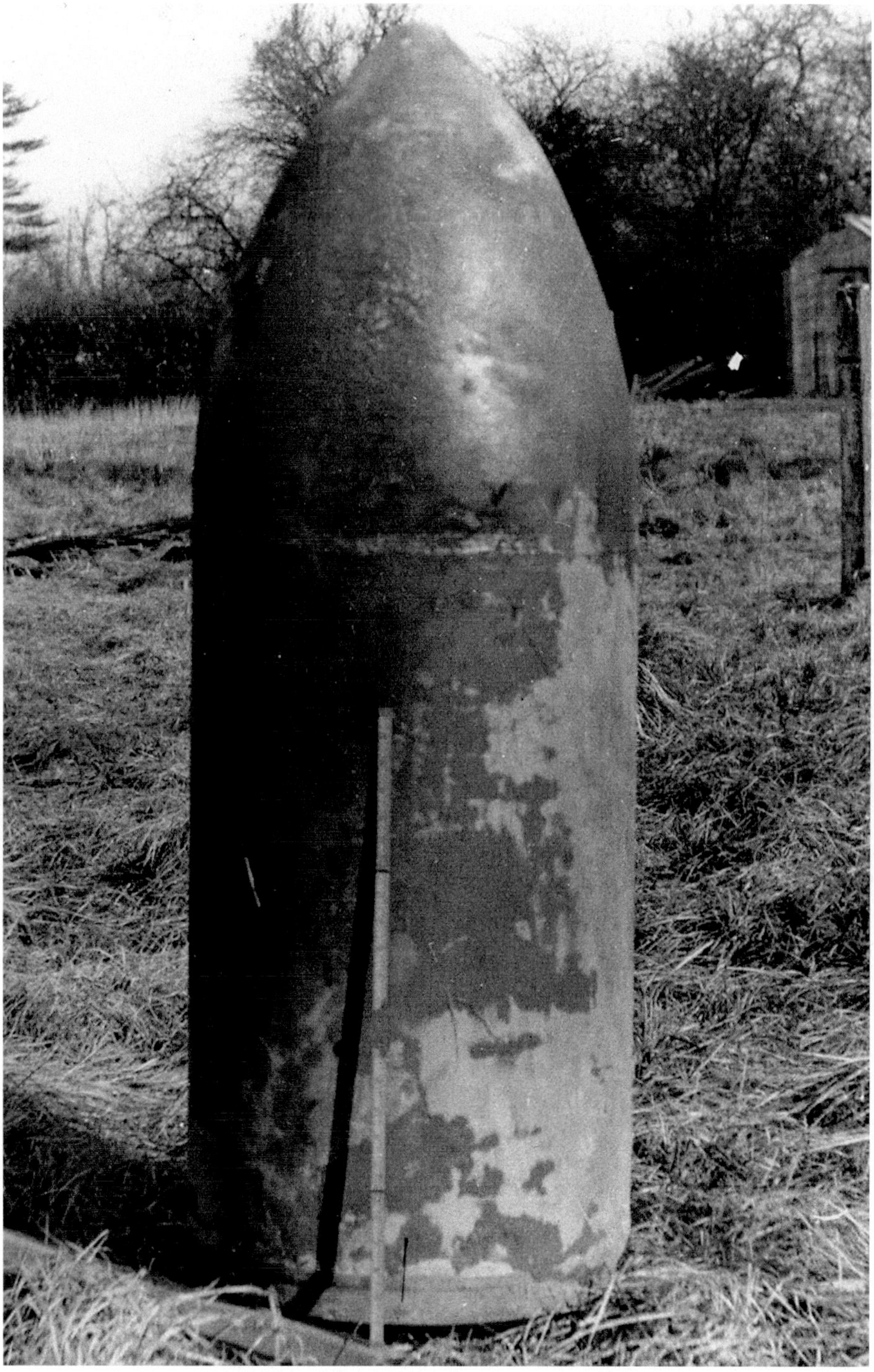

The bomb after removal (note the 2ft ruler).

Air Raid Damage in Heswall, Wirral, 29 May 1941

Damage to Vernons Garage, Pensby Road, Heswall, which was caused by a high-explosive bomb.

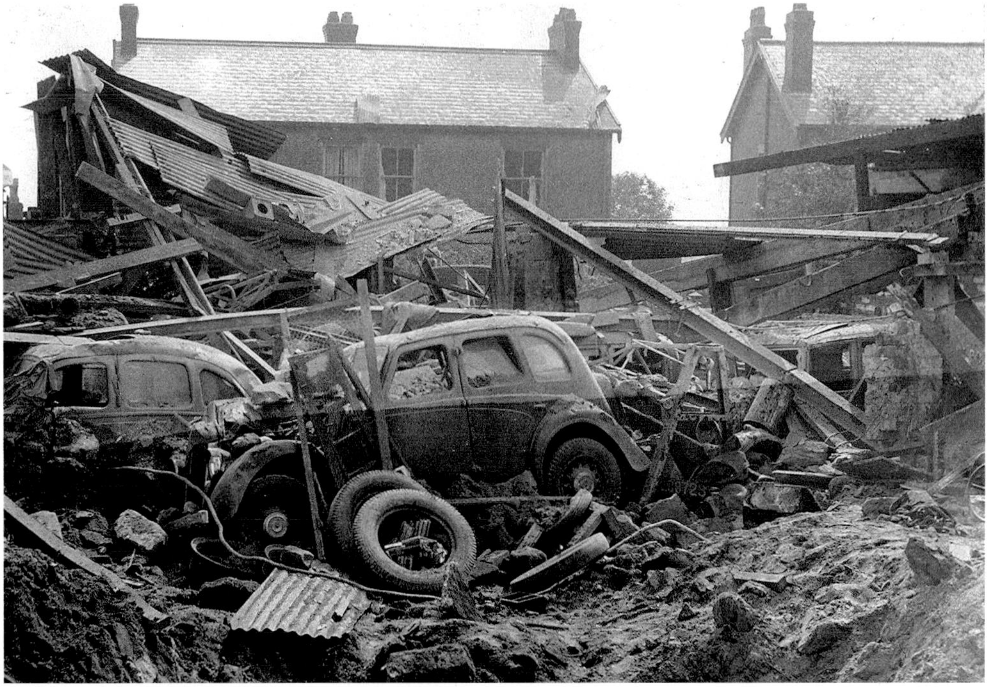

Some of the damage done to Vernons Garage.

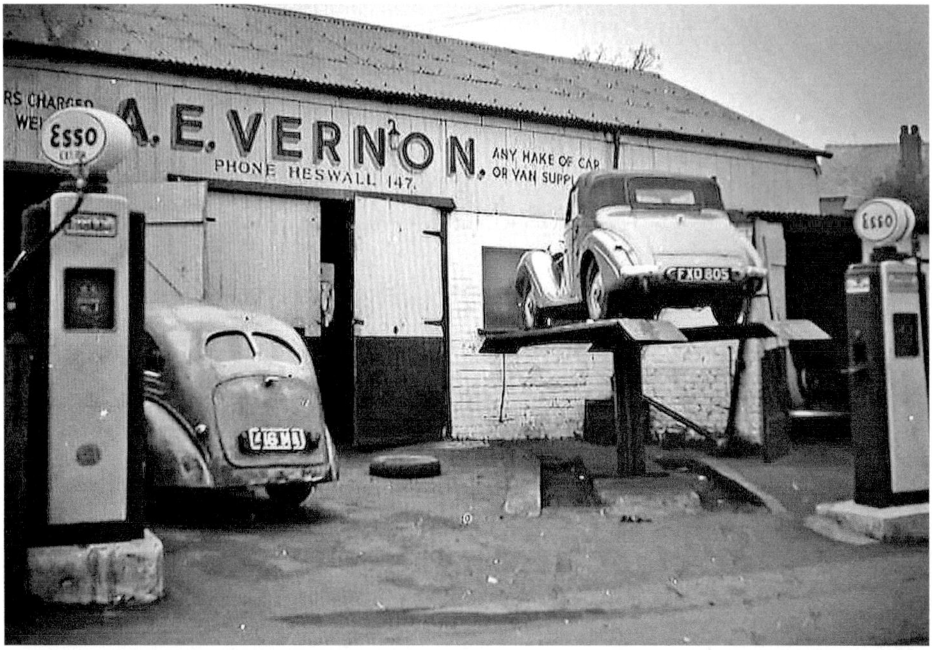

Vernons Garage pre-war. (Vernons Garage c/o Sophie Stievenard)

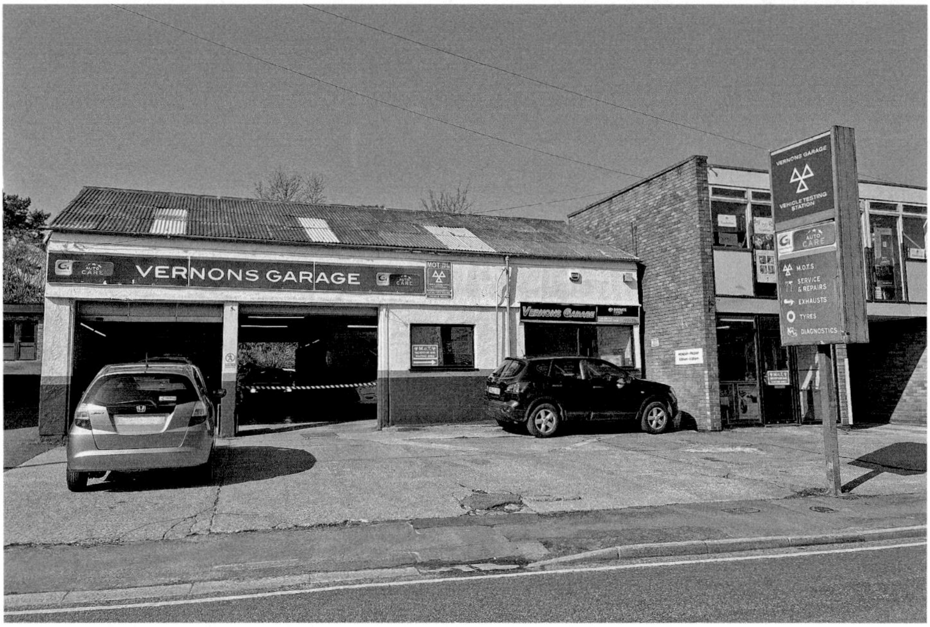

Vernons Garage in the present day. (Vernons Garage c/o Sophie Stievenard)

Air Raid Damage at Heswall, 1 June 1941

Damage caused by a high-explosive bomb at Village Road, Heswall. The shop shown opposite subsequently caught fire and was burned out.

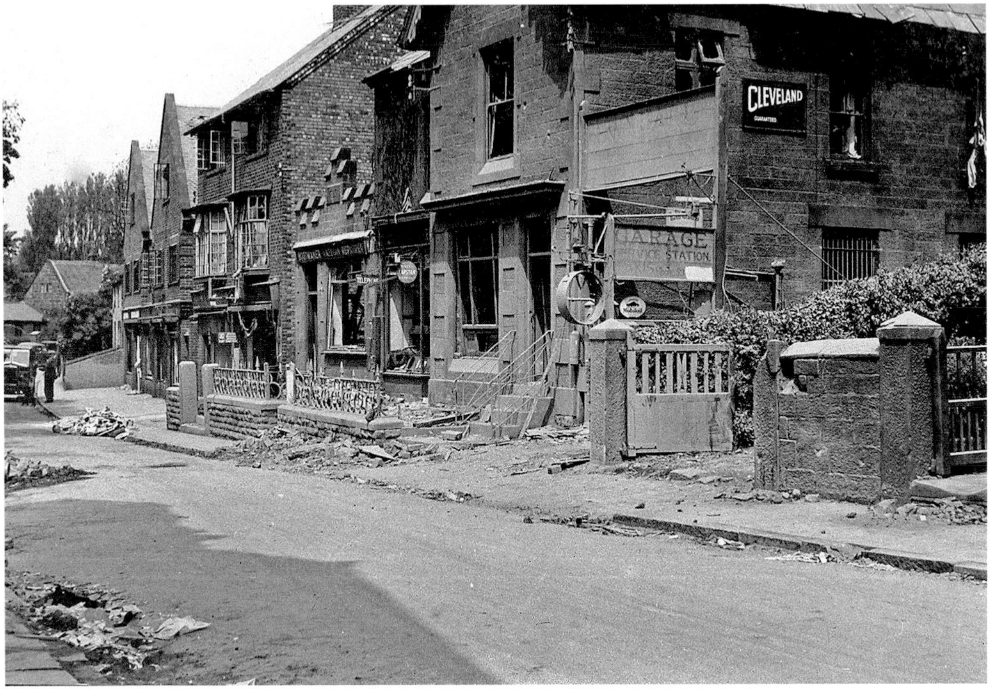

Damage caused by a HE bomb at Village Road, Heswall.

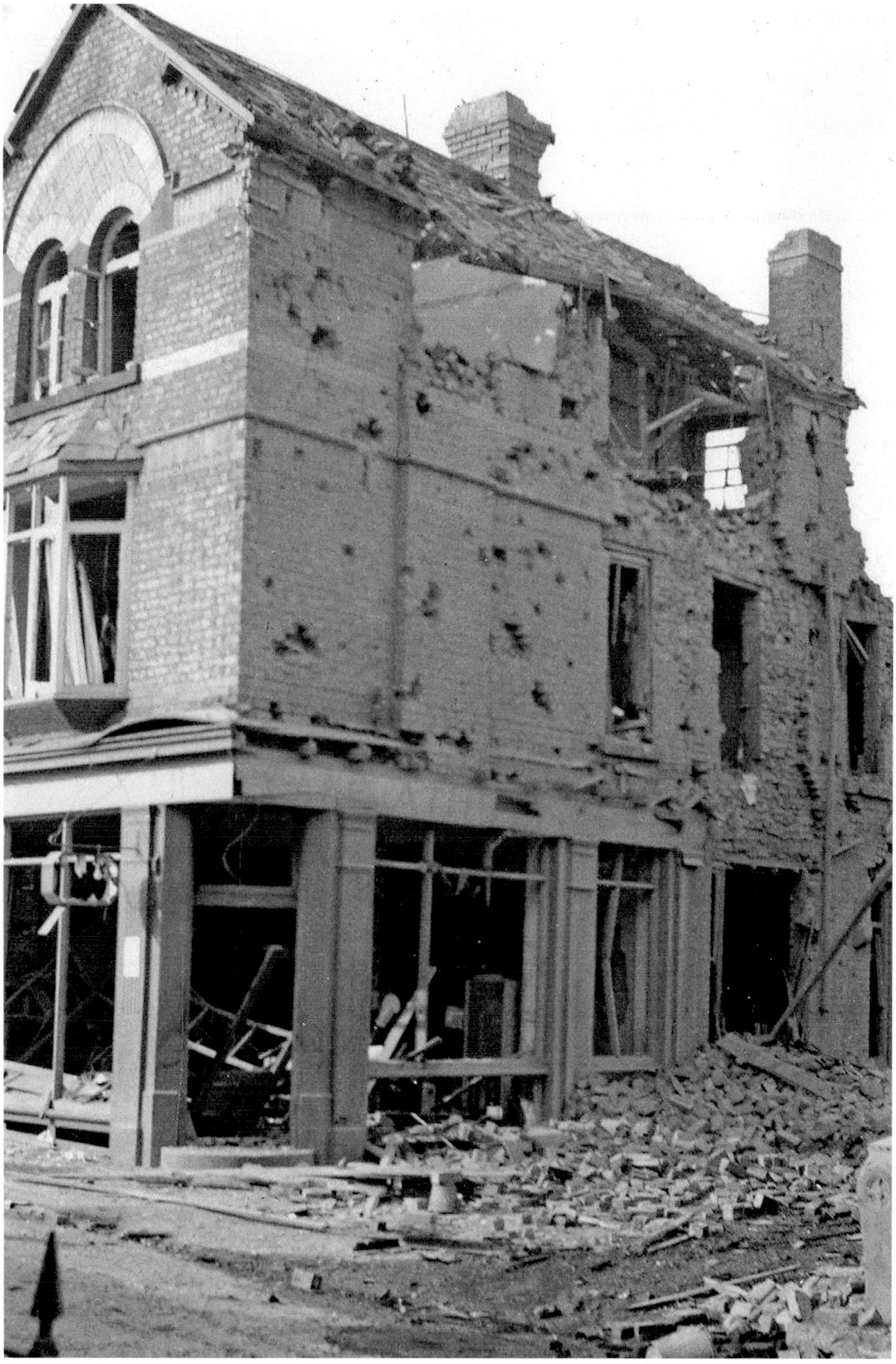

Shop premises in Village Road, Heswall.

Air Raid Damage at Heswall, 1 June 1941
A photograph that shows damage caused by a high-explosive bomb to a house named 'Riversdale' in Telegraph Road, Heswall.

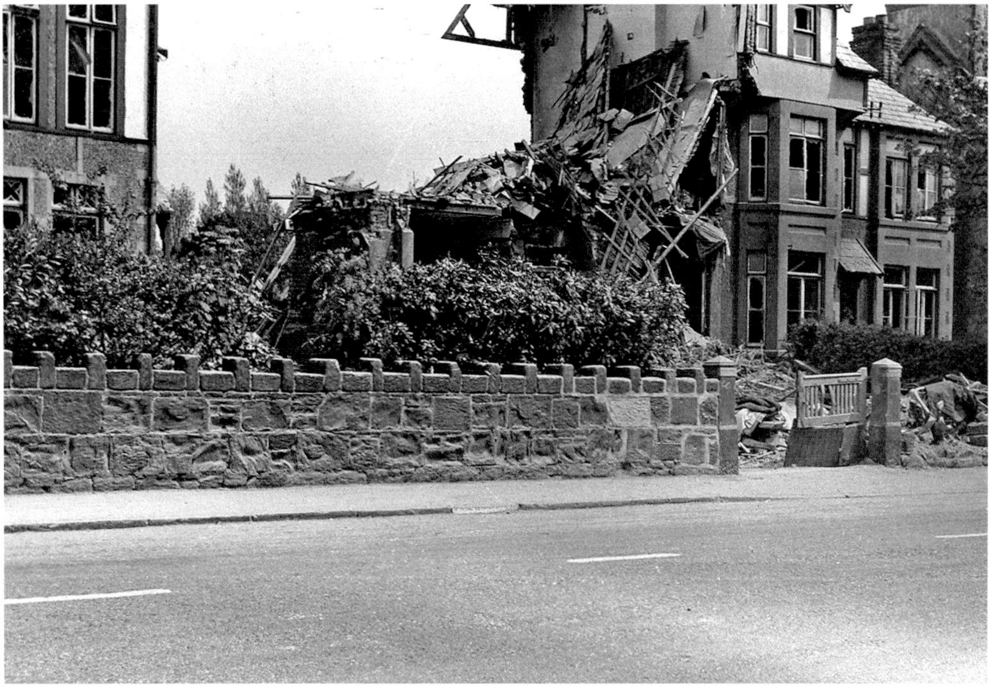

German 1-ton bomb at Okells Farm, Landican, Wirral (undated)

A German 2,200lb bomb, which was 6ft long and a semi-armour-piercing type. The bomb was dropped in a field at Okells Farm, Landican, Wirral.

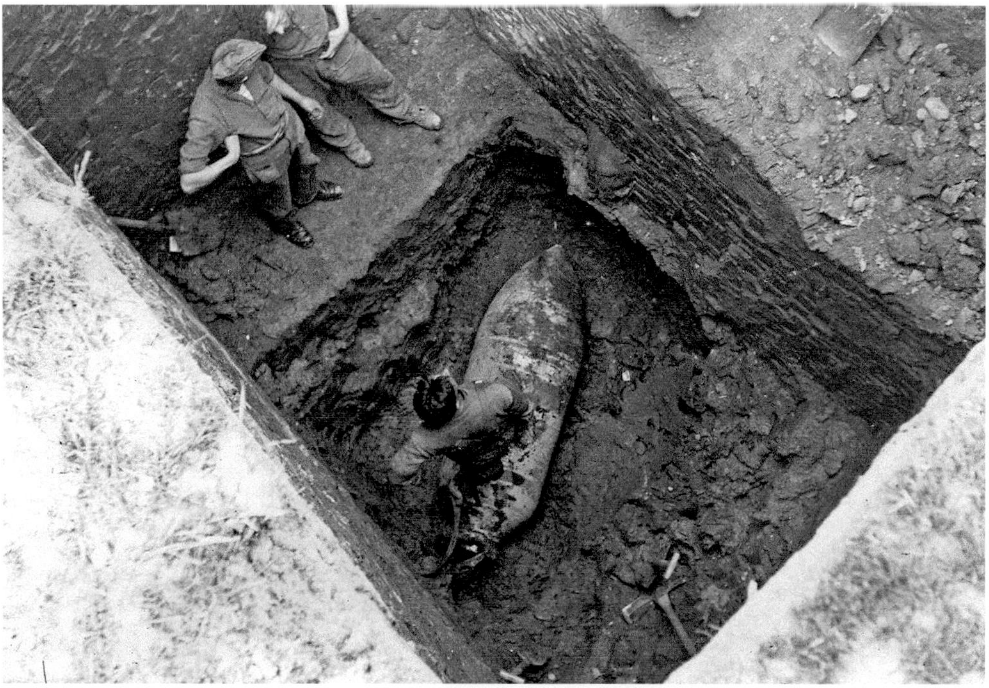

This shows the depth at which this massive bomb ended up after landing in a field.

Air Raid Damage at Higher Bebington, Wirral, 22 October 1941

Photographs showing damage to a house caused by a bomb. Note the corrugated iron indoor shelter shown on the left of the photo below; a woman and her dog were inside when the bomb hit and sustained only slight injuries. This shelter had already been moved when the photograph was taken.

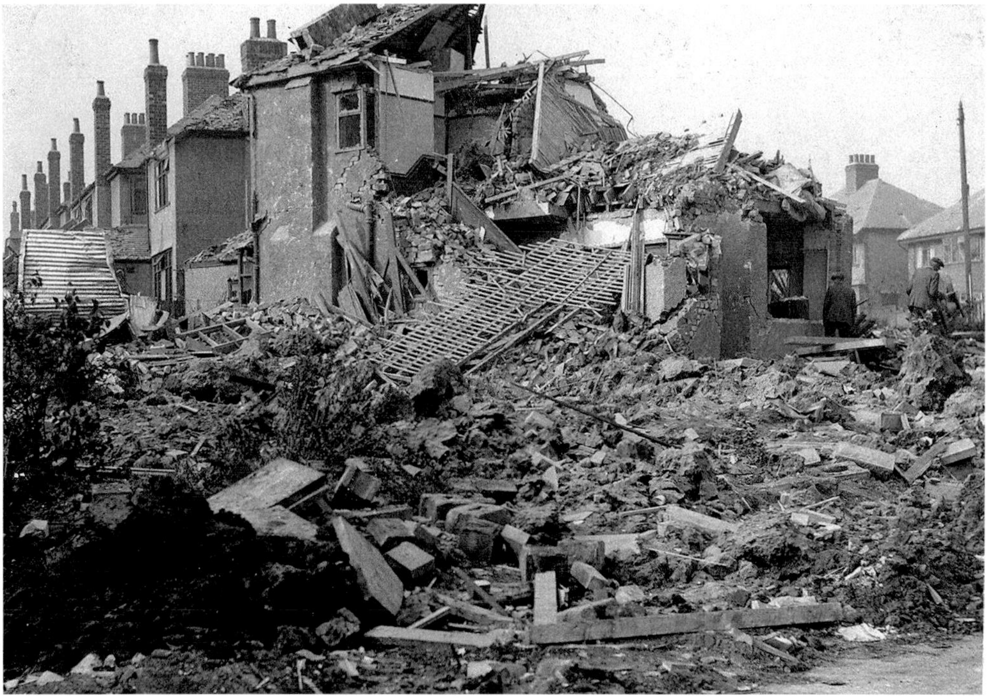

A bomb landed among the houses, causing minor injury.

A Sad Story of a New Cinema in Birkenhead

The Ritz was one of the biggest and most majestic cinemas in the North West when it was built on a 1-acre site at the junction of Claughton Road and Oliver Street in Birkenhead in 1937. It was built in the art deco style out of Portland stone and had a striking external feature: a 70ft glass and steel tower that overlooked one corner of the building above the main entrance doors.

Disaster struck just three years after its opening when, on 21 December 1940, after the showing of *Stardust* with Linda Darnell and *The Girl in Room 313* with Florence Rice had ended, organist Harold Hunt valiantly played on as an air raid took place outside:

> The Ritz Cinema was severely damaged by a German bomb, which came through the roof, exploding just in front of the circle. It killed 10, including Sally Eglington, aged 24, the Cinema's head usherette, and there were over 100 casualties. A second bomb destroyed the rear wall of the building. The front of the building and the foyer areas were untouched.[29]

The cinema eventually reopened in 1947 after renovation work. The original Compton organ was replaced by a Christie organ from the La Scala cinema in Glasgow, and the cinema was later renamed the Essoldo. It closed in 1969 and became a bingo club, which then closed for good in 1997. The building was demolished in October 2000, and the land is now used as a car park.[30]

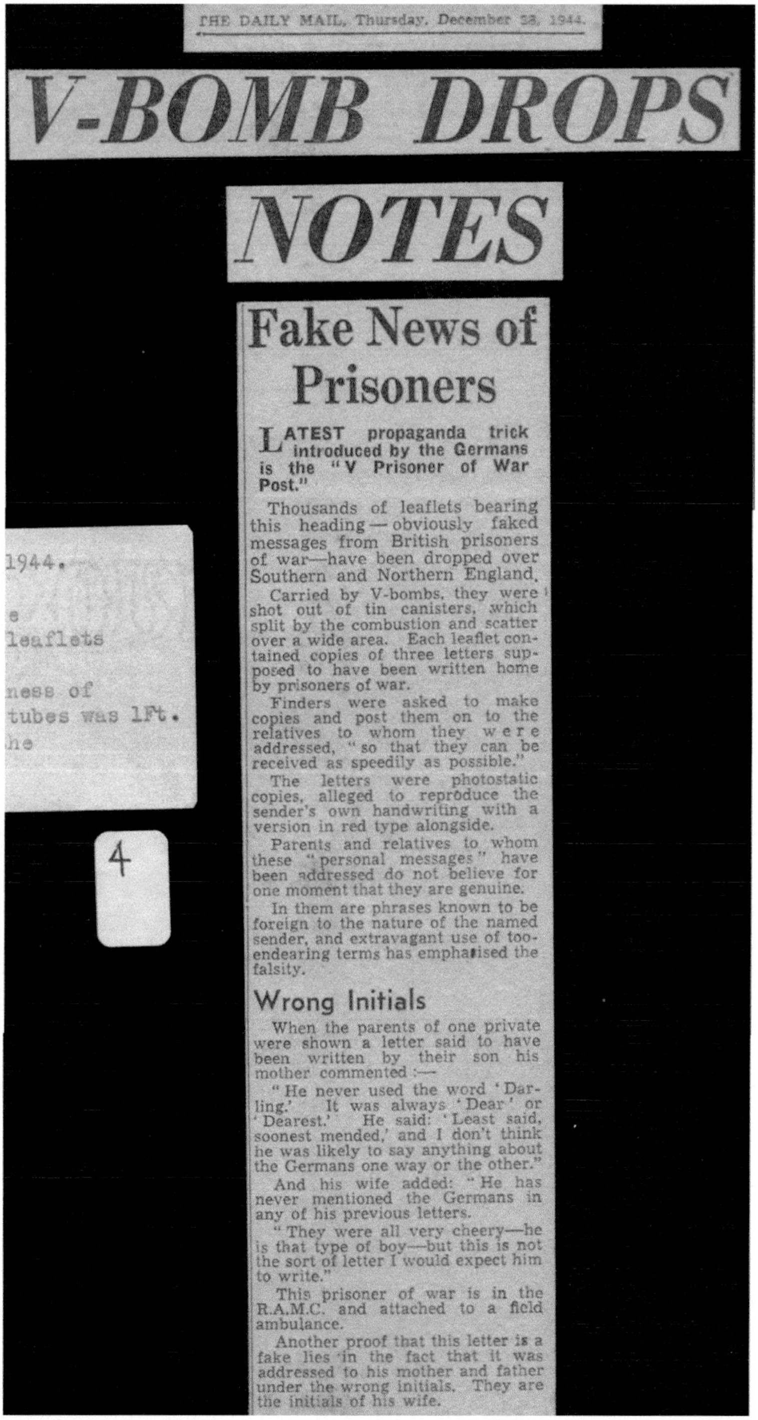

THE DAILY MAIL, Thursday, December 28, 1944.

V-BOMB DROPS NOTES

Fake News of Prisoners

LATEST propaganda trick introduced by the Germans is the "V Prisoner of War Post."

Thousands of leaflets bearing this heading — obviously faked messages from British prisoners of war—have been dropped over Southern and Northern England.

Carried by V-bombs, they were shot out of tin canisters, which split by the combustion and scatter over a wide area. Each leaflet contained copies of three letters supposed to have been written home by prisoners of war.

Finders were asked to make copies and post them on to the relatives to whom they were addressed, "so that they can be received as speedily as possible."

The letters were photostatic copies, alleged to reproduce the sender's own handwriting with a version in red type alongside.

Parents and relatives to whom these "personal messages" have been addressed do not believe for one moment that they are genuine.

In them are phrases known to be foreign to the nature of the named sender, and extravagant use of too-endearing terms has emphasised the falsity.

Wrong Initials

When the parents of one private were shown a letter said to have been written by their son his mother commented :—

"He never used the word 'Darling.' It was always 'Dear' or 'Dearest.' He said: 'Least said, soonest mended,' and I don't think he was likely to say anything about the Germans one way or the other."

And his wife added: "He has never mentioned the Germans in any of his previous letters.

"They were all very cheery—he is that type of boy—but this is not the sort of letter I would expect him to write."

This prisoner of war is in the R.A.M.C. and attached to a field ambulance.

Another proof that this letter is a fake lies in the fact that it was addressed to his mother and father under the wrong initials. They are the initials of his wife.

The *Daily Mail* warning of a propaganda war on Britain.

6

The War's Final Days

As we approach the end of the book, we reach December 1944, with just over four months remaining for Hitler to do his worst before his time runs out. The air over Germany is throbbing with the sound of Allied aircraft, the Nazis are seeing the devastating damage that they have themselves caused to the Allied countries, and the Allies are getting closer. But Hitler has one last throw of the dice: wonder weapons in the form of jet- and rocket-powered bombs. He was hoping to turn the losses around with the use of his 'vengeance weapons'. One of the first of these was the V-1 flying bomb, also known by the nicknames 'doodlebug' and 'buzz bomb'. This was a pilotless weapon built with the range to fly to Britain and strike London, which most of them did. The amount of fuel dictated where they would drop when it ran out over the intended area. The V-1s caused a lot of death and destruction. They didn't all fall on London; the first came down on Swanscombe, Kent, on 13 June 1944, and the last one at Orpington, also in Kent, on 27 March 1945 (Hitler committed suicide on 30 April 1945). During the V-1's short lifespan, 6,725 were launched at Britain. Some 2,340 hit London, causing 5,475 deaths and 16,000 injuries.

Meanwhile, Nazi propaganda minister Joseph Goebbels had been sending forged letters purporting to come from Allied prisoners and letters from Hitler to random addresses, explaining just how much better off Britain would be under his leadership. Luftwaffe planes had also been dropping them. Now he had another vehicle to transport his propaganda: the V-1. We have some examples of these leaflets from a V-1 that landed in a field near Kelsall. The leaflets were in 1ft-long tubes, made of cardboard ¼in thick. Also found at this scene were miniature copies of the German propaganda booklet 'The Signal'.

Propaganda Letters Found in Kelsall, 24 December 1944

At 06:22 hours on Christmas Eve 1944, a loud explosion was heard over Kelsall and numerous windows in the village were shattered as a V-1 came down. This was the most westerly impact site in England, although the intended target had been the industrial areas of Manchester, some 30 miles to the north-east. The weapon could cause damage up to a mile away from impact.

Early that morning, around fifty Heinkel bombers flew over the North Sea near Hull, all releasing V-1s aimed at Manchester:

> A small number failed and fell straight into the sea; they didn't stay in the air very long, such was their speed. They were somewhat difficult to intercept or shoot down, and our northern air defences were not properly geared up to tackling the V1 threat.[31]

However, the crafty RAF pilots learned to fly alongside them and flick their wings, which caused the V-1s to veer off course and increased the chance of them detonating on safe areas. Only one of the V-1s landed within the Manchester Special Civil Defence Area, beside the River Mersey near Stockport. The others were scattered across several counties, including Shropshire, Northamptonshire and Cheshire.

Several of the V-1s, including the Kelsall doodlebug, were designed to carry canisters of propaganda documents. The canister was rigged to eject from a tube near the flying bomb's tail at the moment its pulse jet motor cut out before the final descent:

> The canister's contents would then scatter over the locality, to be picked up by curious local residents. Some of the paperwork was just propaganda, for example, more minor issues of Signal magazine, but another item found at Kelsall was the V1 POW Post. This sheet included a copy of a letter purporting to be from a POW held in Germany. The finder was asked to forward the letter to the POW's family in England, who would then likely refer to it in their next contact with their loved one via the Red Cross. This would be intercepted by Intelligence officers at the POW camp, and the location of the V1's impact could be deduced from the paper trail.[32]

The police had been instructed, as a result, to pick up any of this material they could find near sites of impact and deter the locals from responding to any.

The Kelsall bomb left a massive crater at Street Farm and Lower Street Farm, Kelsall. The V-1 dropped in a grass field, about ¾mile from the main Chester–Northwich Road and the farmhouse, damaging the roofs of Street Farm's buildings when it landed. Slates were blown off, windows shattered and leaflets were scattered over the area. Surprisingly, the Street Farm workers were uninjured, although

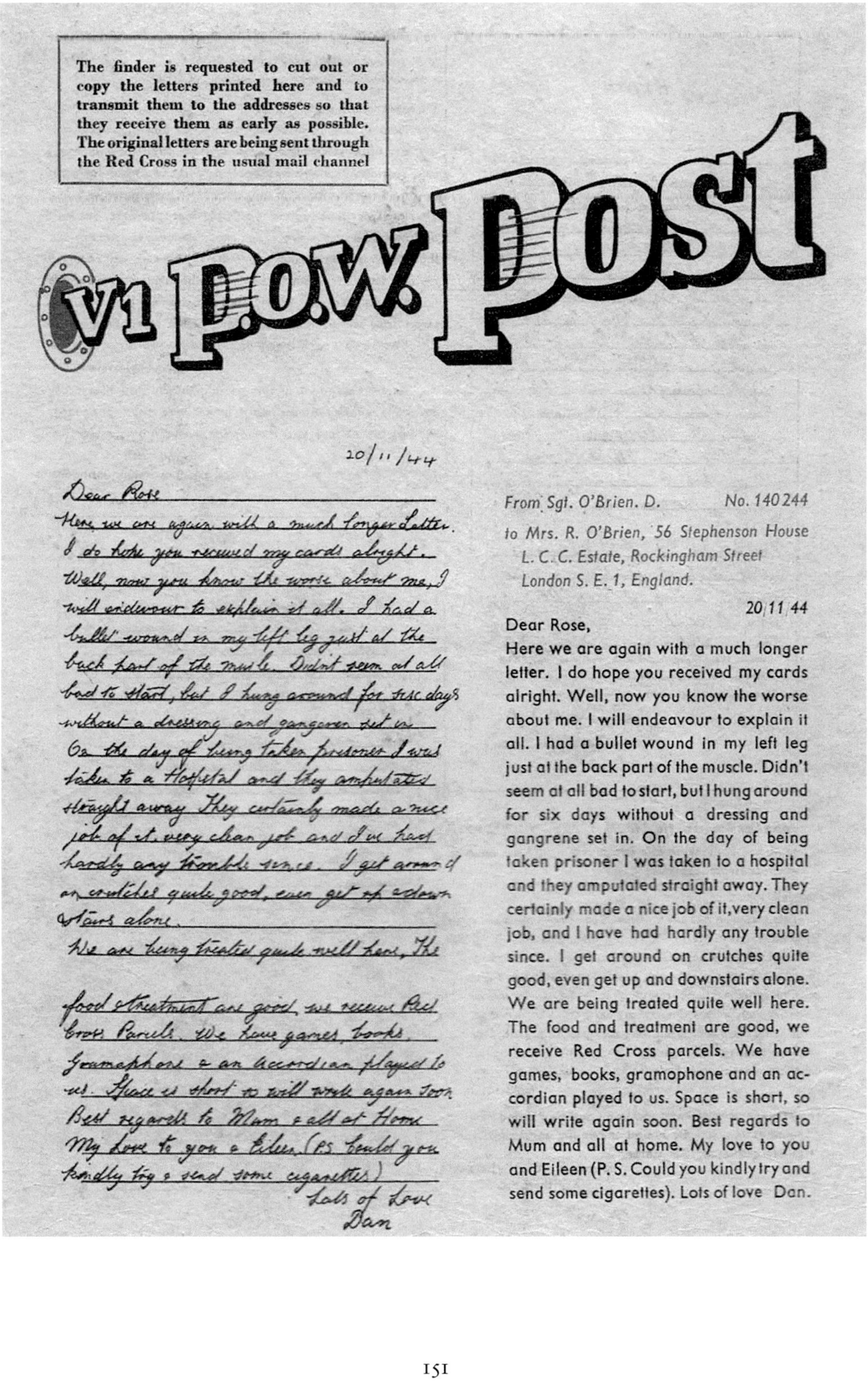

The finder is requested to cut out or copy the letters printed here and to transmit them to the addresses so that they receive them as early as possible. The original letters are being sent through the Red Cross in the usual mail channel

V1 P.O.W. Post

20/11/44

Dear Rose

Here we are again with a much Longer Letter. I do hope you received my cards alright. Well, now you know the worse about me, I will endevour to explain it all. I had a bullet wound in my left leg just at the back part of the musle. Didn't seem at all bad to start, but I hung around for six days without a dressing and gangreen set in. On the day of being taken prisoner I was taken to a Hospital and they amputated straight away. They certainly made a nice job of it. very clean job and I've had hardly any trouble since. I get around on crutches quite good, even get up & down stairs alone.

We are being treated quite well here. The food & treatment are good. we receive Red Cross Parcels. We have games, books, Gramaphone & an accordian played to us. Space is short so will write again soon. Best regards to Mum & all at Home. My Love to you & Eileen (P.S. Could you kindly try & send some cigarettes)

Lots of Love
Dan

From Sgt. O'Brien. D. No. 140244

to Mrs. R. O'Brien, 56 Stephenson House
L. C. C. Estate, Rockingham Street
London S. E. 1, England.

20 11 44

Dear Rose,

Here we are again with a much longer letter. I do hope you received my cards alright. Well, now you know the worse about me. I will endeavour to explain it all. I had a bullet wound in my left leg just at the back part of the muscle. Didn't seem at all bad to start, but I hung around for six days without a dressing and gangrene set in. On the day of being taken prisoner I was taken to a hospital and they amputated straight away. They certainly made a nice job of it, very clean job, and I have had hardly any trouble since. I get around on crutches quite good, even get up and downstairs alone. We are being treated quite well here. The food and treatment are good, we receive Red Cross parcels. We have games, books, gramophone and an accordian played to us. Space is short, so will write again soon. Best regards to Mum and all at home. My love to you and Eileen (P. S. Could you kindly try and send some cigarettes). Lots of love Dan.

From Albert Burton No. 140 144 *4/12/44*

to Mr. and Mrs. Burton, 94 Fairfield St.,

Hopetown. Darlington, Durham/England.

Dear Mum and Dad,

I am writing this from the same old place and I hope you are all in the pink at home. I am still in hospital here, but I am feeling quite well again and hope to be on my feet again before so long. It is a bit monotonous lying in bed like this. but I suppose I will get over it as usual and turn up like a bad penny again, you can remember me saying that a few times. Did you write Hilda when you received my first letter. The letter card before this, which I wrote had no date on it, so you will now know which one it is. I hope you have a happy Xmas and a much better New Year, and it is a pity that I can't let the New Year in.

Love Albert

As Commandant of this camp I inform you that every care is taken for the health of your son and that regarding his welfare you may spend Xmas with no worries.

Bürger

Oberst and Lager-Kommandant

From Alex Sawyers No. 140 276 *1/12/44*

to Mrs. A. Sawyers, Steeple Bumpstead

Lower House, Essex/England

Hello, my Darling,

This message has been allowed in order to wish you and all at home a Merry Xmas and a Prosperous New Year, and I sincerely hope Darling that we will soon be together again. I am alright now, my wounds are almost better and I am walking about a lot now. So don't you be worrying, Joan, I am looking forward to when I receive a letter to hear how you are keeping. Well, Darling, keep smiling, tell everybody at home I was asking for them. Hope this finds you o. k., honey, all my love,

kisses Alex.

This is a special line to let you know that he is doing very well and is very fit. His wound is healing satisfactorily. With best wishes for Christmas

C. James Capt. Rame

British M. O.

V 1/3

several deaths and injuries did occur across the region in the Christmas Eve 1944 V-1 air raid.

Note the date: December 1944, by which time the war was well and truly lost by Hitler, making this a last-ditch approach to the British people.

Other V-1 Bombing Sites

The raid on 24 December 1944 wasn't just on Kelsall; there were several other parts of Cheshire that were also hit by V-1s at the same time.

Blue Bell Wood, Henbury

The bomb was dropped in a grass field at a point 500 yards from Henbury Hall, breaking some windows in the hall and damaging trees. The trees, some 40 yards from the bomb crater, were pitted with pieces of metal from the bomb.

Manor Farm, Ollerton

The bomb fell in a green-cropped field at a point 200 yards from Manor Farm, damaging the roofs of the farm buildings.

Hardings Land, Macclesfield Forest

The bomb dropped in a grass field on a hillside. Blasts from the bomb-damaged roofs broke the windows of farmhouses and cottages in this district but the drystone walls that were used as field boundaries did not appear to have been affected by the blast.

Westwood Farm, Matley, Hyde

This bomb dropped on a stone-built farmhouse and killed two people: a 17-year-old farmer's son and his 70-year-old grandmother.

About 150 yards from Westward Farm was The New Inn, which faced the bomb blast. When the bomb dropped on the farm, the leaded windows of the upstairs front bedroom were blown inwards.

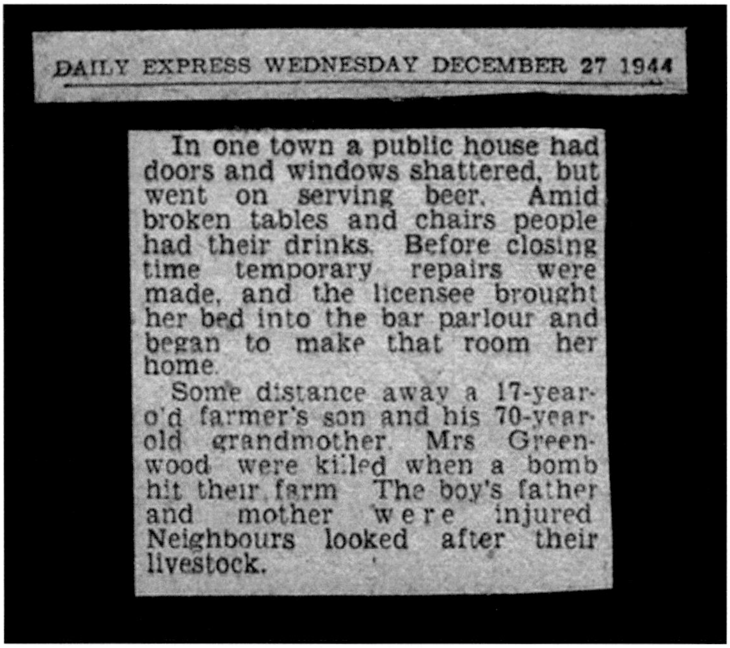

DAILY EXPRESS WEDNESDAY DECEMBER 27 1944

In one town a public house had doors and windows shattered, but went on serving beer. Amid broken tables and chairs people had their drinks. Before closing time temporary repairs were made, and the licensee brought her bed into the bar parlour and began to make that room her home.

Some distance away a 17-year-old farmer's son and his 70-year-old grandmother, Mrs Greenwood were killed when a bomb hit their farm. The boy's father and mother were injured. Neighbours looked after their livestock.

An excerpt from the 27 December 1944 edition of the *Daily Express*, which mentions the Westwood Farm V-1.

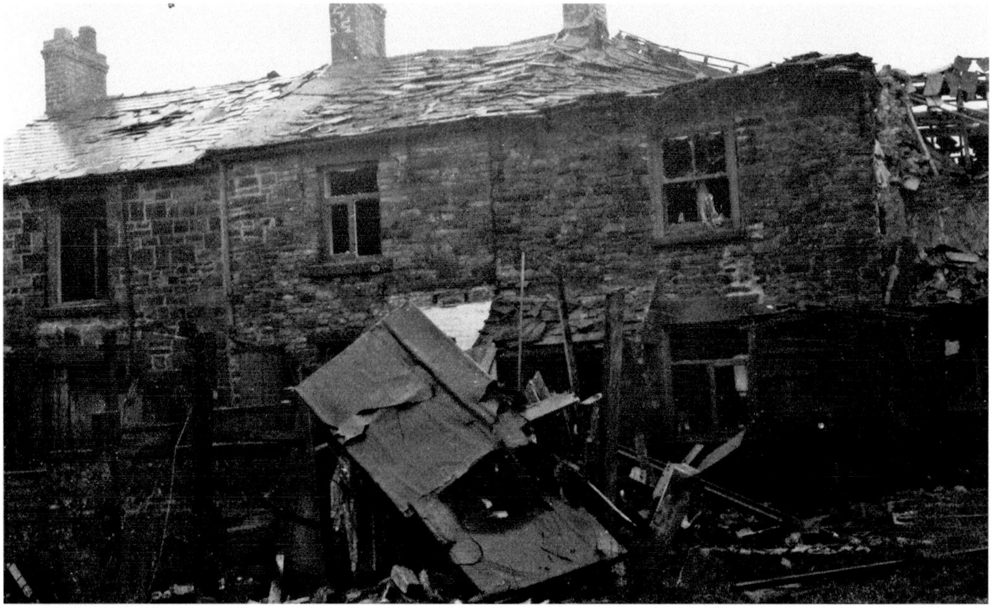

Westwood Farm: a direct hit.

Notes

1 From a War Photography Leaflet issued by the War Office.
2 Dr Brian Barton; www.irishtimes.com/culture/heritage/dublin-s-lights-used-by-luftwaffe-for-belfast-blitz-says-historian-1.2612171
3 Historic England Research Records, Starfish Bombing Decoy Sf37, www.heritagegateway.org.uk/Gateway/Results_Single.aspx?resourceID=19191&uid=415b17b4-be70-47e7-a9b6-d78eba25bda8
4 Paul Hurley, *A to Z of Crewe* (Amberley, 2019).
5 Paul Hurley, *The Changing Railways of Britain* (The History Press, 2019).
6 Sources for this section include www.carlscam.com/warmem/bentley.htm and www.crewehc.co.uk/pyms-lane, as well as the war memorial.
7 I want to thank Paul Chiddick of the excellent 'Chiddick's Family Tree' and local historian Andrew Lamberton for allowing me to utilise much of the research they conducted. https://chiddicksfamilytree.com/2024/04/17/danger-uxb-the-story-of-six-brave-royal-engineers-who-died-at-nantwich
8 With thanks to Paul Chiddick and Andrew Lamberton.
9 Paul Hurley, *Winsford Through Time* (Amberley, 2009).
10 https://altrincham.todaynews.co.uk/events/2015/12/22/when-german-bombs-brought-horror-to-altrincham-75-years-on-from-day-blitz-death-destruction
11 Thanks to Mr Martin McEwen Jr, now the owner, for providing the photos of the premises and information regarding his father.
12 Imperial War Museum and *Warrington Guardian*.
13 With thanks to Paul Chiddicks and Andrew Lamberton.
14 Thanks to: https://myadventures3.blogspot.com/2023/04/sutton-valence-to-boughton-monchelsea.html
15 https://freepages.rootsweb.com/%7Erichardsonsmith/history/COCH%20History/barrowmore-hospital.html; other sources (see next note).
16 Ibid.
17 The research in this article comes from various sources including: https://freepages.rootsweb.com/~richardsonsmith/history/COCH%20History/barrowmore-hospital.html; www.barrowmore.co.uk/about-us/history-of-barrowmore/; Chester Health Service History; captions within the images folder; period newspapers with other research facilities.
18 National Museums Liverpool/Liverpool Blitz 70, also later *The Liverpool Echo*.

19 With thanks to the *Heswall Magazine* for permission to quote from their article, 'Heswall WW2 Bombing', written by Roger Lane and Jenny McRonald.
20 Ibid.
21 The details of this piece are researched from the Public Record Office; period newspapers; and the Wirral.net site: https://oldwirral.net/files/Ju88_Crash_at_Brom.pdf
22 PRO; also Wirral.net https://oldwirral.net/files/Ju88_Crash_at_Brom.pdf
23 Ibid.
24 Ibid.
25 The Liverpool Museums and New Ferry online, https://newferryonline.org.uk/history-of-new-ferry
26 Ibid.
27 https://portsunlightvillage.com/history
28 Ibid.
29 https://cinematreasures.org/theaters/35659
30 Thanks to Historic England for permitting the use of quoted snippets. https://historicengland.org.uk/images-books/photos/item/NWC01/01/2445; also, Chester Cinemas (www.chestercinemas.co.uk/ritz-cinema-birkenhead); www.liverpoolmuseums.org.uk; and UK Picture Palaces site.
31 www.sandstoneridge.org.uk/news/v1-flying-bomb-on-ridge-1944.html; The Sandstone Ridge Trust and Dave Trevor; and *Flying Bombs over the Pennines* by Peter J.C. Smith (1988), with other sources.
32 Ibid.

Bibliography and Sources

Cheshire Police Museum, featuring three albums of bomb damage with written captions.

Home Office, Order Number 1, Control of Photography, 10 September 1939. From a War Photography Leaflet issued by the War Office.

Historic England Research Records.

Roger Lane and Jenny McRonald, 'Heswall WW2 Bombing', *Heswall Magazine*.

Smith, Peter J.C., *Flying Bombs Over the Pennines: The Story of the V-1 Attack Aimed at Manchester on December 24th 1944* (N. Richardson, 1988).

The Liverpool Museums and New Ferry online.

Websites

www.carlscam.com/warmem/bentley.htm

www.crewehc.co.uk/pyms-lane

www.mywesleyanmethodists.org.uk/content/chapels/cheshire/wheelock-wesleyan-chapel

www.messengernewspapers.co.uk/news/14140128.remembering-the-christmas-blitz-sale-battered-by-air-raids-75-years-ago

https://freepages.rootsweb.com/%7Erichardsonsmith/history/COCH%20History/barrowmore-hospital.html

www.tattenhallhistory.co.uk/newton-farm

https://myadventures3.blogspot.com/2023/04/sutton-valence-to-boughton-monchelsea.html

https://newferryonline.org.uk/history-of-new-ferry

https://oldwirral.net/files/Ju88_Crash_at_Brom.pdf

www.chestercinemas.co.uk/ritz-cinema-birkenhead

https://cinematreasures.org/theaters/35659

www.bbc.co.uk/news/uk-england-stoke-staffordshire-14958770

https://altrincham.todaynews.co.uk/events/2015/12/22/when-german-bombs-brought-horror-altrincham-75-years-on-from-day-blitz-death-destruction/

https://historicengland.org.uk/images-books/photos/item/NWC01/01/2445

www.heritagegateway.org.uk/Gateway/Results_Single.aspx?resourceID=19191&uid=415b17b4-be70-47e7-a9b6-d78eba25bda8

www.sandstoneridge.org.uk/news/v1-flying-bomb-on-ridge-1944.html

Acknowledgements

Many thanks to the Museum of Policing in Cheshire for permission to reproduce these photographs from their archives, together with their comments, and particular thanks to Will Brown, Museum Researcher, for his help. To Sophie at Vernons Garage, thank you for kindly providing old and new images of the garage. Likewise, Mr Martin McEwen Jr, now the owner of the premises of McEwens Garage, for providing the modern and pre-war photos of the premises and information regarding his father. Thanks to the *Heswall Magazine*, and Paul Chiddicks for his assistance, as well as Nantwich local historian Andrew Lamberton. We would also like to thank Amy Rigg and Jezz Palmer at The History Press for their invaluable advice and support. And finally, thanks to the hard-working police photographers of the Cheshire Constabulary who took the old photographs used in the book.

All images from Cheshire Police Museum unless otherwise stated.

About the Authors

Paul and Rose are married; Rose researches their books and Paul writes them.

Paul Hurley has been a freelance writer, author and journalist since retiring from the police and is a member of the Society of Authors. To date, he has written an award-winning novel and a police autobiography; three books on railway subjects for The History Press; and one railway book and twenty-eight other books on local Cheshire history for Amberley.

Rose is a first-class researcher and has provided the information used in this book. She has also co-authored two books with Paul on Cheshire and its dark past. Her final occupation before retirement was as a senior project director and she was previously vice president within a financial institution.